THEODORE ROOSEVELT AND THE GREAT WHITE FLEET

American Sea Power Comes of Age

by

KENNETH WIMMEL

BRASSEY'S

Library of Congress Cataloging-in-Publication Data

Wimmel, Kenneth, 1933–
    Theodore Roosevelt and the great white fleet : American seapower
    comes of age / Kenneth Wimmel.
        p.   cm.
    Includes bibliographical references (p.   ) and index.
    1. United States—History, Naval. 2. Roosevelt, Theodore, 1858–1919.
    3. United States. Navy—History. I. Title.
    E182.W565   1998
    359'.00973—dc21   97-40372

ISBN 1-57488-239-2 (alk.paper)

Printed in the United States of America on acid-free paper that meets the American National Standards Institute Z39-48 Standard.

Brassey's
22841 Quicksilver Drive
Dulles, Virginia 20166

10 9 8 7 6 5 4 3 2 1

This book is dedicated to my mother,
who taught me to love books,
and to my father,
who loved the United States Navy, though he
never wore its uniform.

We can steer a course, but who's to set one?
—Long John Silver

TABLE OF CONTENTS

PREFACE

Some readers, especially those possessing a scholarly cast of mind, may be disappointed by the absence of references to sources in this account. To them, I can only offer this note of explanation. I agree with the British historian John Keay that "spattering a narrative history with numbered references, whilst it may invite scholarly regard, is inhibiting for the writer and can be irritating for the reader." Historians as varied and highly regarded as Emil Ludwig in his biography of Napoleon, Harold Nicolson in his account of the Congress of Vienna, A. J. P. Taylor in his study of Bismarck, and Alan Moorehead in his history of the Russian Revolution have chosen to omit notes on sources.

The basic facts in this narrative are not in dispute among historians, and my purpose is not to kindle such a dispute by offering startling new evidence or a radical reinterpretation at variance with the standard histories. By combining information scattered among a variety of published works (many long out of print), along with a dash here and there of previously unpublished material, I do hope to stimulate the reader's interest in an important but often ignored chapter of American history. Perhaps the reader will also be moved to consider these events, and Theodore Roosevelt's role in them, in a new light.

PROLOGUE
"DID YOU EVER SEE SUCH A FLEET AND SUCH A DAY?"

—⟨ℰℐℰ⟩—

For two days an Atlantic storm roiled the waters of Hampton Roads and threatened to spoil the spectacular show the navy had arranged for its commander-in-chief. On the eve of the appointed day, however, a cold west wind blew away the clouds, and Monday, December 17, 1907, dawned clear and calm. Sixteen battleships, resplendent in fresh white and buff paint, rode serenely at anchor as the wintry day broke. The fleet had been assembling for two weeks from points scattered along the east coast. *Louisiana* departed from the Brooklyn Navy Yard on December 3 for the short voyage south. *Illinois* left Newport, Rhode Island, on December 6 with a draft of two hundred newly recruited apprentice seamen aboard. On the same day, *Kansas, Georgia,* and *Kearsarge* sailed from Philadelphia. *Kansas* was the newest of the battleships, having been put into commission the previous April.

The flagship, *Connecticut,* had departed New York on December 4 to head south for the mouth of the Chesapeake Bay. Though not the newest ship, *Connecticut* had been in commission less than eighteen months. Like seven other ships of the fleet, it displaced sixteen thousand tons and carried a main battery of four twelve-inch guns. Fully half the fleet was made up of modern, first-class battleships that incorporated the latest developments in naval technology. The two oldest ships, *Kearsarge* and *Kentucky,* were only seven years older than the newest ships, but they were smaller and represented an older generation of warship design. The differences in the ships underscored the rapid pace of naval technological innovation that had transformed the world's navies over the previous quarter-century.

According to official announcements, the fleet's orders were to sail around South America on a "practice cruise" to rendezvous with the

The Great White Fleet departing Hampton Roads on December 17, 1907.

U.S. Naval Historical Center photograph

much smaller Pacific Fleet at Magdalena Bay in Baja California. But everyone knew that the president's intention was that it sail clear around the world. A fleet of colliers larger than the battle fleet itself was already at sea carrying coal to strategic locations where the battleships would replenish their fuel supplies. Colliers were enroute to Pearl Harbor and Manila to preposition coal supplies for the trans-Pacific voyage. Others were at sea headed for Trinidad, Rio de Janiero, Punta Arenas, Callao, and Magdalena Bay to establish fuel replenishment depots for the long haul around South America to the west coast.

It would be the largest fleet of battleships ever to circumnavigate the globe. It had not yet been dubbed the Great White Fleet. Contemporary news accounts referred to the Atlantic Fleet or the Battle Fleet, and books published by participants used the same terminology. Only long after the cruise ended would someone hit upon the catchy name which caught the public's fancy and stuck. In contrast to the usual secrecy that surrounds movements of warships, this fleet's voyage was designed to attract maximum notice in the news media. A press center had been created aboard *Connecticut* to cater to the needs of the pool of newsmen invited to sail as passengers.

The fleet provided the reporters with copious statistical information. The aggregate personnel complement was 12,793 officers and men. The ships' batteries totalled 360 guns ranging in size from six-inch to thirteen-inch bore. Firing a single salvo from all the guns would have cost fifty thousand dollars, which, many reporters noted, happened to be the size of the president's salary for one year. The fleet carried huge quantities of provisions, measured in tons, so much that foreign naval attachés decided that "the American navy pampers its men too much." There were more than seventy animals aboard the various ships as mascots, including twenty-five goats, thirty-two dogs, twelve parrots, and a donkey. Thousands of gallons of gray battle paint were aboard to transform the gleaming white ships to their wartime color in the unlikely event that they were ordered into battle.

By December 14, the sixteen battleships were anchored in Hampton Roads. Officers and sailors on shore leave thronged Newport News and Norfolk. The hotels were filled to capacity by relatives and friends of crew members who came from all over the country to bid farewell to their loved ones who were embarking on a voyage that promised to last for months, perhaps years. They were joined by visitors from towns and villages surrounding Hampton Roads who were attracted by news reports about the great spectacle of sixteen battleships and a swarm of lesser craft, all in one anchorage. One "local homespun-clad peanut grower from the interior" was quoted as observing, "A'in't been so many folks out since the day the Monitor fought the Merrimac." Sailors, on what promised to be their last liberty in a U.S. port until they reached California, crowded Norfolk on Saturday night. On Sunday morning, special services were held in the city's churches.

Promptly at eight o'clock on Monday morning, the presidential yacht, *Mayflower*, hove into sight and steamed to its anchorage at the head of the double line of warships. It had departed the Washington Navy Yard the day before for the leisurely voyage down the Potomac and into the Chesapeake Bay. Aboard were the president and his wife, accompanied by a large official party. For Theodore Roosevelt, this was one of the supreme moments of his presidency, a moment to be savored. The magnificent fleet was almost entirely his creation, tangible evidence of his devotion to the United States Navy and a monument to his untiring years of service devoted to its strengthening and modernization. His prime purpose in ordering the fleet to sail around the world, he later wrote, was to impress the American people with the strength and capabilities of their navy. But he had other purposes in mind, too.

As soon as *Mayflower* anchored, the fleet's commanding admiral, ac-

companied by his four squadron commanders, came aboard for breakfast with the president. Rear Admiral Robley "Fighting Bob" Evans had
long been Roosevelt's "favorite captain." Like Roosevelt, he had
emerged a hero from the war with Spain. He had commanded the battleship *Iowa* in the battle outside the harbor of Santiago de Cuba when
a Spanish fleet was destroyed and the war, in effect, was won. Evans was
near the end of his career and had already announced his intention to
retire from the navy. Command of this superb fleet for its departure and
the first leg of its record-breaking voyage constituted a fitting cap to an
outstanding career. At a farewell banquet in his honor at the Lotos Club
in New York, the quotable Evans, a favorite with newspapermen, had
told his audience, "You will not be disappointed with the fleet, whether
it proves a feast, a frolic or a fight." Evans had consulted with Roosevelt
in Washington only a few days earlier, so their breakfast together just
before departure was more a formality and social meeting than an occasion for the commander-in-chief to issue orders to his fleet commander.

Breakfast with the president was rapidly completed, because the
commanders had to hurry back to their ships for the fleet's ten o'clock
departure. They paused long enough on *Mayflower*'s quarterdeck to have
their photograph snapped with the president. The morning sun sparkled on the water as anchors were winched up and catted, and the ships
prepared to get underway. Sailors in dress uniform manned the rails,
bands struck up "The Girl I Left Behind Me," engine bells clanged, and
ensigns fluttered in the breeze. From *Mayflower*'s halyards, signal flags
flapped the message: "Proceed on your assigned duty."

With the presidential yacht in the van, the warships formed a single
column as they got underway and headed for the entrance of the bay.
On shore, throngs of onlookers cheered and waved handerchiefs. The
porch of the Old Point Comfort Hotel was crowded with guests who
did not want to miss this once-in-a-lifetime spectacle. Heads filled every
window of the hotel. At Horseshoe Point, where the Chesapeake Bay
met the open Atlantic, *Mayflower* slowed to a halt and Roosevelt appeared on the bridge to review the passing fleet. The long column of
battleships stretched as far as the eye could see as they steamed past at
a stately ten knots. As each battleship passed the yacht, it fired a twenty-
one gun salute. The final crash of the guns boomed over the water as the
last ship began to round Cape Henry and enter the Atlantic. Roosevelt's

intense delight bubbled to the surface as he paced *Mayflower*'s bridge, watching the departing ships disappear one by one around the Virginia Capes. "Did you ever see such a fleet and such a day?" he exclaimed as *Mayflower* turned and headed back toward Chesapeake Bay for the return trip to Washington.

Even as he gave voice to his satisfaction, Roosevelt was aware that the departing battleships, as new as they were and as imposing as they might appear, had already been rendered obsolete, or nearly so, by the relentless and accelerating march of technology. Only a little more than a year before the battle fleet's departure from Hampton Roads, the British battleship *Dreadnought* had sailed out on its sea trials in the English Channel. At 17,900 tons, *Dreadnought* displaced less than two thousand tons more than *Connecticut,* and its main batteries were twelve-inch guns like *Connecticut*'s. But *Dreadnought* mounted ten guns in its main battery as compared with only four in *Connecticut* and other American battleships. The British ship was the "all-big-gun ship" visualized and debated by naval experts for several years.

Moreover, *Dreadnought* represented a revolution in marine propulsion. It was powered by steam turbines rather than the reciprocating engines that powered all the other warships of the world. Steam turbines permitted the ship to maintain top speed for extended periods, whereas a fleet powered by reciprocating engines was bound to have at least some of its ships suffer breakdowns after only a few hours of operating at flank speed. *Dreadnought* was several knots faster than *Connecticut,* and—a sort of bonus—its steam turbines operating at maximum speed consumed less coal than the older reciprocating engines. *Dreadnought* could show its heels to any fleet of existing battleships that might outgun it. If it chose to fight, its main battery was the equal of any three existing battleships'. As Theodore Roosevelt realized, *Dreadnought* represented the latest quantum leap in a naval technological revolution that had been underway for more than a quarter-century. It would soon render all other battleships obsolete.

Dreadnought had been built in great secrecy and with extraordinary speed. Launched just four months after its keel was laid, it sailed out on sea trials one year and one day after keel-laying, whereas battleships normally required three years or longer to build. The British were prodded by a developing naval arms race with Germany that threatened

Britain's long dominance of the sea. But Roosevelt knew that they were also prodded by developments in the United States during his administration. In March, 1905, Congress authorized the president to have constructed "two first-class battle ships, carrying the heaviest armor and the most powerful armament for vessels of their class." Their main batteries would consist of eight twelve-inch guns, double the number on existing battleships. Two even more modern ships were authorized in 1906 and 1907. Each was to carry ten twelve-inch guns. Like *Dreadnought,* they would be "all-big-gun ships." The keel of one of the new ships, *North Dakota,* was laid in Quincy, Massachusetts, on December 16, the day before the Great White Fleet sailed from Hampton Roads. The United States, however, would not duplicate the extraordinary speed of the British shipbuilders who constructed *Dreadnought.* None of the new American "dreadnoughts" would be commissioned until 1910.

Nevertheless, Roosevelt knew that the four new American battleships under construction would enable the United States to maintain the position it had only recently attained as a naval power. In 1907, Britain dominated the world's oceans as it had for decades, if not centuries. The British were determined to maintain their lead over Germany, which was working hard to close the gap with Britain. Some experts ranked Germany second and the United States third, while others, using different criteria, reversed that ranking. By other measurements, perhaps more important than fleet size or composition, the United States was the equal of, if not superior to, both Britain and Germany as one of the great powers. In the manufacture of steel—perhaps the single most important measure of industrial and therefore war-waging capacity—the United States produced more than Britain and Germany combined. The war with Spain had drawn the United States out of its traditional continental isolation into the arena of world politics, and its already gigantic and still-growing industrial muscle gave it influence and authority in international affairs. Theodore Roosevelt believed that the nation needed a first-rate navy to protect its interests, discharge its responsibilities, and maintain its status and prestige as a leading world power.

As *Mayflower* steamed up the Potomac to return to Washington, Roosevelt could look ahead to his final year as president. Immediately after his election in 1904, he had pledged that he would not be a candidate for reelection in 1908. As president, Roosevelt chalked up a number of interesting "firsts." He was the first president to ride in an automobile and the first to dive beneath the surface in a submarine. He was the first president to travel outside the United States while in office. He was the first to go aloft in an airplane, although the flight occurred after he left office.

When he stepped down from the presidency, Roosevelt left several legacies, any one of which would be a cause for pride for most presidents—he would be remembered as trust-buster, builder of the Panama Canal, preserver and protector of the environment, and peace-maker. He was awarded the Nobel Prize for Peace in 1905 for mediating the end to the Russo-Japanese War; only one other president, Woodrow Wilson in 1919, has become a Nobel Laureate. No other legacy gave Roosevelt greater satisfaction than the strong navy he fought to establish.

His years of public life coincided with a period of revolutionary change that transformed the American navy. Within little more than a generation, it moved from the centuries-old era of wood and canvas to steel and steam. Roosevelt did not, of course, bring about this revolution single-handedly. But the dynamic, questioning, impatient figure of Theodore Roosevelt, like a recurring theme in a symphonic movement, turns up repeatedly in the history of the United States Navy during those important decades.

Roosevelt came to the presidency armed with more extensive knowledge of naval history, more hands-on experience operating a navy, and a deeper understanding of naval technology than any other president, before or since. His influence on the American navy and on the attitude of the people of the United States toward their navy was crucial, even long before he became president. He prodded his fellow politicians into supporting the navy, he badgered an often-reluctant navy into accepting all the technological changes being thrust upon it, and he instilled in his countrymen an abiding understanding that their country's security and responsibilities demanded a strong navy. More than any other single person, he was responsible for the United States Navy coming of age.

Among the goals he set for himself during his last year in office was to gain congressional authorization for several more "dreadnoughts" to ensure that the navy would remain a formidable fighting force for years to come. In the decades that followed his departure from the presidency, the navy experienced ups and downs. But it never again descended to the depths of decay, obsolescence, and humiliating ineptitude it had reached in the nineteenth century before Theodore Roosevelt entered public life.

1

"TEEDY'S DRAWING LITTLE SHIPS!"

The report issued by the Naval Committee of the House of Representatives at the end of January, 1880, was detailed and bluntly worded. "Small as the number of our naval vessels is as compared with the other navies of the world," it said, "it is infinitely smaller in real fighting power, and it is time for Congress and the country to face the fact." The report went on to review the condition of the United States Navy, vessel by vessel. The largest and presumably the most formidable ships protecting the country were five "first-rates," wooden sailing vessels dating from before the Civil War. They were so old and in such a state of disrepair that "we class them as non-combatants." Of twenty-seven "second-rates," three were "unfinished on the stocks, rotten and worthless," seven were in such poor condition that they were not considered worth repairing, and only nine were regarded as fit for service. The list went on through the third-rates, the fourth-rates, and the iron-clads. There were twenty-seven vessels in the last group, of which four were "rotten and worthless," several were unfinished, and the fourteen considered serviceable were each armed with only two obsolete smooth-bore cannon. "There is not a single rifled gun on our iron-clad fleet," the report pointed out. It concluded, "in the opinion of the committee, the time has arrived when it is a national duty to begin construction of a new Navy."

The sharply critical report attracted attention, as intended by its author, Representative Benjamin Harris of Massachusetts, who served as chairman of the Naval Committee. The *New York Times* published a long news item about Harris's investigations with the headline "Our Worthless Naval Forces." *The Nation*, bemoaning "the satirical semblance of a navy that we possess," opined that "this state of affairs is only less ridiculous than it is melancholy." Both publications joined others in urging Congress to pass the bill that Representative Harris introduced along with his report that would authorize funds to begin a long-term construction program to rebuild the navy.

Scarcely fifteen years earlier, the navy had emerged from the Civil War as one of the largest and strongest in the world. It was a somewhat peculiar navy, it is true, that had developed in response to the peculiar demands of that peculiar war. The navy had been configured to discharge three main responsibilities: conduct riverine operations along the Mississippi and its tributaries to support the army, blockade southern ports, and chase down a handful of Confederate commerce raiders on the high seas. There were no major fleet actions and no threat of such actions, because the Confederacy did not possess a navy worthy of the name. But the war had been notable in naval history, because it had been the occasion for the first battle between steam-driven, ironclad warships. In 1865 when the war ended, the United States Navy was staffed by officers and men trained and tested in battle. The same could not said of the navy of any other major power. It was one of the largest in the world and a force to be reckoned with.

The end of the war brought an end to interest in the navy on the part of Congress and the American population in general, as the ending of wars had done in the past. There seemed little justification for spending money on a navy when so many other important priorities existed. No discernible threat to the country's security from any other country needed to be met. No significant American merchant marine existed to protect. In 1860, American overseas trade was overwhelmingly carried in American flag vessels. But the threat of Confederate commerce raiders during the war caused American shipping companies to shift their ships to foreign flags, and American traders to ship their cargoes in foreign ships. In 1865, American-owned ships that had been shifted to foreign registry during the war were not permitted to revert to American registry, and the American foreign trade that burgeoned after the war continued to be carried mostly in foreign bottoms. The attention of the general population shifted from winning a war to developing the incredible industrial and agricultural potential of the United States. The public was not interested in matters outside the country. There was no apparent need to spend money on a navy. The formidable navy of 1865 was ignored and allowed to wither away.

Soon after Ulysses S. Grant took office as president in 1869, he was told by the Navy Department that not one ship was ready for sea. It would take five months, the president was informed, to make even one ready in all respects to get underway. But little was done during Grant's two terms to rectify the situation. Secretaries of the navy after the war were politicians appointed because of their political connections. They took no interest in the service they supposedly headed. It was said of Richard W. Thompson, who was appointed by Grant's successor, Rutherford B. Hayes, that he knew nothing about ships when he was appointed and had never even been aboard one. Thompson was a politician from Indiana, and he was not Hayes's first choice for navy secretary, or even his third or fourth choice. He was appointed because Hayes owed a political debt to the governor of Indiana. The story, perhaps apocryphal, was told that after taking over as secretary, Thompson went aboard a ship for the first time. He peered into the ship's hold and exclaimed, "I'll be blessed! Why, the durned thing's hollow!" In 1876, as the whole country triumphantly celebrated its centennial, a survey of the world's navies published in Britain included such powers as Brazil, Turkey, Peru, and Austria, but failed even to list the United States. The American navy was omitted, the report explained, because its guns were "condemned all over the world and superseded," while the American navy's "system of armor plating is also unsound."

The decline and obsolescence that government and public neglect fostered were abetted by the leadership of the navy itself. Sailors, especially naval sailors, are conservative by nature, because life afloat is a good deal more chancy than life ashore. A battle or a storm at sea is a dangerous place to test new, untried ideas, because lives are literally at stake. Sailors tend to cling to the tested and to be wary of the new and untried, and in 1865, there was a plethora of new and untried ideas about warships being discussed and published around the world. The senior officers of the American navy in 1865 had come to maturity in the old prewar sailing navy, and when the war ended, they instinctively reverted to that familiar milieu. Many probably were personifications of the stereotype of the reactionary old mossback, unthinkingly resistant to change and innovation. But there were several understandable reasons for their wish to revert to the familiar world of an earlier naval era.

The war had proven that wooden sailing ships were no match for steam-powered ironclads, especially in the restricted waters of rivers and bays. But the ironclads developed during the war were awkward, ungainly vessels that had been designed for use on inland waters. They sat low in the water so that their engines would have the added protection of being below the waterline. They therefore had little freeboard and little reserve buoyancy. The original *Monitor* had been lucky to make the voyage safely from New York to Hampton Roads to fight the *Merrimac*. It sank a few months later in a storm off Cape Hatteras. The monitors built during the war were useful as gun platforms on rivers to support the army, but they were dangerous craft in which to venture out on the open sea. Monitors had proven useful during the war, so the navy continued to depend upon them as important elements of the fleet, even though they were useful only for harbor defense.

Steam-powered ironclad warships, whether monitors or some other design, were dirty, uncomfortable ships compared with the familiar sailing vessel. Space for the crew and their comfort were sacrificed to the needs of the machinery and its fuel. For centuries, the wind had served as the means of propulsion, and there was no need to curtail space in the hull for the crew and their provisions to accommodate engines and fuel. With the introduction of the steam engine, living accommodations were given second priority after the needs of the propulsion plant. The engine rooms were hot, filthy dens below the waterline. Every surface was coated with a film of oil mixed with coal dust, and the space reverberated with the ear-splitting din of machinery. Temperatures could reach 150 degrees Fahrenheit. Coaling ship was a detested exercise. It was back-breaking labor, and it left the ship and its crew filthy. It is no wonder that old-time sailors from the prewar navy, faced with a long cruise on the high seas, preferred a sailing vessel with its billowing canvas and white, holystoned decks to the cramped quarters of a noisy, dirty, unseaworthy ironclad.

Ships of the middle decades of the nineteenth century were hybrids. When steam-powered ships were introduced before the Civil War, they were essentially sailing vessels fitted with auxiliary engines. Designs evolved into what were primarily steamships fitted with masts and sails as auxiliary power. It had been growing apparent that steam would soon replace sail completely, especially in warships. Most senior American naval officers resisted this obviously inevitable march of technology. Vice Admiral David Dixon Porter, a hero of the Civil War and the son of a naval hero of the War of 1812, succeeded David Farragut as Admiral of the Navy in 1870. He issued an order that "constant exercise shall take place with sails and spars." Handling sails was regarded as good physical exercise for the crew that also fostered teamwork, conferring on sailors benefits similiar to those of close-order drill on military units ashore. Porter decreed that "commanders of fleets, squadrons and of vessels . . . do all their cruising under sail alone." Moreover, he wrote, "they must not be surprised if the coal consumed is charged to their account." He sought to reduce the size of the steam propulsion plants on the ships that had them, and he arranged to replace four-bladed propellers with two-bladed ones because the latter were more efficient for sailing ships. Porter and the other senior officers wanted ships that could still circumnavigate the world by sail alone, "without once touching their coal." Most officers afloat were probably quite happy to let the filthy coal lie undisturbed in its bunkers and the noisy engines be silent.

By 1880, neglect from without and resistance to change from within had produced the "worthless navy" described by Representative Harris. His authorization bill to begin reconstruction passed the House in February. Unfortunately, it was defeated in the Senate in April. Nevertheless, 1880 was the year that presaged a change in the navy's fortunes, even if the upward arc out of the abyss did not actually begin until later. In November, a new president was elected, and although he remained in office only a few months, his election marked the beginning of an improvement in the navy's condition.

When Benjamin Harris was waging his unsuccessful crusade on behalf of the navy in early 1880, Theodore Roosevelt was entering his final months as a student at Harvard University. Roosevelt was an excellent scholar who earned top grades during his first three college years. During his senior year, however, his attention was increasingly distracted from his studies. First of all, he had fallen in love with a lovely girl named Alice Lee. His courtship was met by apparent indifference on Miss Lee's part, and young Roosevelt lived in an agony of doubt and suspense for months. In January, he was overjoyed when Alice accepted his proposal of marriage, and they became formally engaged in February.

Another distraction was a book he had started to write in December about naval operations during the war with Britain in 1812. He had been prompted to write it by a book on the subject by a British scholar, which he had found in the Porcellian Club's library at Harvard. Roosevelt decided it was an inadequate account of that naval war, and he resolved to write his own. He was determined to write a detailed account that was historically and technically accurate, despite his meager knowledge of such subjects as navigation and ship-handling. With his already customary drive and determination, he set about becoming an expert on the technical details of naval warfare under sail. As the academic year neared its end, the time he spent with his fiancée and on his naval research reduced the number of hours he spent weekly on his regular studies from his usual thirty-six to fifteen.

Roosevelt's interest in naval history had begun in his boyhood. Two of his uncles on his mother's side of the family had served as officers in the Confederate navy, and their tales of their adventures in the war thrilled young Theodore. His uncle Irvine Bulloch had served as navigation officer aboard the famous Confederate raider *Alabama* and had been aboard when it was sunk. His uncle James Bulloch had served the Confederacy in England, arranging purchase of *Alabama* and the other ships that served as commerce raiders. James Bulloch lived to a ripe old age, residing after the Civil War in a kind of exile in England, where Roosevelt visited him. When he was serving as president, Roosevelt told his military aide, Archie Butt, that his uncle James Bulloch appealed to him more than any man he had ever met.

Despite the distractions of his senior year, Roosevelt graduated magna cum laude from Harvard, ranking twenty-first in a class of one hundred seventy-seven. He had already decided he wanted to pursue a political career, and he planned to study law as preparation. He had completed two chapters of *The Naval War of 1812*, but it was laid aside for the moment as more urgent matters claimed his attention. He divided his time in the summer between Alice and a hunting trip with his brother to the western prairies. It was his first introduction to the western open spaces and their cowboys, hunters, and other men of action whom he came to admire. He and Alice were married on October 27, his birthday, and settled down in New York City. Roosevelt began law studies at Columbia Law School and made a start on his political career by gaining membership in the Twenty-First District Republican Association.

He also resumed work on his neglected naval history, burying himself in the Astor Library where he pored over tomes of naval history and lore through the winter of 1880 and into the spring of 1881. He worked on the book at home, puzzling out the details of navigation and the handling of sailing ships in battle. He sent off orders for technical manuals and histories and received shipments of books by the crate. A friend from Harvard days, the novelist Owen Wister, has described Roosevelt the author as he often appeared to visitors in his New York brownstone. He worked, wrote Wister, "mostly standing on one leg at the bookcases in his New York house, the other leg crossed behind, toe touching the floor, heedless of dinner engagements and the flight of time. A slide drew out from the bookcase. On this he had open the leading authorities on navigation, of which he knew nothing." As a member of an old, prominent New York family, Roosevelt had an active social life. He and Alice were out for dinner or other engagements several evenings a week. They were members of the "Four Hundred" invited to Mrs. Astor's famous ballroom. Often, on evenings when they were due at one or another New York mansion, Alice would find him at his bookcase, totally absorbed in his studies, drawing diagrams of ships to work out what happened during a battle. According to Wister, she would exclaim at his apparently oblivious back, "we're dining out in twenty minutes, and Teedy's drawing little ships!"

The Roosevelts spent the summer of 1881 on a tour of Europe that began in Ireland and ended in Italy. In England, they spent time with Roosevelt's maritime uncle, James Bulloch. Roosevelt carried his book manuscript along and worked on it during odd free moments before or after such activities as climbing the Matterhorn in Switzerland. In the fall, he returned to his studies at Columbia Law School. On October 17, he wrote in his diary, "Am working fairly hard at my law, hard at politics, and hardest of all on my book." Actually, he was losing interest in his law studies as he devoted all his attention and energy to the book and the Twenty-First District Republican Association. He became a candidate for a seat in the New York state assembly, and to the surprise of many, was elected in November. On election day, after casting his own vote, he became so absorbed in his work on the book at home that only when someone stopped by to greet "the rising star" did he realize his political career was fairly launched.

By December 3, the completed manuscript was sent off to the publisher, G. P. Putnam's Sons. Roosevelt had produced a very learned work, bristling with technical details and statistics, and written in precise, scholarly prose. He later wrote that when he had finished the first two chapters at Harvard, he decided that they were "so dry they would have made a dictionary seem light reading by comparison." In the preface, however, the dry scholar let himself go. He seized the occasion to give his views in forceful language about the disgraceful condition of the contemporary navy as compared with the victorious force of 1812. "It is folly," he wrote, "for the great English-speaking Republic to rely for defense upon a navy composed partly of antiquated hulks and partly of new vessels rather more worthless than the old."

The book appeared in the spring to excellent reviews. The *New York Times* rejoiced that "a rising young politician like Mr. Roosevelt has wider scope for his mind than wire-pulling and has made at least one period of American history the object of serious study." The reviewer summed up: "The volume is an excellent one in every respect, and shows in so young an author the best promise for a good historian— fearlessness of statement, caution, endeavor to be impartial, and a brisk and interesting way of telling events." Theodore Roosevelt was twenty-two years old. His political career was launched and his credentials as an expert on naval affairs established.

When James Garfield assumed the presidency on March 4, 1881, he had not yet filled all his cabinet seats. One of the men he was consider-ing for a cabinet post was William Henry Hunt, a goateed judge from New Orleans. Garfield had never met Hunt, who was almost totally unknown to both Garfield and his political advisors. If he was known for anything, it was his four marriages. He had been recommended by the outgoing president, Rutherford B. Hayes. Hunt was a northerner who had migrated to the south, and during the Civil War he had been a "Unionist southerner." Garfield wanted someone from the south in his cabinet for political reasons, and Hayes recommended Hunt as a "safe southerner." Which cabinet post he occupied was of secondary importance. He was first considered for the Department of the Interior, but on the day after his inauguration, Garfield appointed him secretary of the navy.

Hunt was delighted with the position. His son had served as an officer in the Union navy, and he had entertained Admiral Farragut and his officers at his home in New Orleans during the Civil War. Probably unknown to Garfield, he took a deep interest in the navy. He quickly learned of the disgraceful condition in which the navy had sunk, and he began a campaign to rebuild it by appointing a Naval Advisory Board to draw up a plan of action. One of its members was an outspoken navy commander from Virginia named Robley Evans. He put forth a radical proposal: any new ships the Board might propose should be built of steel. Some members of the Board opposed Evans's idea and argued, erroneously as things turned out, that the steel needed for ships could not be produced in American steel mills. Moreover, they pointed out correctly, steel was a great deal more expensive than iron.

The Board submitted its report on November 7, 1881. It focussed on two recommendations. The United States should build sixty-eight new ships, and most of them should be built of steel. The Board recommended construction of cruisers and gunboats rather than battleships, because it decided that the purpose of the navy was protection of commerce, "showing the flag" in foreign ports, and coastal defense, not major fleet actions against other naval powers. Other unstated reasons for avoiding any recommendation to build first-rate line-of-battle ships may have been their cost and the widespread opposition in the country at large to constructing any ship called a "battleship."

Garfield had been in office barely four months when he was shot in the Washington, D.C., railroad station in July. He died in September. He was succeeded by his vice-president, who was regarded as a typical product of the machine politics of post–Civil War New York. Chester Alan Arthur had risen through the ranks of Republican state politics by being a consistently loyal party man. In 1877, he had been replaced as Collector of the Port of New York by Theodore Roosevelt's father, who was not a politician and considered politics a tainted pursuit. Like all new presidents, Arthur would want to name his own cabinet, and as a typical "spoilsman," he was expected to replace Garfield's cabinet with his political supporters and cronies. To people like Theodore Roosevelt and Benjamin Harris, eager for a top-to-bottom reform of the navy, Arthur's succession to the presidency threatened to stall the movement toward reform begun so promisingly by William Hunt. It seemed likely that any new secretary of the navy would be another in the line of political hacks occupying the office since 1865 who "let the admirals run the navy."

Only a few months after taking office, Arthur eased Hunt out of the Navy Department by naming him minister to Russia, a move that Hunt considered equivalent to dismissal from office. One of Hunt's last official acts, taken in April, 1882, was to create the Office of Naval Intelligence, the first American government agency created to collect military information abroad. Hunt was in poor health, and he died in Russia early in 1884.

The choice for his replacement in the Navy Department appeared to confirm reformers' fears that the emergence of a "new navy" would be postponed indefinitely. The new secretary was William E. Chandler, a forty-six-year-old politician from New Hampshire. He had served in the Navy Department during the Civil War when he was still in his twenties, and as assistant secretary of the treasury under President Andrew Johnson. He had been active in Republican politics ever since. Chandler had gained the reputation of being "a shrewd and not over-nice political manager." He was credited with engineering in 1876 the election triumph of Rutherford B. Hayes, who lost in the popular vote but secured the presidency in a political compromise between the two parties that produced cries of "the Stolen Election."

Garfield had nominated Chandler to the post of solicitor general, but the Senate refused to ratify his nomination. He was opposed by a coalition of southern Democrats who remembered the stolen election, and certain conservative Republicans who considered Chandler unqualified for the post. His nomination to a cabinet post by Arthur received decidedly mixed reviews. The *Boston Post* said, "The attempt to foist Chandler upon the country in an official capacity has been defeated once and should be again." The liberal *Nation* acknowledged that he was "a man of capacity," but declared that "his appointment borders upon the grotesque. What the President hopes to accomplish by it is a mystery." The influential and Democratic New York *World* announced that "he will be forgiven much of the mischief he has done and much of the mischief he undoubtedly meditates, if he succeeds in getting us a navy."

Chandler's nomination was confirmed by the Republican Senate by a vote of sixteen to twelve, and he took office in April, at about the same time that *The Naval War of 1812* appeared. He moved into a splendid office, described as "one of the most beautiful in the world," in the just-completed State, War and Navy Building next door to the White House. It was the largest office building in the world at that time. The walls of his office were of rare marbles, there was "rich ornamentation" in sea motifs everywhere, and above the door was a slab of lapis lazuli from Pompeii. His term of office, his political enemies predicted, would be an orgy of corruption, favoritism, and graft.

Chandler confounded his critics. He took charge of his department immediately and continued the course of reform begun by Hunt. His staff was favorably impressed by the new secretary's policy of literally leaving his office door open for anyone, staff or visitor, who wished to see him. Most of the visitors were seeking favors, and often they were not connected with the navy. His staff might have noticed that the secretary worked at a battered old stand-up desk, where he received his visitors on his feet. Conversations were conducted with all parties standing. The old pol had learned that conversations so conducted were much briefer than if they were held with all parties comfortably seated, especially if the visitor was pleading for a political favor.

The problems afflicting the navy that Chandler faced were not confined to the obsolete, worthless ships of the fleet. There was a surfeit of officers, especially in the higher ranks—more than were needed to fill the required billets. Senior officers were kept on the active roster into their seventies and even eighties, to be removed only by death. One correspondent, who explained that he had "no axe to grind, no friends who want anything," warned the new secretary that "Admiral Porter [then almost seventy years old] runs the entire navy from his headquarters, a private room over the stable in the rear of his residence." A procession of the chiefs of the department's bureaus could be seen entering that room every morning to conduct the department business, the writer claimed. There was a glut of navy shipyards, many lying idle or nearly so but maintained with a full staff. Many were incapable of building or maintaining modern warships. Contractors, bureau officials, and members of Congress conspired to waste public funds repairing worthless ships.

Chandler attacked all these problems with vigor. He made speeches pleading for public support to persuade Congress to authorize construction of new ships. In August and September, he went on an extended cruise along the east coast to visit shipyards and see for himself their condition. Against predictable opposition in Congress, especially from members whose districts were affected, he was able to close shipyards in New London, Connecticut, and Pensacola, Florida. He reduced the size of the officer corps by more than four hundred men.

On August 5, Congress passed a law that constituted a first, if rather limited, step toward rectifying the problems of the fleet. It decreed that the cost of repairing wooden ships could not exceed thirty percent of the cost of building a new vessel of the same size and material. For years, repairing worthless ships had been a means of justifying the existence of superfluous shipyards and putting money into the pockets of unscrupulous navy contractors. For example, *Kearsarge,* a famous vessel which had sunk the celebrated Confederate commerce raider *Alabama,* had been built in 1861. Over the years, more than $1.1 million had been lavished on it for repeated repairs—much more than the original cost of the ship—although it had long ago become obsolete. It was but one of many such ships. The new law meant that a great many of those vessels would finally be scrapped. Years after Chandler left office, he said, "I think I did my best work in destroying the old navy." At Chandler's urging, the new law also provided for the creation of a second Naval Advisory Board to continue the work begun by Hunt's board. Included in the law was authorization to construct two new steel cruisers. Unfortunately, the authorization was rendered meaningless when the appropriations bill for the navy failed to provide any funds for the two ships.

Chandler endeavored to include a cross section of experience and expertise in the membership of the new Naval Advisory Board. He chose Commodore Robert W. Shufeldt as chairman, a senior-level officer with a reputation as both a naval officer and a diplomat. The other officers he appointed represented various levels of experience. Two civilians were included, a naval engineer and a naval architect. The group was charged not only with formulating recommendations about the ships to be constructed for the new navy, but also with overseeing the construction itself.

The board had to grapple with a host of daunting questions on which it was not easy to reach agreement. What kind of ships should it recommend? A revolution in warship design and construction had been underway in Europe for several decades, and new, radical designs succeeded each other every few years. If the board's members were too conservative in their judgment, the ships they recommended might well be obsolete by the time they were commissioned. If they opted for the latest, untried designs and technology, the ships might prove to be useless, or worse.

The quickest means of getting new vessels into the fleet would be simply to purchase them abroad, probably from Britain. That idea was rejected out of hand. American warships must be American-built. But perhaps the designs could be purchased abroad or adapted from new foreign ships, to gain time and to ensure that they would incorporate the latest proven technology. Again, the board's members agreed that they must recommend American-designed vessels. However, while it would be all very well to recommend an American-designed and -built fleet, could American steel mills and foundries produce the high-quality steel, the armor plate, the guns that modern ships required? Could American shipyards build them? Finally, how many ships should the Board recommend be built, and of what size? If its recommendations were too ambitious and costly, Congress might balk and sanction nothing at all, and the whole process would have to begin anew.

The board decided to adopt the reasoning of the first board and recommend construction of cruisers. Their decision was prompted in large part by the navy's mission as it had long been traditionally construed in the United States. The navy existed to protect American commercial shipping around the world—in time of peace, mostly from pirates. In time of war, it should engage in commerce raiding and coastal defense. For the latter responsibility, coastal forts and ironclad monitors were regarded as sufficient. To protect American shipping from commerce raiders, fast and therefore lightly armored ships with a large cruising radius were deemed best. Little if any thought was given to any need to seek out and engage an enemy fleet in a major action. In his *Autobiography*, Roosevelt commented scornfully on what he considered a timid policy: "We built some modern cruisers to start with, the people who felt that battleships were wicked compromising with their misguided consciences by saying that the cruisers could be used 'to protect our commerce'—which they could not be, unless they had battleships to back them up." This board decided that the first board had recommended constructing too many ships. The United States ultimately would need a great many, but as a first step, this board limited its recommendation to three steel cruisers and one small dispatch boat. It recommended one cruiser in the 3,000-ton range and two of 2,000 tons. They would be "protected cruisers," not "armored cruisers." This meant that their decks would be covered with relatively thin armor plate to protect the machinery below from the plunging shells of enemy fire, but their hulls would not have armor plating. Armored cruisers were protected by armor plating on both their decks and their hulls above the waterline. The four new ships would be steam-driven, of course, but they would carry auxiliary masts and sails to provide maximum cruising range. The board further recommended completion of three double-turreted monitors that had been under construction for several years. Work had been suspended six years earlier, because the ships were regarded as already obsolete, and debate had raged whether they were worth completing. The board decided they could be useful for harbor defense. Its report was submitted in December, 1882.

The board could find no one interested in submitting a bid to design the four new ships. Perhaps the time limit it gave—sixty days—was too short to allow completion of plans. It arranged to design them itself. The designs were mainly the work of a young graduate of the Naval Academy named Francis T. Bowles, who had recently studied naval architecture in Britain. He later became the navy's chief designer. In May, construction bids were solicited. Eight companies submitted bids. In early July, the Navy Department announced that the contracts to construct all four ships had been awarded to a shipyard in Chester, Pennsylvania, owned by a man named John Roach. The announcement triggered a storm of protest in Congress fueled by charges of corruption and cronyism.

John Roach's life had been a success story to rival the "Pluck and Luck" novels of Horatio Alger and the other dime novels so popular in the nineteenth century. He arrived in the United States at the age of sixteen, a penniless, nearly illiterate immigrant from Ireland. He was able to land a job in an iron works in New Jersey that paid twenty-five cents a day. He lived frugally and saved as much money as he could while he learned how to make castings for marine engines. With his savings he succeeded in establishing an iron works in Brooklyn, New York, to manufacture marine engines and other heavy machinery. By 1868, he owned several iron works and foundries. He moved into shipbuilding and sent a representative to Britain to study how the British built iron ships in their huge shipyards on the River Clyde. In 1871, he established a shipyard at Chester, on the Delaware River. It quickly grew to become the largest and busiest in the United States. He specialized in the construction of iron ships and built more of them than all his competitors combined. During the 1870s, the Roach shipyard was sometimes building ships at the rate of one a month. Roach gained the reputation of being an innovative builder of top-quality ships and the leading American builder of vessels made of iron.

The storm of protest that descended on John Roach's head when the construction contracts were announced was triggered in part by the fact that all four contracts had gone to the same builder. The other bidders had assumed that the four contracts would be parcelled out among several shipyards. The sealed bids for each contract were opened by William Chandler in his office in Washington in the presence of the bidders. For each contract, Chandler revealed, Roach had submitted the lowest bid. When Chandler finished, and it was known that Roach had landed all four contracts, one of the other shipbuilders jumped to his feet and with a flushed face cried, "Mr. Secretary, are you going to give all these contracts to one man?" Chandler replied, "I don't see how I can help it."

As the other bidders and everyone else knew, John Roach was a close personal friend and business associate of William Chandler. During the 1870s, Chandler had operated as lobbyist for Roach in Washington, to gain government contracts. Worse, Roach had on several occasions contributed money to Chandler's political campaigns and had even extended substantial personal loans to Chandler. Roach, and presumably Chandler, had anticipated the possibility of protest if he were awarded the contracts.

Roach was attacked by Democrats in Congress as embodying all the corruption that had flowed from twenty years of Republican control of Congress and the White House. His government contracts obtained during the scandal-ridden Grant administration were recalled and denounced. Grant's navy secretary, George Robeson, had awarded contracts to Roach. It was said of Robeson then that he was "a first-rate judge of wine, a second-rate trout fisherman, and a third-rate New Jersey lawyer." Congress rang with cries of "Roach, Robeson, Robbers!" Interestingly, George Robeson was now a member of Congress serving on the Appropriations Committee. Outraged Democrats charged that Roach had forged an unholy alliance with the shady Republican politico who had helped him get those earlier contracts in order to loot the treasury again. Chandler's reputation as a wily political operator fueled suspicions that there must have been collusion and pay-offs for four of the biggest, most important naval construction contracts in several years to be awarded to one of the navy secretary's best friends.

A few early historians of America's Gilded Age painted very unflattering portraits of Chandler and Roach and their relationship. Allan Nevins, in his biography of Grover Cleveland, portrayed the two as unscrupulous rascals who conspired to fleece the government. Nevins called Chandler "a hack politician" and Roach "an illiterate, elderly, infirm ironmonger" who was "indifferent to fine technical skill." Roach's surviving letters to Chandler, usually written in pencil and nearly illegible, are so riddled with misspellings and bad grammar that Nevins's opinion of his writing ability appears at least partially justified. However, even Roach's critics would not have accused him of indifference to superior workmanship. His shipyard had rapidly become the busiest in the country precisely because Roach insisted on producing a top-quality product. Moreover, only a small portion of his total business came from government contracts. In recent years, since the publication of Nevins's book in the 1930s, historians, and especially naval historians, have been more sympathetic toward Roach. They have focussed on his many accomplishments and technological innovations, while refuting the charges of corruption leveled against him.

Roach was a successful businessman in an era of unfettered laissez-faire capitalism when Social Darwinism was becoming a popular philosophy. He no doubt had to be ruthless in his business affairs to succeed, as he had to take care to keep in the good graces of politicians sympathetic to businessmen. He had, it was true, turned a profit from government contracts during George Robeson's term as navy secretary. However, his critics could uncover no evidence of wrongdoing in the matter of the Chandler naval contracts. Roach's bids had been the lowest by a wide margin. The total amount he had bid for the four contracts was three quarters of a million dollars less than the estimates given by the Naval Advisory Board of the total probable cost of the four ships. Roach's shipyard was obviously the best-equipped to undertake what everyone knew would be a technological challenge. The entire bidding process had been handled with scrupulous attention to legal requirements and procedures. In sum, Roach did not need surreptitious intervention to gain the contracts. On the contrary, awarding them to anyone else would have required rigging the process against Roach.

Three days after the contracts were awarded, Roach wrote a long private letter to Chandler. Marshalling his meager skills in spelling and grammar, he explained that he had seriously debated whether to bid on the contracts at all, because he wished to avoid embarrassment to Chandler:

I have been discusing in my own mind whether I should have anything to do with the Navy Department while you ware at its head. It has been well-known that you ware my friend. But I so truely say I never wished you to have the position for a personal benefit to me. In your private capacity I know of no one if in trouble I would go sooner than to you. But in your public capasity, I do not want a single favour.

He offered a personal guarantee: "I pledge my selfe to you that every precaution in my power to see that there is no extra bills and that you can proudly say when the work is done that no private Endevidual garded his own interest with more vegilence and care than you have in this instance garded the interest of your department." Nevertheless, the suspicions and accusations, once begun, would not die, and construction of the new navy got off to a sour start.

The problems of Roach and Chandler were compounded by complaints about the ships' designs. The Naval Advisory Board, not Roach, was responsible for design, but doubts about whether the vessels would prove to be useful as warships grew in Congress, and these doubts and the charges of corruption fed one another. Many people in the Navy Department resented the intrusion of an advisory body from outside the department into what was regarded as the navy's business, even if the Advisory Board included senior naval officers. The navy's chief constructor predicted that the two smaller cruisers "will practically be failures" as sea-going ships, while the largest cruiser might prove capable of attaining its highest planned speed, but "there is a very grave question how long she will keep it up, from the fact that, not being sheathed with wood and copper, she will foul very quickly and her speed will be reduced." Doubters said it would prove impossible to produce steel of the strength specified in the contracts for the ships' hulls.

The Advisory Board had decided that the ships should carry two-thirds sail power rather than the full sail power that had always been required for navy ships. Cries of protest came from within the navy. Henry Steers, the civilian naval architect who was a member of the Advisory Board, described typical reactions from naval officers:

A number of naval officers asked me, "why do you not give the ships more sail power?" Said I, "very well, we will give it. But what do you give up for it? Sixty tons! You get rid of sixty tons of coal, and you take that sixty tons of weight and put it on the spars." A naval officer said to me, "Steers, why do you not have a larger sail power?" I told him why. I left him, and another naval officer of equal standing the very next moment said to me, "Steers, why do you put so much sail on these boats? Why do you not cut it down?"

Amid the crossfire of protest, doubt, sniping, bickering, and charges of corruption, construction of the four ships got underway late in 1883. They came to be called the ABCD ships, because even before their construction contracts were awarded, they were given the names *Atlanta, Boston, Chicago,* and *Dolphin. Chicago* was the largest cruiser. It was designed to displace 4,500 tons with a speed of fourteen knots and armament of four eight-inch, eight six-inch, and two five-inch guns. *Atlanta* and *Boston* were each to displace three thousand tons with a speed of thirteen knots and batteries of two eight-inch and six six-inch guns. *Dolphin,* the small dispatch boat, would displace 1,500 tons, be capable of fifteen knots, and carry one six-inch gun. Even as construction was getting underway, many people were already taking it for granted that the ships would be failures.

Construction proceeded slowly, because Roach and his shipyard faced technological challenges never before encountered by American industry. Robley Evans's insistence that the new ships be made of steel had been opposed by some members of the Advisory Board, for good reasons. Until after the Civil War, steel was very expensive to make, so it was used only rarely in manufacturing. In 1850, Britain was the largest producer of iron in the world. Its annual iron production was 2.5 million tons, but the British produced only about sixty thousand tons of steel in a year. The Bessemer process, which significantly reduced the cost of producing steel, was patented by Sir Henry Bessemer in 1857. In the United States, the first Bessemer steel plant opened in 1864. By 1867, only about twenty-two thousand tons of steel were produced in the entire country. As late as 1873, Britain produced more than three times the amount of steel produced in the United States. During the 1860s and 1870s, the Bessemer process was used by American steel producers mostly to manufacture steel for the railroads that were expanding so rapidly all over the country. That kind of steel was inappropriate for ships' hulls. The steel needed for ships required the open-hearth and crucible method of production developed in Britain in the 1860s by two German immigrant brothers named Siemens. In the early 1880s, it was still used only rarely in the United States. In 1883, steel was not yet widely used for manufacturing in the United States, and the idea of constructing a steel-hulled warship was revolutionary.

Building a steel hull was not Roach's only daunting challenge. The guns and armor plating for the ships required even more specialized steel. The navy's first six-inch breech-loaded rifled cannon was not designed until 1878, and a model was first tested at the proving grounds at Annapolis only in 1882. Nobody in the United States had ever produced a rifled breech-loaded naval gun with a bore larger than six inches. Nor had anyone ever manufactured armor plate, and nobody could. Chandler appointed a Gun Foundry Board and sent one of its members to examine naval ordnance production in Britain and France. The eight-inch guns for the three cruisers and the armor plate for their decks had to be obtained in Britain, because they simply could not be produced in the United States. Only after the ABCD ships had been built and placed in commission did American steel companies create the capacity to manufacture large-bore ordnance and armor plate.

Roach oversaw every detail of construction. His extensive experience building metal ships enabled him to detect flaws in the designs, which forced delays in construction, because the Naval Advisory Board that was responsible for design had to be consulted each time a flaw was found. At least fifty changes in the design of the *Dolphin* alone were made by the Board after construction began, twenty-three of which required ripping out completed work. Roach complained that all the changes were slowing the pace of construction to a crawl and adding to his costs—the problems of cost overruns and extended deadlines so familiar to the twentieth-century Pentagon. The slow pace of construction confirmed in doubters' minds the notion that the ships would prove useless.

The Congressional elections of 1882 had given control of the House to the Democrats, while the Republicans narrowly retained control of the Senate. The result was political deadlock on many issues, and few matters before Congress suffered more than Roach's construction contracts. The naval appropriation bill shuttled between the two bodies through the spring of 1884 without agreement being reached. Central to the debate was the question of whether the ABCD ships would prove to be a big mistake and should therefore be scrapped even before they were completed. In July, a temporary measure was passed just before adjournment for the summer to extend for six months authority to pay only expenditures already approved. When Congress reconvened in December, the question still could not be resolved.

Chester Alan Arthur, in declining health, had lost the Republican presidential nomination at the summer party convention to James G. Blaine, who in turn was defeated in the November election by Grover Cleveland. For the first time since before the Civil War, a Democrat would occupy the White House, and he would have the good fortune of support from a Democratic Congress. As they assumed power, the Democrats vowed to clean up the corruption and waste they claimed the Republicans had tolerated and abetted during the quarter-century they had been in power in Washington.

Dolphin, the smallest and most easily constructed of the four ships, had been launched in April, 1884. It failed its first sea trial in November, just after the presidential election. It did not generate the horsepower specified in the contract, and its propeller shaft had broken, all due to faulty design. Members of Congress began calling for John Roach's financial scalp. By December, Roach had spent more than half a million dollars on the four navy ships for which he had not been reimbursed because of the deadlock in Congress over naval appropriations. *Dolphin's* failed sea trial ensured that no money would be forthcoming.

Roach's shipyard faced bankruptcy, and Roach himself was on the verge of a nervous breakdown. He appealed to Chandler for financial relief to stave off bankruptcy, and the secretary was able to arrange partial payment of what was due him from reserve funds. But William Chandler was a lame-duck cabinet officer, and he could do no more for Roach. When he left office in March, none of the four ABCD ships was completed. *Dolphin* was being readied for a second set of sea trials. *Atlanta* had only just been launched, while *Boston* and *Chicago* were still under construction on the ways at Roach's shipyard in Chester.

Dolphin's second sea trials were held ten days after Chandler left office. Roach was delighted with the result. The ship exceeded its anticipated speed of fifteen knots, despite being tested in a near-gale and rough seas. It just missed generating the horsepower specified in the contract, but in view of the speed it attained and the weather conditions then existing, that deficiency seemed minor. "The ship is a grand success," Roach wrote to Chandler, "and all are highly pleased with her." The Naval Advisory Board recommended that the vessel be accepted by the navy. Roach could look forward to payment of what was due him on the contract and would consequently avoid bankruptcy.

The report on the test and the board's recommendation hit the desk of the new secretary of the navy less than one month after he took office. William C. Whitney was a very wealthy lawyer and financier. Much of his wealth had come to him through his marriage. When he married in 1869, the man who became his brother-in-law was Oliver Hazard Payne, one of the owners of the largest oil refinery in Ohio. In 1870, Payne threw in his lot with John D. Rockefeller and merged his company with the recently created Standard Oil Company. He became treasurer of Standard Oil and one of its largest shareholders after Rockefeller himself. His father—William Whitney's father-in-law—was elected a senator from Ohio in the same year that brought Grover Cleveland to the presidency and Whitney to the Navy Department. Senators were then elected by state legislatures, and there were charges that Oliver Hazard Payne had bribed members of the Ohio legislature in order to ensure that there would be a "senator from Standard Oil" in Washington.

Any taint of corruption and bribery that might have been associated with his brother-in-law or father-in-law, however, did not extend to Whitney. His reputation as a lawyer was exemplary. He and his wife nevertheless enjoyed access to Standard Oil's burgeoning millions, and in Washington they set the social standard. They bought a mansion in the capital for their residence, and the dinners, receptions, and balls they hosted outshone those held anywhere else in Washington, including the White House.

Like his Democratic colleagues in the new administration, Whitney regarded himself as a reformer who must root out the corruption and waste engendered by the Republicans during their years of power in Washington. He had replaced as secretary of the navy the slippery politico who for years had been the *bête noire* of the Democratic party. The ABCD ships were the best-known, most controversial, and—who knew?—possibly the most successful product of William Chandler's term of office. Here on Whitney's desk was a report about the first of those ships to undergo tests. The new secretary read it with minute care, and he pounced on the fact that the ship had not generated the required horsepower. He declared that *Dolphin* had failed its test again. He called for new tests, and he appointed his own board to assess the results.

Commodore Schufeldt, the chairman of Chandler's Advisory Board, interpreted the new secretary's rejection of his board's favorable recom-

himself and the other members of his board. He wrote to Chandler: "The Advisory Board seems to have been subjected to criticism which, perhaps, however ill-deserved, might be expected . . . I hope that the time will come to the country when a public man can do his duty without being subjected to the suspicion of being corrupt, but I despair of its advent in my time." Jolted by Whitney's decision, Roach wrote to Chandler:

> The man in Washington is not going to confine himself to the law and the contract, nor to seeking that justice be done by the Government, but is determined to prove the ships a failure and has selected his own men for that purpose. They will go into the smallest details and keep their findings secret so that no explanations are given. I see nothing ahead of me but persecution and injustice which will wear me out and, for aught I know, ruin me.

Chandler advised Roach to calm down. He said he considered Whitney "a fair and courageous, though cautious man" who was not acting out of revenge or a desire to ruin Roach.

The new sea trials were held on Long Island Sound in June. *Dolphin* again made fifteen knots, and this time it exceeded the required horsepower. The chairman of Whitney's board told the secretary the ship had performed satisfactorily, but Whitney rejected his assessment. He dismissed the ship as "a mere pleasure craft." The test, he pointed out, had been conducted in calm, smooth seas. Under those conditions, the ship should have reached seventeen knots or more, he said. "I want to know whether she is structurally weak or not," he told the members of his board. They caught his meaning and submitted a thoroughly unfavorable report, citing many "structural weaknesses."

The adverse report was given wide publicity that stressed that the first of the ships designed and built during the previous administration suffered from structural defects. The Chandler Advisory Board became incensed by the publicity that reflected badly upon it, and it counterattacked. It issued a report that contradicted, point by point, the Whitney board's report. For example, the Whitney board's report charged that one of *Dolphin*'s storerooms was supposed to be lined on all four walls with tin to prevent rats from entering, but only three walls were lined. The Chandler board in rebuttal pointed out that the fourth wall was the steel hull of the ship. But the rebuttal did not receive the publicity given the original report.

Chandler became convinced that Whitney was not acting in good faith, and he fired off a series of letters to the New York *Tribune* that accused Whitney of persecuting John Roach. But Roach was not Whitney's real target, Chandler claimed. His real target was Chandler and his Advisory Board and the previous administration. Vicious partisan politics was at the bottom of the controversy, Chandler charged. Whitney was unmoved by the attack, and in July he obtained a ruling from the attorney-general that the *Dolphin* contract was void because the ship did not meet specifications. By this ruling, all the money paid to Roach for *Dolphin* was recoverable by the government, and the ship could be held as security for repayment. Chandler attacked Whitney's move in another series of letters in the press, but to no avail.

Dolphin became a cause célèbre, the center of a vicious political battle fought in the pages of the daily press. Newspapers took sides according to their political orientation. Partisan Republican papers defended Chandler and Roach as innocent victims of a political vendetta begun by the new administration, while Democratic papers applauded Whitney as a courageous, scrupulously honest reformer.

John Roach was devastated by the turn of events. On July 13, Henry Steers, the civilian naval architect who was a member of Chandler's board, wrote to Chandler: "Mr. Roach is weak mentally, physically and financially. I am afraid that the Attorney-General's report will finish him. His mind is about gone." He was not totally ruined financially, but he was 71 years old and in poor health. Since the late 1870s, he had been diagnosed with cancer of the mouth. For a while, it had appeared to be in remission, but now it grew worse. He was unable to continue. On July 18 he closed down his shipyard, which was placed in the hands of receivers.

Early in 1886, *Dolphin* was subjected to her "last trial trip," a 340-mile journey from Newport to Cape Hatteras in "the worst season of the year." In high winds and rough seas, the little ship made fourteen knots. The weather worsened until a sixty mile-per-hour gale was blowing. The captain kept the ship at full speed in "conditions highly unfavorable to the crew," until the entire vessel was awash. After several hours, the captain agreed to slow down to half-speed. *Harper's Weekly* reported that "her seamen came back with profound respect for her sailing qualities and very little has been said by the Board of Experts about her structural weakness." The captain reported finding several flaws in the ship, but he attributed them to faults of design, not construction.

Though his shipyard was closed, John Roach had the satisfaction of seeing one of his ships vindicated in the public press. However, he never recovered from the financial and professional blows he had suffered from the controversies over the ABCD ships. His health continued to decline, and he died on January 10, 1887. His son, who had worked at his side for years at Chester, was able to gain control of the shipyard two years after his death and reopen it.

The navy finally accepted *Dolphin* in the summer of 1886, in an arrangement that included cancellation of a debt of twenty-five thousand dollars that the government owed John Roach. The government took over construction of the three cruisers after Roach closed down his shipyard. It found that even the largest naval shipyard, at New York, was incapable of completing the ships, and Whitney took control of Roach's shipyard until the ships could be finished by naval constructors. Progress was no more rapid than it had been previously. *Atlanta*, which had been launched while Chandler was still in the Navy Department, was not commissioned until 1886. *Boston* and *Chicago* did not join the fleet until 1889.

Despite the controversies that marred their beginnings, the ABCD ships became famous as the United States' first steel warships and the first ships of the "new navy." *Chicago* was especially admired as possessing trim lines and a noble silhouette. Critics of the ships complained that they were not the equals of the most formidable warships of the European maritime powers, but they had never been designed to stand up to the heavily armored battleships being produced by Britain, France, and Italy. It was true that their engines were of an obsolescent design, but the cruisers were able to make sixteen knots, a speed that only a few warships were able to attain in the 1880s.

They went on to long, honorable careers. Within a few years of being commissioned, they shed their masts and sails. The three cruisers, together with another built later, formed a "White Squadron" which visited Europe in 1891 to show the maritime powers the new American navy. *Boston* was part of Commodore George Dewey's tiny squadron that won a spectacular victory over a Spanish fleet in Manila Bay in 1898. *Dolphin*, the "mere pleasure craft" that could not pass its sea trials, was part of the fleet that destroyed a second Spanish fleet at the battle

Squadron of Evolution

The three ABC cruisers, with the gunboat *Yorktown*, form a "squadron of evolution" in 1889 to show Europeans the new American navy. *Chicago* is in the foreground.

U.S. Naval Historical Center photograph

of Santiago Bay. *Atlanta* and *Chicago* were laid up for scheduled repairs and so could not take part in the brief war with Spain. In 1903, John Davis Long, who served as secretary of the navy during that war, wrote of the three cruisers, "For ships of their date and class, they are today efficient vessels." *Dolphin* was on hand at Hampton Roads in 1907 for the departure of the Great White Fleet.

Atlanta was sold in 1912, the first of the four ships to be taken off the navy's rolls. *Dolphin* remained in commission until 1921, then had a second career in South America until 1927. *Chicago* lasted until 1936, its last years spent as a barracks ship at Pearl Harbor. *Boston* had the longest life of all. It survived until 1946 when it was towed out to sea and sunk after serving at San Francisco as a receiving ship for transient sailors during World War II.

The Naval War of 1812 quickly sold out a first, then a second printing. In 1883, Roosevelt wrote a new preface for a new edition. It was hailed by naval experts and historians in both the United States and Britain as an authoritative work. Within two years of its publication, it had been adopted as a textbook in several colleges. Even today, it is regarded as the definitive work in its field. In 1886, the navy ordered a copy placed aboard every American warship. The name of a young politician from New York, not yet thirty years old, became familiar to the officers of the emerging "new navy." William Sims, who became Roosevelt's naval aide during his presidency and later the admiral commanding American ships in Europe during World War I, wrote of the book years later, "it was listened to by the American people, and it profoundly affected the attitude of the nation toward its navy."

2

"POOR LITTLE POORHOUSE"

In January, 1865, General William Tecumseh Sherman was contemplating a pleasant prospect. His army's devastating march to the sea from Atlanta to Savannah, through the heart of Georgia, had just been completed. At his headquarters in Savannah, he was devising a plan to capture his next prize, one more glittering than either Atlanta or Savannah. Charleston was the premier city of the Confederacy, the "cradle of sedition and rebellion" to ardent Unionists, the city where the first shots of the Civil War had been fired. Sherman's orders were to wheel his army sharply to the left and advance northward up the coast to capture Charleston.

On January 15, Sherman's council of war was joined by a middle-grade naval officer named Stephen B. Luce. Though only thirty-seven years old, Luce had already served in the navy nearly a quarter century, having joined as a midshipman at age fourteen. A thoroughly seasoned sailor who had learned his profession during years of cruising in the old sailing navy, he was the author of a book, *Seamanship*, that was considered the standard text in its field.

In 1865, Luce was a lieutenant-commander in command of a gunboat, *Pontiac*, that was part of the Union naval force blockading Charleston. He was ordered to report to Sherman in Savannah, because Sherman needed a gunboat for his plan to capture Charleston. *Pontiac*, Sherman told Luce, was to steam forty miles inland up the Savannah River, to cover the river crossing by the left wing of Sherman's army as it advanced into South Carolina to encircle Charleston. "You navy fellows have been hammering away at Charleston for the past three years," Sherman told Luce. "But just wait until I get into South Carolina. I will cut her communications, and Charleston will fall into your hands like a ripe pear."

Years later, Luce recalled the meeting. "After hearing General Sherman's clear exposition of the military situation, the scales seemed to have fallen from my eyes. 'Here,' I said to myself, 'is a soldier who knows his business!' It dawned on me that there were certain fundamental principles underlying military operations which it were well to look into; principles of general application whether the operations were conducted on land or at sea."

Luce took *Pontiac* up the Savannah River on his assigned mission, and he watched the execution of Sherman's plan with fascination. Everything worked as Sherman had predicted. The city was surrounded and cut off. On February 17, it was evacuated by the meager Confederate forces still capable of organized resistance, and it was occupied by units of Sherman's army. Soon after, Luce walked the empty streets of the captured, deserted city. "Charleston fell into our hands just as General Sherman said it would, severing her communications," he later wrote. "There was, then I learned, such a thing as a military problem, and there was a way of solving it; or what was equally important, a way of determining whether or not it was susceptible of solution." In February, 1865, the Confederacy was entering its final death throes, and Sherman's capture of Charleston may have been less a product of brilliant strategy than the inevitable outcome of a victorious army moving against an already defeated enemy. Moreover, Luce recalled his meeting with Sherman nearly forty years later in a lecture. His recollection of it as being such an epiphany for him at the time may have been affected by events later in his life. Nevertheless, it is true that after the war, Luce became an enthusiastic and dogged proponent of what he called "postgraduate study" by naval officers in "the science and art of war."

When the war ended, Luce continued his naval career. He was described as "a lean, wiry man of medium height, with thin features between iron gray sidewhiskers, a prominent hawk-like nose, thin lips and determined chin, and piercing gray eyes." He was promoted to commander in 1866 and served as commandant of midshipmen at the Naval Academy under Admiral David Dixon Porter. For the next fifteen years—the dreary years of the navy's decline—he received the usual mixture of assignments ashore and afloat, the latter in increasingly decrepit ships. He lobbied tirelessly for better training for officers and in particular for the creation of a school for "post-graduate study."

He faced an uphill fight. Most of his fellow officers scoffed at the idea that experienced, seasoned naval officers should go back to school for formal study of their profession. Congress and the civilian leadership of the navy were indifferent. In 1877, when he was in command of *Hartford*, which had been David Farragut's flagship during the Civil War, Luce wrote a long letter to the secretary of the navy. He proposed that the navy create a school to offer naval officers "a post-graduate course consisting of the higher branches of their profession." His timing could not have been worse. The secretary of the navy to whom his letter was addressed was the Honorable Richard W. Thompson—the secretary who had discovered with surprise that ships were hollow. Luce's proposal was simply ignored.

By the early 1880s, Luce held the rank of commodore in command of the Training Squadron based in Rhode Island. He was in his middle fifties, with forty years of naval service behind him. Obviously, retirement was not far off. His campaign to establish a professional school for naval officers had fallen flat. Those among his fellow officers with any interest in professional study were struggling to keep abreast of the technological changes that were being thrust upon them in dizzying profusion. Few had the time or inclination to look into Luce's "science and art of war" or the possible implications these innovations might have for naval tactics and strategy.

The pages of the only professional journal published for naval officers reflected this preoccupation with technical subjects. The creation in 1873 of the United States Naval Institute was one of the few bright spots for the navy during the dismal post–Civil War years, but it was not the work of the navy. An organization independent of government, the institute was established by a group of naval officers and interested civilians to investigate and disseminate information of professional interest to naval officers. Luce was involved in its creation. Its founders decided it should publish a professional journal, which they first called its *Record* and, later, its *Proceedings*.

Even the Naval Institute's journal ignored Luce's crusade. For the first ten years of its publication, the institute's *Proceedings* carried scarcely an article that related to Luce's "science and art of war." Its pages were filled with abstruse, densely technical discussions of such subjects as steam propulsion plants, muzzle velocities of large-bore artillery, and the strength and resilience of armor plating. Naval officers had their hands full struggling to master the increasing complexity of the tools of their profession, and they had no time left to consider how those tools ought to be used.

At the battle of Trafalgar in 1805, the flagship of Admiral Lord Horatio Nelson was *Victory*, a 100-gun first-rate ship of the line. *Victory*'s keel had been laid in 1759, and the ship joined the fleet in 1765. Standing on its quarterdeck in 1805, Nelson won one of the most spectacular and significant victories in naval history. In the 1880s, any government that sent out its admiral in a forty-year-old warship to do battle in a major fleet engagement would have been courting disaster. Any warship that old would have been destroyed in minutes by any recently built ship, even a much smaller one. A revolution in warship design and construction had been underway for several decades, and by the 1880s it was accelerating.

Although the controversies that dogged the construction of the ABCD ships were prompted to a large degree by petty political and bureaucratic jealousies, they were also the product of this revolution. How warships should be designed and built involved questions that produced honest differences between men of good will. The members of William Chandler's Naval Advisory Board could look around the world and behold a bewildering variety of warships built during the previous ten years. Design and construction of warships—their size, shape, armament, and range—were in such a state of flux and uncertainty that no one could be certain whether the latest theories about naval architecture would produce a ship that would revolutionize naval warfare and render all other ships obsolete, or one that would be an expensive and embarrassing failure. The revolution that was underway was caused by five technological innovations introduced during the nineteenth century: steam propulsion, the screw propeller, explosive shells, rifled cannon, and armor plating. Each of these inventions had affected development of the others. Together, they created a ferment in the world's navies that was bubbling fiercely in 1883.

The steam engine was successfully combined with waterborne craft as early as the first decade of the century. Only two years after the battle of Trafalgar, Robert Fulton's *Clermont* demonstrated the practicality of the steamboat. Although an eye-witness described *Clermont* as "looking precisely like a backwoods sawmill mounted on a scow and set on fire," its maiden voyage was a sustained achievement superior to the initial effort by the first steam locomotive or the Wright brothers' first airplane. Gulping cords of firewood, it chugged up the Hudson River from New York City to Albany and back in sixty-two hours, making an average speed of five miles per hour. With only a few improvements, it was put into regular service between the two cities. Within a few years steam engines were powering ocean-going ships. In 1819, an American steamship, *Savannah,* made a voyage from the United States to Russia. In 1827, the first all-steam crossing of the Atlantic was accomplished by a British ship.

It was inevitable that steam engines would be placed on warships. The first was *Demologos,* an American ship designed by Robert Fulton and built in 1814 for the war with Britain. An obvious problem of early ocean-going steamships, immediately recognized by Fulton and others, was the vulnerability and fragility of their wooden paddle wheels. They worked fine on the calm, protected waters of inland waterways, but the big paddle wheels were easily damaged or even totally destroyed in a storm at sea. The problem was compounded for a warship. Paddle wheels mounted on the sides of the hull were almost certain to be the first part of a ship damaged by enemy fire. Fulton tried to solve the problem in his design for *Demologos* by giving the ship twin catamaran-like hulls and mounting the paddle wheel inboard between the hulls. The ship proved impossible to steer, and the experiment was a failure. *Demologos* never took part in a battle.

The solution to the paddle wheel problem turned out to be an invention dating from ancient times. Archimedes, the Greek mathematician and inventor, experimented with the screw propeller in the third century B.C., but it needed a source of power stronger than human muscles to work. It fell to a Swedish immigrant to the United States, John Ericsson, to combine Archimedes's idea with the steam engine to provide power for large ocean-going ships. In 1843, the U.S.S. *Princeton,* a ten-gun sloop designed by Ericsson, was launched as the first propeller-driven steam warship.

For several decades thereafter, steam power was regarded as only an auxiliary to sails, to be used for leaving and entering harbor, perhaps for getting out of an area of calm at sea, and for maneuvering during battle. For ordinary cruising, navies still relied on the wind. Nineteen years after designing *Princeton,* Ericsson produced a more famous warship of revolutionary design, *Monitor*, which took part in the first battle between ironclads during the Civil War.

Princeton was a naval innovation, but it was made of wood, which left it vulnerable to another naval innovation of the nineteenth century. Exploding shells had been thrown from mortars in the eighteenth century, but smoothbore naval cannon relied on solid iron shot to demolish wooden hulls. In 1819, a French army major, Henri-Joseph Paixhans, developed the first large explosive shell designed to be fired from a cannon. In 1824, Paixhans's experimental shells were tested with devastating effect against a moored frigate. But the seaman's fear of fire at sea—probably the greatest fear of the sailor in a wooden sailing vessel—made navies reluctant to carry explosive shells aboard ship along with the gunpowder they already carried. It was not until 1853, during the Crimean War, that the vulnerability of wooden ships to explosive shells was demonstrated with dramatic effect in battle. A Turkish squadron in the Black Sea was set afire and totally destroyed by a Russian fleet using explosive shells.

The threat of explosive shells to wooden ships was increased by the development of rifled artillery at about the same time Paixhans was inventing his shell. In the eighteenth century, American farmers armed with Kentucky long rifles (which were actually manufactured in Pennsylvania) had demonstrated the superiority of rifles in range and accuracy over the smoothbore muskets used by British troops in the American Revolution. But adapting the rifling principle to large-bore artillery posed problems. Forcing an iron cannon ball down the barrel of a cannon was much harder than ramming a small, soft lead bullet down the barrel of a rifle.

The solution was artillery loaded from the breech. French and Italian inventors worked on the problem in the 1840s. The French perfected an "interrupted screw" device that had originally been an American invention. By the time of the Crimean War in the 1850s, breech-loaded rifled artillery was used with effect on the battlefield, and it was being adapted for use aboard ship. A ship armed with rifled cannon could remain outside the range of a ship armed only with smoothbore artillery and destroy its enemy at its leisure.

Traditional black powder, used for centuries, proved to be dangerous when used in the new, ever larger, ever more powerful rifled artillery pieces. It burned too fast. The huge quantities of powder needed in

large-bore rifled cannon to throw large shells long distances instantly
built up gasses to a pressure that would burst the breech of the strongest
cannon anyone could forge. Foundries experimented with various tech-
niques to strengthen the breech of an artillery piece. In the early 1840s,
President John Tyler and a large party of officials went for a cruise down
the Potomac River from Washington to witness the firing of a huge new
naval cannon mounted on the bow of John Ericsson's ship *Princeton*. Its
inventor boasted that it would render all existing artillery obsolete. The
gun, loaded with black powder, exploded, killing several high-ranking
officials, including the secretary of the navy. The president escaped injury only because he happened to be below deck at the time of the explosion. The answer to the problem was slower-burning powder, which
was developed in Germany a few years later.

By the late 1840s, something obviously had to be done to protect
combustible wooden ships from the lethal armament being developed.
The answer was armor plating. An American inventor, Robert L. Stevens, designed a floating battery in the early 1850s intended to protect
American harbors from enemy fleets. The "Stevens Iron Battery"
would have a steel hull, iron plating, and heavy artillery protected by
side armor, and it would be propelled by a steam engine and a screw
propeller. Stevens even included tanks attached to the side of the battery
which could be flooded during battle to lower the battery in the water,
thereby using the water itself as protection. It was another revolutionary
idea in a period crowded with revolutionary ideas, but Stevens's battery
was never built. Similar batteries were built by the British and French
and used during the Crimean War to reduce Russian coastal batteries
on the Black Sea, but they were not really ships.

The first seagoing ironclad warship was the French *Gloire*, built in
1859. *Gloire* had a traditional wooden hull protected by iron plates. Two
years later, the British built *Warrior*, the first iron-hulled warship. In the
spring of 1862, the practicality of armor plating was tested in a Civil
War battle at Hampton Roads between two hastily built ironclads, *Monitor* and *Virginia* (which was originally named *Merrimac* before the Confederacy converted it to an ironclad and renamed it). They fought to
a draw, because both ships' iron plating was too strong for their
smoothbore artillery to penetrate. After bouncing shots off each other
for several hours, both withdrew from the battle. European naval experts studied the battle with intense interest. Within a matter of weeks,

the British admiralty ordered a 131-gun first-rate to be cut down, armor plated, and fitted with turrets, like *Monitor.* Less than a month later, Britain laid down the keel of *Prince Albert,* the first iron-clad armored turret warship. The pace of the naval revolution, a seesaw race between armament—offense—and armor—defense—was accelerating.

By the late 1860s, naval architects in Europe were experimenting with a variety of radical warship designs that incorporated all the new inventions. They were forced to make tradeoffs among range, speed, armament, and armor. The cruising radius of a sailing ship was limited only by the crew's endurance and the provisions it could carry. During the Napoleonic Wars, the Royal Navy ships blockading Napoleon's Europe stayed at sea for months at a stretch. The range of a steamship was determined by the amount of coal it could carry and the rate at which its engines consumed the fuel. But fuel consumption was also a factor that determined the ship's speed, a crucial matter for a warship. A fast, fuel-gulping ocean greyhound would have a much smaller cruising range than a slower ship powered by smaller engines that consumed less fuel, but it would have the advantage over the slower ship in battle. Large-caliber guns, their ammunition, and heavy armor plating had to be carried. Their weight affected a ship's speed and range and had to be taken into account when designing the ship's propulsion plant. A floating fortress, protected by thick armor and bristling with heavy cannon, might be invulnerable, but it was bound to be slow, and its range of operation very restricted, compared to a more lightly armed and armored ship.

The lumbering floating fortress would be useless for attacking an enemy's navy or commercial shipping halfway around the world. That required fast cruisers with extended range, but how fast must they be? During the Civil War, the navy built *Wampanoag,* a cruiser designed to be a commerce raider able to catch the fastest merchant ship. *Wampanoag* was huge and fast, but it possessed a narrow hull almost filled by its immense engines. It attained a speed in excess of seventeen knots, which was unheard of in a warship in the early 1860s. It was the fastest ship in the world, and twenty years passed before anyone built another warship that could equal its speed. But it was not completed until 1868—too late to be of use in the war. Moreover, naval experts, while admiring its greyhound lines and speed, complained that it gulped fuel at such a rate as to make it impractical as a warship. Its engines took up so much space in its narrow hull that there was little room for anything else, including the fuel to operate them. The navy abandoned the ship as an innovative, instructive, admirable, but ultimately unsuccessful experiment in warship design.

The placement of armament, a warship's raison d'être, prompted naval architects to the most radical experimentation, and exotic designs blossomed in the 1870s. Steam propulsion had caused the basic shape of a ship to change. For centuries, the bows and sterns of sailing ships towered high above their low midsections. On steamships, the high forecastles and poops disappeared. The midship section, low on a sailing ship, housed the propulsion plant in a steam ship and sprouted a high citadel.

On steam-driven warships with the new configuration, designers experimented with "casemate" ships, like the Confederate *Virginia*, with the high central citadel forming a fort with the guns protruding through gunports. Other designers followed the example of *Monitor* and mounted the guns in turrets. Sometimes they were sited along a ship's centerline fore and aft of the citadel, sometimes diagonally and extending over the ship's side on sponsons to provide a wider field of fire. The turret offered the obvious advantage of providing a wide, sweeping field of fire, but its critics argued that it could easily be jammed by enemy fire and put out of action. They devised the "barbette," a circular armored breastwork surrounding a gun that, unlike a turret, was open above. The gun could be swivelled around to sweep through large arcs of fire as in a turret, but the barbette could not be jammed like a turret. Every few years, warships sporting new, striking, and exotic shapes emerged from naval shipyards. The range of naval ordnance increased at a prodigious rate.

The last decades of the nineteenth century were the years of the Pax Britannica, when Britain ruled the oceans of the world. The only wars being fought were "little" colonial wars against primitively armed tribesmen in Africa and Asia. The Royal Navy saw to it that the oceans of the world were peaceful avenues of commerce, not arenas of battle. The decades of peace were a boon to most people, but not to naval architects. There were no actual wartime conditions under which to test all the new designs and technology being introduced in the world's navies. No one could be absolutely sure which ideas about warship design worked and which did not. It was obvious that naval tactics would have to change radically. What worked with sailing fleets armed with smoothbore cannon firing solid iron shot would not work with steam-powered, armored battleships armed with long-range ordnance firing explosive shells.

Some theorists speculated that future naval battles would be decided not by guns but by two other weapons. One, the torpedo, did indeed prove to be a revolutionary weapon. A British inventor, Robert Whitehead, built the first torpedo in the 1860s. Whitehead's "automobile torpedo" was powered by compressed air, carried a large explosive charge, and ran underwater. It almost immediately raised fears and prompted efforts to defend against it. The most heavily armored battleship could not withstand the tremendous blast, intensified by the pressure of the water itself, inflicted by a torpedo below the waterline. The torpedo boat—small, fast, maneuverable, and therefore difficult to hit—was developed to carry the new weapon. Theorists visualized swarms of fast, cheap, little torpedo boats swiftly slipping under the gunfire of a fleet of heavily armored, very expensive battleships and sinking them. Much thought was given to defense against the torpedo and the torpedo boat.

One new defense was a new kind of ship, the torpedo boat destroyer. It was slightly larger than the torpedo boat and armed with both torpedoes and guns. Another defense for capital ships, at least while they lay at anchor and were most vulnerable to attack, was the torpedo net. It was a thick steel mesh swung out from the ship on long booms and lowered into the water so that the net completely encircled the ship. A torpedo net for a large ship weighed tons. The idea was that a torpedo fired from a torpedo boat executing a swift, surprise attack on an anchored warship would strike the net and explode before it could reach the ship. As warships shed their masts and sails, many ships' captains and admirals welcomed the advent of the torpedo net. Swinging out the booms and rigging the net replaced sail handling as exercise for the crew and a test of teamwork and seamanship. Captains vied with each other to see which ship's company could rig its torpedo net in the fastest and smartest manner.

The other weapon considered possibly decisive, the ram, dated from ancient Greek and Roman galleys. It was like some exotically shaped animal of eons past that had somehow survived to modern times long after it should have become extinct. It became a staple in naval tactical thinking in the late nineteenth century through a fluke. The battle of Lissa was fought in 1866 in the Adriatic Sea between Austrian and Italian fleets. It was one of the few fleet actions to occur in the last decades of the nineteenth century. The battle was a confused melee in which Austrian ships managed to ram several Italian ships and sink them. The Austrians thereby won the battle, despite having a smaller fleet than the Italians. In the confusion of proliferating warship designs and the absence of actual battle experience to test them, naval theorists and architects eagerly studied the battle to extract its lessons. They seized on the ram as the decisive weapon. For several decades thereafter until into the twentieth century, the bows of large warships were fitted with rams, giving the ships of the 1890s and early 1900s their distinctive look, with bows that sloped forward rather than backward, in a rake. Navies even built ships designed for the principal purpose of ramming.

By the 1880s a basic warship design was beginning to emerge, recognizable as the battleship and cruiser that would become the two most widely adopted warships for the next sixty years. The ship was armored and steam-driven, with a central citadel, or perhaps two, from which towered several tall funnels that spouted billowing clouds of black smoke when the ship steamed at top speed. The guns of the main battery were mounted in turrets sited fore and aft of the central citadel. Battleships were heavily armored and carried the largest guns. Their cruising range was limited, because they were intended to remain mostly in home waters as the backbone of the fleet, defending the country from attack. Cruisers, less heavily armored and gunned, were faster than battleships and able to range much farther from home. They would be the eyes of the fleet. In wartime, they would serve as commerce raiders, and in peacetime they would range the world, "showing the flag" in distant ports and protecting their country's commercial fleet from pirates.

The admirals were reluctant to abandon sail altogether, especially in cruisers, because it provided an increase in cruising range. But masts and rigging interfered with the field of fire of a ship's main battery housed in the turrets, and even the most reactionary admiral had to admit that the day of the sailing navy had passed. In 1873, Britain put the first all-steam warship, H.M.S. *Devastation,* into commission. Displacing over nine thousand tons and boasting four twelve-inch guns in two turrets as a main battery, *Devastation* might be considered the first battleship, or at least the earliest direct predecessor of the familiar twentieth-century battleship.

In the 1880s, a naval officer with forty years of service, like Stephen Luce, had witnessed changes in the tools of his profession every bit as sweeping as those that have occurred in the twentieth century. The capital ship of 1881 simply bore no resemblance at all to the capital ship of the navy Luce had joined in 1841. Luce's fellow officers struggled to understand and adapt to these changes, or in many cases, to ignore or resist them. Luce was consumed by a different vision. Ever since his encounter with General Sherman, he had become convinced that there are basic, immutable principles of war, unaffected by time or changes in technology. The new technology demanded new tactics, and Luce agreed that the technology and the tactics it demanded must be studied. But he firmly believed that the military or naval commander who also understood and applied those eternal, basic strategic concepts would triumph. Such commanders would understand the interrelationship of war on land and at sea. Luce's self-assigned mission was to create an institution where naval officers, and others, could gather together to discover those principles and teach them to the next generation of officers.

In William Chandler, Luce finally found a secretary of the navy willing to listen to his ideas. When Chandler decided to look into the scandal of superfluous, useless naval shipyards, he assembled a board to investigate and appointed Luce its president. Luce's board recommended closing the yards at New London, Connecticut, and Pensacola, Florida. They were closed over congressional objections. Luce's work apparently pleased Chandler, and the secretary was ready to listen when Luce enlisted two influential allies on his behalf.

Admiral David Dixon Porter had already served as the senior naval officer in the service, the Admiral of the Navy, for more than a decade. He was appointed by Ulysses S. Grant, with whom he had served in the Civil War. Porter commanded the riverine forces that supported Grant's campaigns in Kentucky and Tennessee. When Grant became president, he would have appointed Porter secretary of the navy, but he could not, because Porter was still an officer on active duty. He gave Porter the senior officer position from which he effectively ran the navy. One naval historian has described Porter as "a loose cannon" who was "sometimes intemperate in thought and language." He was outspoken, dogmatic, and often reactionary in his views, as in his resistance to steam propulsion. However, Porter was forward-looking enough to embrace Luce's proposal for a professional school for naval officers. He promised Luce he would bring the matter up with Chandler, although he claimed that he was being ignored in the navy department under Chandler and could not even guarantee that he would be able to get an appointment to speak with the secretary.

Luce's other ally, who was probably more influential with Chandler, was Nelson Aldrich, a Republican senator from Rhode Island. Luce wanted to locate his school—if it was ever established—in Rhode Island on the shores of Narragansett Bay. During the Civil War, the Naval Academy was temporarily relocated from Annapolis to Newport, and Luce served a brief tour of duty there during the war. In the 1880s, the Training Squadron he commanded was based at Newport. He decided Newport would be a better location for his school than Annapolis, the other logical location, because the climate was more bracing and healthful, and the sheltered but expansive waters of Narragansett Bay offered an excellent setting for all kinds of naval instruction and research.

Nelson Aldrich was in his second term representing Rhode Island in the Senate. A phlegmatic, somewhat inscrutable politician, he was nevertheless influential in the inner circles of the Republican party. He was bound to have the ear of a political operator like Chandler, and like any other politician, he was in favor of locating a planned military installation in his state if that was where the navy wanted it. He was a natural political ally of Luce, who wrote to him, "The interests of the Navy and the people of Newport running in the same direction, we can pull together to our mutual advantage."

Newport had become the summer playground of such New York millionaires as the Vanderbilts and the Astors, and some of Luce's fellow officers thought it would be a poor choice for a naval training school. The nonstop social activities of the millionaires would be an irresistible distraction. The officer-students, they feared, would spend their time disporting on the beaches and in the millionaires' "summer cottages" with the belles of Newport, rather than studying the immutable strategic principles of war. But Luce argued that few naval officers could afford to move in the same social circles as the Vanderbilts, so it was unlikely they would receive invitations to balls and dinner parties in the Newport mansions.

In April, 1883, Luce delivered a lecture entitled "War Colleges" at the Naval Institute in Annapolis. He reviewed various professional schools established by armies in Europe and the U.S. Army and outlined his proposal for a school for naval officers. The text was published in the Naval Institute *Proceedings,* and in August, Luce sent a copy to Senator Aldrich. A few months later, in early 1884, Admiral Porter was able to arrange a meeting with Chandler where Luce could present his ideas in person. The meeting lasted several hours. Luce marshalled all his arguments in favor of a Naval War College and named Newport as the best location for the school. He asked for a staff of five officers to constitute its "academic board." He described his proposed institution as a "school of application" where new tactical ideas could be tested. He displayed his familiarity with the latest thinking in naval tactics when he asked that "there be attached to the school a steam sloop of the most modern design fully equipped for torpedo service" and "as soon as practicable, a torpedo boat of high speed as well several steam cutters equipped for ramming." In other words, the school would be a practical asset for the navy.

Chandler was convinced by Luce's presentation. "Warfare has now become so much a matter of science and precision," he said, "that it would be utter folly not to set all the younger officers to studying modern developments." He appointed a board, chaired by Luce, to consider the question of establishing "post-graduate courses or schools in the Navy." The board convened aboard Luce's flagship at Newport in May, and submitted a long, detailed report on June 13. It of course recommended establishment of a Naval War College "where our officers will not only be encouraged but required to study their proper profession: war." More specifically, the report explained, "naval expeditions which have ended in disaster that could have been foretold through an intelligent study of the problem, and the great naval battles, which illustrate and enforce many of the most immutable principles of war, should be carefully examined and rendered familiar to the naval student." On October 6, Chandler issued a General Order creating the college and appointing Luce its first president.

The War College would be housed in a rambling stone building in a state of disrepair on Coaster's Harbor Island in Narragansett Bay, off

Newport. It had once been Newport's poorhouse. Luce had had his eye on it as the home for his war college for several years. He had arranged for the city of Newport to deed it over to the state of Rhode Island. With help from Senator Aldrich, he persuaded the state to transfer it to the federal government for use by the navy. Admiral Porter inspected the building when the navy assumed charge of it in 1882. He said he found it "so foul from occupation by paupers that it is unfit for human habitation." By 1884, it had been cleaned up sufficiently to serve as the headquarters of the commandant of the Training System. By Chandler's order, it was transferred to the new War College. By October 1884, when Chandler issued his order to create the War College, Luce held the brevet rank of rear admiral and commanded the Atlantic Fleet. Toward the end of the month, he was ordered detached to take over the War College. Most of his colleagues probably considered him crazy. At his request, he was moving from one of the most senior, most coveted commands in the navy to take charge of an institution staffed by five officers in a run-down building. At the end of October, he took formal departure from his flagship as it lay in Narragansett Bay off Coaster's Harbor Island. He was rowed over to the island accompanied by a small group of officers. When they departed to return to their ship, the darkness of a gray New England October evening was descending. In the twilight, Luce stood with his messboy on the steps of the bleak, empty building he had chosen for his beloved college. He placed his hand on the door jamb and announced, "poor little poorhouse, I christen thee United States Naval War College."

The new college's first class did not convene until nearly a year later, in September, 1885. Luce had recommended that the class contain fifty officers holding the rank of commander or higher. It turned out to be comprised of eight officers, all lieutenants. Most of them were from the Torpedo Station on nearby Goat Island and "considered they had been shanghaied." Their course lasted only one month. The college's main—perhaps its only—teaching aid was a plan of the battle of Trafalgar that hung on a wall in the lecture room. A newspaper reporter sent to interview Luce and write about the navy's new school looked around the lecture room and remarked to the new president, "Ah, I see you are still talking about Trafalgar."

Luce remained in charge of the Naval War College less than two years. In September, 1886, he resumed command of the Atlantic Fleet.

He retired three years later. But he continued to remain in close touch with his creation until the end of his life, badgering and cajoling support from a mostly reluctant navy. He died in 1917 at the age of ninety. A much younger and more junior officer who had come to admire Luce offered this epitaph when he died: "He taught the navy to think."

Perhaps he did, but the navy was slow to absorb his teachings, and the Naval War College has never really fulfilled Luce's hopes and dreams of creating an institution to serve as the navy's intellectual center. Certainly, in 1885, the navy needed intellectual stimulation. Many in the officer corps derided the very idea of a War College. One senior admiral, when he heard about Chandler's order to create the War College, snorted, "*Teach* the art of war! Well, I'll be damned!"

Published accounts of the War College's creation and early history have usually portrayed its critics as anti-intellectual know-nothings. But they also included thoughtful people in no way opposed to "postgraduate education" for naval officers. One such was Francis M. Ramsay who in the early 1890s was appointed chief of the Bureau of Navigation, one of the most powerful and senior posts in the service. He had been a foe of Luce and the War College practically since its inception, and he was not above using petty bureaucratic maneuvering to shut the War College down. He may have been mean-minded and vindictive in his actions, but he was not a know-nothing. In 1893, when the position of president of the War College was vacant and the institution's future appeared to hang in the balance, Ramsay explained some of the reasons for his opposition in a letter to the officer being considered for the post of president:

> I am strongly in favor of the higher education of officers and am ready to assist in it in every way in my power, but I do think the present War College System has very much the appearance of a farce. I find that the last series of lectures were not only unfavorably criticized but very much laughed at. . . . Some of the officers who heard the lectures had [already] read everything that they heard at the College. We have the means of furnishing officers with excellent post graduate courses and we can do it in a much better manner than has been done at the War College.

The college's most fruitful and influential years were probably just before and after World War I when it developed "Plan Orange," the strategy to fight a war with Japan. "Orange" undoubtedly affected the thinking of all the senior American naval officers of World War II.

The Naval War College was conceived, like a university, to serve a dual purpose: It was to be both a research center and a school. Perhaps because of its location at Newport, it has never become closely involved in the navy's inner councils as a source of important planning or research. It might have fared better if Luce had consented to place it at Annapolis or, even better, in Washington, close to the navy's centers of power. As a research institution, the War College has always been behind the times. In Luce's era, it accepted uncritically the conventional idea that the ram was an important naval weapon. The range of naval ordnance was increasing so prodigiously that it should have been obvious that future battles would be fought with the ships so widely separated that there would be little opportunity for ramming.

In the twentieth century, the War College as an institution was slow to grasp the coming importance of the aircraft carrier. During the years between the world wars, the War College was mostly engaged in endlessly refighting the battle of Jutland, the inconclusive clash of battleships in World War I. As late as 1940, the War College maintained that "naval aviation should be based ashore because at an air station it is far less vulnerable than aboard ship." The submarine was mostly ignored as an offensive weapon during the interwar years. War games held at the War College during this period used submarines mostly as scouts or screens for battleships. Right up to the outbreak of World War II, the War College as an institution considered the battleship the backbone of the fleet. The navy quite properly continued to build battleships during the interwar years, because the aircraft carrier had yet to prove itself. As a research institution, however, the War College should have paid more attention to the obvious potential of the carrier.

As a school, the War College has never been a magnet for naval officers. It has never been able to strike a satisfactory balance between the minutiae of contemporary naval technology, the preoccupation of most junior and middle-grade officers, and the broad intellectual and historical search for the "immutable principles of war" envisioned by Luce. Most middle-grade officers, eager to ascend the ladder of promotion, regard the latter as a waste of professional time and effort, because they know the navy as an institution considers it so. The navy is proud of an officer with a Ph.D. from a famous university. It cherishes the badges of intellectual achievement rather than the achievement itself.

Most naval officers consider a year at the War College as, at best, a welcome year of shore duty to spend with their families or, at worst, a waste of time. A year at the War College has long been considered mainly a matter of "ticket-punching," an assignment an officer must have in his service record if he is to attain flag rank. Admiral Hyman Rickover, the "father of the nuclear navy" and one of the service's leading intellectuals, considered a year at the War College profitless. The officers of Rickover's nuclear submarine force were long noticeable by their absence from the ranks of War College students. The presidency of the War College has long been a sinecure reserved as the last comfortable assignment for an admiral before retirement, rather than a post eagerly sought by a highly regarded younger officer moving toward the top of his profession.

The failure of the War College to fulfill Stephen Luce's vision is not proof that his vision was flawed. The navy has turned to civilian "think tanks" like the Rand Corporation for the studies and theory that Luce wanted his War College to provide. Perhaps the navy will some day produce another Stephen Luce who will succeed in molding the War College to fill the intellectual lacuna Luce saw and tried hard but unsuccessfully to fill for the navy.

The War College's first years were especially difficult, and it probably would not have survived at all except for the presence of the man who succeeded Luce as president. Like Luce, he believed passionately in the mission of the Naval War College. Less than four years after taking over from Luce, his lectures at the college were brought together and published as a book which instantly became the most influential book on naval warfare ever published. He was honored and feted on both sides of the Atlantic, and his writings profoundly affected the thinking not only of naval strategists but of politicians and statesmen as well. The association of the War College with his name probably saved the college from extinction and even gave it a measure of fame. It is probably also true that if Stephen Luce had not brought him to the War College, he would today be forgotten, because his book would never have been published. He became a friend of Theodore Roosevelt and exerted a significant influence on Roosevelt's ideas, not only about the navy but about the role of the United States in world affairs. His name was Alfred Thayer Mahan.

3

"A Very Good Book"

Theodore Roosevelt spent the weekend of May 10 and 11, 1890, reading straight through from cover to cover a thick book of naval history
that had just been published. It was Alfred Thayer Mahan's *The Influence
of Sea Power upon History, 1660–1783*. Roosevelt today would be called a
speed-reader, devouring as he did enormous quantities of printed matter. Every morning, he raced through several daily newspapers, flinging each page aside onto the floor as he finished it. When he rose from
the table, he was surrounded by a pile of crumpled newsprint. Books
he sometimes zipped through at a single sitting. He was known to go
through three books in a single evening and be ready to discuss their
contents.

He read Mahan's book with his usual speed and total absorption. By
virtue of *The Naval War of 1812*, Theodore Roosevelt in 1890 was a well-
known, respected naval historian, while Alfred Mahan was an unknown
naval captain in the twilight of a solid though undistinguished career.
Roosevelt's book was being used as a text at the Naval War College,
which Mahan headed as president. Mahan was the author of one book
about naval operations during the Civil War, published the year after
Roosevelt's book appeared, that was workmanlike but unremarkable
and little-known.

In 1890, Roosevelt was serving as a member of the federal Civil Service Commission in Washington, having been appointed in 1889 by
President Benjamin Harrison. He had spent the 1880s after graduation
from Harvard pursuing his political career when he was not operating
his cattle ranch and hunting in the Dakota Territory. A terrible blizzard
in the winter of 1886–87 had almost totally destroyed his cattle herd
and nearly wiped him out financially. His beloved wife, Alice, had died
giving birth to a daughter, and Roosevelt had remarried. His second
wife was a childhood sweetheart he had known for years named Edith

Alfred Thayer Mahan

Library of Congress photograph

Carow, and they had begun to produce the large family that Roosevelt so cherished for the rest of his life. He had built the sprawling house at Oyster Bay on Long Island that he called Sagamore Hill, although in 1890 he was living in Washington and able to spend time there only during the hot summer months, when everyone who was able to do so abandoned muggy Washington.

At age thirty-two, Roosevelt was not yet old enough to serve as president of the United States, but a growing number of people were speculating that he just might one day attain that exalted office. He was regarded as a rising figure with a bright future in the Republican party. As a civil service commissioner, he played no role in the continuing debates about reconstruction of the navy or international affairs. But as a rising young politician who was attracting growing attention nationally, he kept abreast of developments in both fields. He had become a close friend of another rising young politician, Henry Cabot Lodge, who in 1890 was serving as a member of the House of Representatives from

Boston. Like Roosevelt, he was a Republican and shared many of Roosevelt's views. Both men were impressed by Mahan's new book.

Roosevelt had met Alfred Mahan at least once, in 1888, when he delivered a lecture at the Naval War College. Mahan by then had replaced Stephen Luce as president, but the invitation was issued by Luce who had become acquainted with Roosevelt when they served together on the New York Board of Education. In a letter to Roosevelt on February 13, 1888, Luce referred to "your admirable work," *The Naval War of 1812,* and told Roosevelt, "There is no question in my mind that your work must be accepted as the very highest authority on the subject." The book "must be our text" for the study of the War of 1812 at the new Naval War College, he wrote. He assured Roosevelt that the College's president, Captain A. T. Mahan, "would be glad to see you at any time, and explain the objects and ends he has in view."

Actually, Luce was hoping for something more from Roosevelt than a visit to Newport. The very existence of his cherished War College was in doubt because of strong opposition in Congress and among certain high-ranking naval officers. Luce was trying to line up political support, and he remembered Roosevelt's connections in the Republican party. "May we not hope," Luce wrote, "that the study you have given to the early history of the Navy will lead you to take some interest in a naval institution now struggling through the ills of infancy?" Perhaps Luce did not realize that Roosevelt's political fortunes were at a low ebb in early 1888. He had run for mayor of New York City and lost, and he held no political office at all. He was still recovering financially from the devastation wrought by the blizzard on his ranch the year before. He was pleased and flattered by Luce's invitation. "I doubt if I have ever received any letter which gave me more genuine pleasure than yours did; it gave me a real pride in my work," he wrote. "Praise coming from you is praise which may indeed be appreciated. . . . I know Captain Mahan by reputation very well; it is needless to say that I shall be delighted to do anything in my power to help along the Naval college." Before heading west to his ranch in the Dakota Territory in August, he visited Newport, where he met Mahan and delivered a lecture on "The True Conditions of the War of 1812." However, with the Democrats in control of both the White House and Congress, there was little he could do politically for the War College.

Given his interest in naval history and his personal acquaintance with the book's author, it was not surprising that he read Mahan's new book as soon as it was published. On May 12, 1890, immediately after finishing it, he dashed off a note to Mahan: "During the last two days I have spent half my time, busy as I am, in reading your book. That I found it interesting is shown by the fact that having taken it up, I have gone straight through and finished it. . . . It is a *very* good book—admirable; and I am greatly in error if it does not become a naval classic." He wrote a laudatory review that appeared in the October issue of the *Atlantic Monthly*. The book, he wrote, was "the best and most important, and also by far the most interesting, book on naval history which has been produced on either side of the water for many a long year." Roosevelt clearly grasped Mahan's underlying meaning and his purpose in writing the book: "He subordinates detail to mass-effects, trying always to grasp and make evident the essential features of a situation; and he neither loses sight of nor exaggerates the bearing which the history of past struggles has upon our present problems." Roosevelt was one of few Americans in 1890 who understood the full significance of the book. Roosevelt and Mahan were very different personalities in many respects, but they were kindred souls in their views about the navy and its proper role. If William Tecumseh Sherman and his plan to capture Charleston caused the scales to fall from Stephen Luce's eyes, Luce's younger colleague and protégé, Alfred Mahan, and his landmark book performed a similar operation for Theodore Roosevelt. According to one of Roosevelt's most thorough and perceptive biographers, when he finished reading it, Roosevelt "flipped the book shut a changed man."

In 1890, Mahan was fifty years old, a captain with thirty-four years of service. His father had been a lecturer in engineering at West Point, who had on his own initiative introduced a course of study on strategy and grand tactics. As a result, young Alfred grew up in the midst of the study and teaching of military history and affairs. He became a student at a private Episcopal school in Maryland and spent two years at Columbia College. Despite a boyhood spent at West Point, he chose the navy rather than the army for a career and graduated from the Naval Academy in 1859.

He spent the Civil War mostly on boring blockade duty. By the end of the war, he had achieved the same rank as Stephen Luce, lieutenant-commander, although Luce was his senior in service time by fifteen years. After the war, he continued an unremarkable career, reaching the rank of commander by the early 1880s. He is described as slender and more than six feet tall, with light sandy hair, a clear complexion, and gray-blue eyes. An early photograph shows a young man with finely drawn, almost feminine features. In later years, he was mostly bald and sported a fashionable goatee. He married in 1872 and became the father of two daughters and one son.

Mahan's fellow officers regarded him as "bookish"—not a very desirable reputation for a professional naval officer in the nineteenth century. He himself later wrote that he perhaps was not temperamentally suited to be a naval officer. By the early 1880s, he thought that he might have done better in some other field. He found sea duty boring, and he could work up little enthusiasm for the technological developments that were transforming warships. In 1879, he submitted an entry in the Naval Institute's annual essay contest. The assigned topic was "Naval Education for Officers and Men." Mahan argued that studies in the humanities—history, foreign languages, and literature—were more important than narrow technical studies to the development of mental faculties, such as judgment, which were required for higher command. His essay took third prize. The entry awarded first prize argued in favor of technical training.

Mahan became acquainted with Stephen Luce early in his career. Both were assigned to the Naval Academy when it was temporarily relocated at Newport early in the Civil War. In 1863, the midshipmen were taken on a training cruise aboard an old sailing ship, *Macedonian,* with Luce in command and Mahan as executive officer. During the last year of the war, he may have seen more of Luce, because he served on the staff of the admiral in command of the force blockading Charleston, of which Luce's ship, *Pontiac,* was a part. In the shrinking navy of the postwar years, the paths of two senior career officers no doubt crossed from time to time. They must have learned that they shared many common interests and convictions.

In 1884, when Stephen Luce received the authority from William Chandler to establish his War College, Mahan was in command of *Wachusett,* a steam sloop stationed on the west coast of South America as part of a tiny force sent to protect American businessmen from potential Latin American revolutionaries. The duty was boring, and the ship was old, obsolete, and decrepit. Mahan recommended that it be taken out of commission, but he was ignored. Sometime in August or September, a welcome reprieve from his tedious exile arrived in the form of a letter from Luce inviting him to join the staff of the War College to teach strategy, tactics, and naval history. Several months before Chandler issued his order, Luce was sufficiently certain it would be done that he began to recruit a staff. Mahan's book about naval operations during the Civil War, *The Gulf and Inland Waters,* had appeared the year before, and it may have had something to do with Luce's invitation. Mahan was appropriately modest in his reply, saying that perhaps Luce was giving him credit for more knowledge than he possessed, and perhaps he was not qualified for the position. But he also wrote that he would "like the position, like it very much."

Unfortunately for Mahan and Luce, William Chandler was on his way out as navy secretary, and William Whitney was on his way in. By the time Luce could become established in his "poor little poorhouse," Chandler was about to leave the Navy Department, and a transfer for Mahan was deferred until a new administration took over in Washington. In November, Mahan took some leave from his ship while it lay in the harbor at Callao, Peru, the port for Lima. He wanted to begin to prepare for his war college assignments by reading history in the library of the English Club in Lima. One of the books he read was Theodore Mommsen's *History of Rome.* He was particularly struck by Mommsen's account of Hannibal's campaigns in Italy. Years later, he wrote that reading about Hannibal marked the beginning of a transformation in his thinking about the importance of sea power: "It suddenly struck me . . . how different things might have been could Hannibal have invaded Italy by sea, as the Romans often had Africa, instead of by the long land route; or could he, after arrival, have been in free communication with Carthage by water." He described the effect of this abrupt insight as "one of those concrete perceptions which turn inward darkness to light—give substance to shadow."

His efforts to get off *Wachusett* and move on to Newport were unsuccessful, because the new secretary of the navy, William Whitney, could see no good reason to transfer him before his tour of duty ended. His request for a transfer elicited a scathing reply from Whitney, who called the request "weak and unworthy." "A good commander," Whitney scolded, "should not complain over assignments." Mahan stayed aboard his ship as it steamed up and down the coast of Central and South America. Not until August, 1885, was he able to take permanent leave of *Wachusett*. He left the ship at Mare Island Naval Shipyard in California, because the old ship was at last taken out of commission. He had had plenty of time to form a plan in his mind about what he would teach at the War College.

He was too late for the first class in September, so he asked Luce's permission to spend time in New York to study up on naval history. In November, he holed up in the Astor Library where Roosevelt had spent months doing research for *The Naval War of 1812*. He emerged in early summer with bundles of notes and went to Bar Harbor, Maine, to spend the summer with his family and work up his notes into lectures. By September, when he arrived in Newport, he "had on paper in lecture form all of my first *Sea Power* book, except the summary of conclusions which constitutes the final chapter." By the time he arrived, Luce had already departed Newport to return to command of the Atlantic Fleet. Mahan replaced him as president of the War College in time for the beginning of its second year of classes, although "it was by default, without special orders that I can remember."

For several years after the War College was officially opened, its continued existence remained in doubt. In Congress, the powerful chairman of the House Naval Affairs Committee was Hilary Herbert of Alabama. He was regarded as pro-navy, but he looked askance at the War College, because he entertained a healthy suspicion about the growth of bureaucracies. In his eyes, the War College was another small government institution that promised inevitably, in the manner of all bureaucracies, to grow ever larger and more expensive. Herbert thought it ought to be "nipped in the bud." With Mahan, who lobbied for the college in Washington, he was friendly, but "whenever he saw me," Mahan wrote, "he set his teeth and compressed his lips . . . he stopped his ears, like Ulysses, and kept his eyes fixed on the necessity of strangling the vipers in their cradle." There was no prospect in 1887 for any appropriations from Congress.

William Whitney's attitude toward the college was unenthusiastic at best. His biographer states that he supported it, at least at first. Mahan wrote that Whitney "from indifference passed into antagonism." By 1887, he showed Mahan "a frowning countenance" and told him, "I will not oppose you, but I do not authorize you to express any approval from me." Perhaps Mahan's request for a transfer from *Wachusett* early in Whitney's term which had so annoyed the secretary had gotten their relationship off on the wrong foot. By 1888, Whitney was writing to his wife about "the infernal War College at Newport." He reduced the length of the course and, to Luce's consternation, merged the War College with the Torpedo Station on Goat Island, half a mile from Coaster's Harbor Island. He sent Mahan off to Puget Sound on the Pacific coast to choose a site for a new naval shipyard.

As the presidential election of 1888 approached, the future of the War College seemed to depend upon the outcome of the election. On September 17, William Chandler, who had been elected to the Senate from New Hampshire, wrote to Stephen Luce: "If Cleveland is [re]-elected President, it [the War College] will be destroyed; at any rate, it will not be allowed to remain in Newport. If [Benjamin] Harrison is elected, we shall take care of the College and locate it at Newport." Harrison was elected, and by the summer of 1889, the exiled Mahan was able to return from Puget Sound. By winter, with a more sympathetic Republican administration in power, funds to build a home for the War College on Coaster's Harbor Island were at last authorized by Congress. Classes were totally suspended in 1890 and 1891 while the new building was under construction. In 1892, the War College reopened in its own quarters. Mahan was on hand to greet a new class of officer-students and deliver his lectures, which by then had become famous. They apparently were received with attention and interest by some of his students and dismissed as irrelevant ancient history by others.

In 1892, two more books by Mahan were published. A biography of David Farragut was a disappointment which failed to garner much attention or money. But the other book, the second of his sea power books, entitled *The Influence of Sea Power upon the French Revolution and Empire, 1793–1812,* was a fitting sequel to the 1890 book. It, too, prompted favorable reviews that sparked brisk sales. In a very laudatory review in the *Atlantic Monthly,* Roosevelt called it "a thoroughly fit companion piece for his former book," and in a review of both books for *Political Science Quarterly,* he described Mahan as "founding a new school of naval historical writing." In Mahan's second sea power book appears what is probably the most famous passage he ever wrote. Its context is Napoleon's frustrated effort to invade Britain. "The world has never seen a more impressive demonstration of the influence of sea power upon its history. Those far distant, storm-beaten ships, upon which the Grand Army never looked, stood between it and the dominion of the world." It is a passage to stir the soul of any true naval person.

By December, 1892, with two admired works to his credit, Mahan had become a famous historian, although he was, as yet, better known and more admired in Europe than in his own country. His own service probably held him in lower regard than the country at large. He received congratulatory letters from a few brother officers when his first sea power book elicited a few admiring reviews in the United States, but as an institution, the navy was curiously indifferent to the budding celebrity in its midst. Early in 1893, it decided that he had been on shore long enough and should go back to sea for a while.

Mahan was in the midst of getting the reconstituted War College back into operation, and he was investigating ideas for a new book, including a request from a publisher to write a naval history of the Civil War. He had plenty of congenial activities to occupy him in Newport, so he was not happy at the prospect of a return to sea duty, which had always bored him. Command of a ship would require all his time and attention and force him to suspend his writing. He sent in a request to be excused and to stay in Newport. The sea duty assignment was actually the decision of Francis M. Ramsay, who had just been appointed director of the Bureau of Navigation, where assignments were made. He was a long-time, outspoken critic of the War College and unsympathetic to anyone associated with it. He curtly turned down Mahan's request by saying, "It is not the business of a naval officer to write books."

Mahan sought help from Theodore Roosevelt and Henry Cabot Lodge to persuade the navy to allow him to remain at the War College until his retirement, which was scheduled to begin in 1896. Before agreeing to help, Roosevelt asked him to explain both the pros and cons of being exempted from sea duty. He responded by outlining his War College activities and the possible writing projects he was considering. He argued that even from the navy's point of view, he would be more valuable in Newport than at sea. He wrote to Roosevelt, "May I not, from the reasons given, be even more useful to the navy by the proposed course than by commanding a ship?"

Roosevelt was persuaded and interceded with the secretary of the navy, who made no promises to change Mahan's assignment but said he took a sympathetic view of the situation. Ramsay, however, was implacable in his determination to get Mahan out of Newport and onto a ship, and a sea duty assignment continued to loom. On April 30, Roosevelt convened a "solemn war council," which included Henry Cabot Lodge and Stephen Luce, to decide how to proceed. Roosevelt realized that the chief obstacle was Ramsay. "A blind, narrow, mean, jealous pedant," he raged in a letter to Mahan. "If I can ever do him a bad turn, I most certainly will. . . . Oh, what idiots we have had to deal with!"

During the months that Roosevelt and his friends worked to keep Mahan in Newport, a change of administration occurred in Washington. In March, Republican Benjamin Harrison surrendered the White House to Democrat Grover Cleveland, who began his second term as president. The new secretary of the navy was Hilary Herbert, who, as chairman of the House Naval Affairs Committee in 1888, had tried to strangle the naval vipers at Newport in their cradle. Herbert felt no personal animosity toward Mahan, and he was not as vehemently opposed to the War College as Ramsay apparently was. But given a choice between the War College and overdue sea duty as an assignment for Mahan, it was unlikely he would opt for the former.

Mahan himself sealed his doom by choosing this particular moment to write an injudicious magazine article guaranteed to antagonize the new administration in Washington. In January, a revolution of sorts occurred in Hawaii. The American sugar planters and missionaries who actually controlled the islands overthrew the indigenous ruling monarchy, with help from American marines landed from the cruiser *Boston*. They then proclaimed the establishment of a republic, which was immediately granted diplomatic recognition by the American minister in Honolulu. The new government sent a delegation to Washington to petition for annexation by the United States. The lame-duck Harrison administration supported the idea and submitted a treaty of annexation for ratification by the Senate. However, Cleveland was a longstanding anti-imperialist, opposed to expansion overseas by the United States. As soon as he took office, he withdrew the treaty.

When the issue of annexation of Hawaii hit the newspapers, Mahan dashed off a letter to the *New York Times* supporting annexation. His reading and thinking about sea power had caused him to reverse his long-held anti-imperialist ideas into enthusiastic support of expansion overseas by the United States. He followed up his letter to the *Times* with a long article published in *Forum* magazine making strong arguments for annexation. It appeared just as Cleveland was taking office and with-drawing the treaty from the Senate. Mahan was a famous historian, and *Forum* was a leading journal of opinion on public affairs. His article attracted widespread attention. He was also a naval officer on active duty, and he had gone too far in publicly airing his private views about government policy. His article could not have appeared at a worse time for his own self-interest. Francis Ramsay was not one to allow such an opportunity to pass.

On May 3, Mahan received orders to take command of *Chicago*, the "C" of the ABCD ships. On the same day, Secretary Herbert explained his endorsement of the transfer in a letter to a friend who had pleaded Mahan's cause with the secretary. "It is my intention, as far as possible, to treat all officers alike," Herbert wrote. He explained that he was not an enemy of Mahan and did not agree with Francis Ramsay's views about naval officers writing books.

> I realize fully the value of the work that Capt. Mahan has been doing, and he has been assigned to one of the best ships in the service. . . . I hope he will be able to devote a considerable portion of his time to liter-ary work. I should regret very much to see Capt. Mahan drop his pen, and I realize that his work is of an exceptional character, but it would be hard to explain to other officers why they should be compelled to go to sea and Capt. Mahan allowed to remain on shore.

There is a measure of irony in the efforts made by Mahan, Roosevelt, and Lodge to keep Mahan in Newport and excused from taking com-mand of *Chicago*. Mahan himself later wrote of his request to remain at the War College that "it was not granted, luckily for me." In the summer of 1893, *Chicago* steamed off to Europe, where Mahan, regarded by Eu-ropeans as a famous historian and brilliant naval philosopher, was feted and lionized, especially in Britain. In August, he was invited by Queen Victoria to attend a royal dinner for Kaiser Wilhelm II. He was received at the Admiralty. At a dinner in his honor at the American Embassy, he met two future prime ministers, Arthur J. Balfour and Herbert Asquith. He was the center of constant, admiring attention. The following March, he reflected in a letter to his wife on the contrast between the notice he attracted in Europe and the relative indifference shown him by his own countrymen. "Except Roosevelt," he wrote, "I don't think my work gained me an entrée into a single American social circle."

His cruise on *Chicago* was not unalloyed pleasure, however. *Chicago* was the flagship of the admiral in command of the European Station. He was Rear-Admiral Henry Erben, a gruff, bluff old sea dog who was the very antithesis of the cerebral, poetry-reading Mahan. Through the summer in Britain, Erben watched with increasing irritation as British movers and shakers clamored for an opportunity to meet his flagship's captain, while he, the admiral, was ignored. Erben also watched as Mahan, his head understandably turned by all the adulation being showered upon him, adopted an attitude of only thinly disguised condescension toward his superior officer.

In October, Erben suddenly called an admiral's inspection of his flagship. Such an inspection included a fitness report of the captain, even though he had been aboard less than six months. Mahan saw the report only in January, and it was a stunning blow. Erben charged that the ship was being poorly run by Mahan. He rated Mahan as only "tolerable" in "Professional Ability" and "Attention to Duty." He wrote that Mahan appeared more interested in reading and writing books than in his naval duties. Moreover, he wrote, Mahan had even told Erben that he was. The report was a damning indictment.

Mahan was incensed by what he considered an inaccurate and unfair blot on his record. Before Erben submitted it, he had given no hint of what he intended to write or offered Mahan an opportunity to reply. Mahan decided to ask the secretary of the navy to arrange an inspection of the ship by a panel of disinterested third parties, to prove that he performed his duties as captain in an exemplary manner. He also asked Theodore Roosevelt and Henry Cabot Lodge to intercede on his behalf with the secretary. When Lodge discussed the matter with Herbert, the secretary expressed sympathy for Mahan, but advised Lodge to tell Mahan not to press for the inspection. It would only call attention to the quarrel and make things worse for everyone concerned. Mahan accepted the advice, and no inspection was made. The damning report remained in his file. Aboard *Chicago*, relations between the two officers were frigid, and they communicated only in writing.

In the summer of 1894, the ship returned to Britain, and Mahan again attracted praise and attention from the admiring English. Again, he was entertained by the queen. The prime minister, Lord Roseberry, hosted a small private dinner. He was the guest of honor at a dinner hosted by the Royal Navy Club, the first foreigner so honored. He dined with Kaiser Wilhelm aboard his imperial yacht during Race Week at Cowes. He was awarded honorary degrees by Oxford and Cambridge. The *Times* compared him to Copernicus. In July, he also received a second unflattering fitness report from Admiral Erben. Relations between the two officers had been poisonous for months, but they had finally managed a truce despite their mutual dislike. In September, Erben left the ship to retire from the navy.

Mahan's two-year cruise aboard *Chicago* was a royal progress through Europe that produced plenty of favorable publicity back in the United States. He later wrote, "This brought my name forward in a way that could not but be flattering, and affected favorably the sale of the books." His compatriots and service colleagues back home began to sit up and take notice. When he returned to the United States in 1895, he became the center of the kind of admiring attention he had attracted in Britain. He was awarded honorary degrees by Harvard, Yale, Columbia, and McGill University in Montreal. When he retired in 1896, two adverse fitness reports in his service jacket counted for very little, because he had become one of the most popular, admired, and influential writers in the world, including the United States.

The Influence of Sea Power upon History, 1660–1783 made a much greater initial impact in Britain than in the United States, for good reason. It offered a convincing explanation, in terms any intelligent reader could understand, as to why Britain—so small in comparison with France or Germany or Russia—was the dominant, most powerful country in the world with an empire on which the sun never set. A reviewer in *Blackwood's Magazine* wrote that the book "might almost be said to be a scientific inquiry into the causes which have made England great." The average British reader, he thought, could learn from it how his "country acquired her present position among nations, and how that position may be maintained." The *Edinburgh Review* described it as a "splendid apotheosis of English courage and English endurance, of English skill and English power." The Royal Navy seized upon it as justification for even greater naval appropriations. At the dinner hosted for him by the Royal Navy Club, Mahan was toasted by a Royal Navy officer who said, "We owe to his books the three million pounds just voted for the increase of the navy."

Not surprisingly, other countries in the world became interested in an account that explained how the world's most powerful nation had achieved that position. Within a few years, Mahan's book was translated into German, Japanese, French, Italian, Russian, and Spanish. By 1894, Kaiser Wilhelm cabled to an American friend of Mahan, "I am just now not reading but devouring Captain Mahan's book and am trying to learn it by heart. It is a first-class work and classical in all points. It is on board all my ships and constantly quoted by my captains and officers." The Kaiser, bilingual in German and English, presumably read the book in its original English.

What, specifically, was it in Mahan's book that made such a profound impression on such disparate people as Theodore Roosevelt, the German Emperor, and a British professor reviewing books for the *Edinburgh Review*? The bulk of the book is narrative history—an account of Britain's naval wars with the Dutch and the French in the seventeenth and eighteenth centuries. Only the first and last chapters are given over explicitly to analysis of the lessons Mahan drew from his study of those wars, but the lessons are derived directly from the history.

Britain won the wars, Mahan argued, because the Royal Navy controlled the sea. By his definition, control of the sea does not mean strewing the world's oceans with warships. It is impossible to exert control everywhere all the time. Control of the sea means the ability to bring to bear at any chosen place and time sufficient force to defeat any force that the enemy might mount. This is Mahan's central, governing concept. The Royal Navy could do that, so British merchant ships could sail the sea lanes secure from any threat by the Dutch or French navies. British overseas commerce could continue to contribute to the country's strength and wealth. It could maintain its ties with its expanding overseas empire. By contrast, enemy ships, both warships and merchant vessels, were denied the use of the sea. They ventured out of port at their peril.

Mahan's thesis was both an explanation and a prescription. It offered lessons and implications for both naval officers and statesmen. For the former, the most important lesson was concentration of force, a principle Mahan consciously borrowed from the Swiss military philosopher Antoine Henri Jomini, the interpreter and analyst of Frederick the Great and Napoleon. The battle fleet should never be divided. Concentration of overwhelming force is paramount. Piecemeal distribution of warships invites their piecemeal destruction. A corollary of the undivided fleet axiom for the United States in 1890 was the need for an isthmian canal across Central America, so that a unified American battle fleet could move quickly between the country's two coasts. Mahan became an ardent advocate of such a canal, and he predicted that the Caribbean would become one of the world's most important commercial sea lanes once it was built, to the great advantage of the United States.

Important, too, for the naval officer was the distinction Mahan made between strategy and tactics. Like Luce, he believed that the basic principles governing strategy are timeless and immutable. He wrote, "from time to time the structure of tactics has to be wholly torn down, but the foundations of strategy so far remain, as though laid upon a rock." Like Luce, he believed that the basic principles of strategy can be deduced from a study of naval history, of the successes and failures of past naval battles and campaigns. Tactics, on the other hand, he recognized must change as naval technology changes. When he was recruited by Luce for the War College, he was assigned to teach both strategy and tactics. He was astute enough to recognize that in the welter of technological change that was transforming navies, no one had any real understanding of how tactics would be affected in the next great sea battle that was bound to be fought, sooner or later. There was no recent experience to examine, except the confused battle of Lissa, which Mahan decided to ignore. When he was holed up in the Astor Library preparing his lecture notes, he wrote to Luce, "We are already deluged with speculations and arguments as to future naval warfare, more or less plausible and well-considered, but I don't see any wise in my adding to that clack. I want, if I can, to wrest something out of the old wooden sides and 24-pounders that will throw some light on the combinations to be used with iron-clads, rifled guns and torpedoes." He prepared lectures on tactics, but when it came time to begin teaching, he was happy to leave the subject to another member of the War College staff.

For the statesman, perhaps the principal lesson was this: If a nation wished to emulate the success of Britain as a dominant world power, a strong navy capable of offensive action was centrally important. In time of war, it must be able to seek out and destroy the enemy's navy. "The proper main object of a navy is the enemy's navy," Mahan wrote. To an American like Theodore Roosevelt, this idea leaped off the page, because it ran counter to the role of the navy traditionally accepted in the United States. In time of war, the American navy was charged with protecting the coast and raiding the enemy's commerce. This was a defensive role. It required coastal forts and a fleet of cruisers that would operate singly rather than as a unit. An energetic, aggressive personality like Roosevelt immediately seized upon Mahan's aggressive, offensive concept as obviously preferable.

Roosevelt also recognized that Mahan's prescription required battleships—the biggest, fastest, most heavily armed and armored ships that could be built. Mahan specifically dismissed commerce raiding as a strategy which could not win a war. It might be useful to harass an enemy and cause him pain, but it could not defeat him. Twentieth-century critics have faulted Mahan, as an expounder of immutable principles, for not foreseeing the effectiveness of submarines. He failed to foresee their importance, especially as used by Germany, in both world wars of the twentieth century. But the failure of German submarines to decide either war's outcome, despite their punishing depredations on cargo shipping, simply confirms Mahan's dismissal of a *guerre de course* strategy as incapable of producing victory.

Mahan's concept of sea power included the idea that not every country—not even every large and powerful country—could be dominant on the sea like Britain. He posited six defining national characteristics—including such matters as a country's geographical location and configuration, and the nature of its population and government—that determined whether it was or could become a seafaring nation. He believed that a country cannot be both a dominant land power and a strong sea power. Britain was obviously his model when he drew up his list of characteristics. Germany, in contrast to insular Britain, enjoys access to the sea only through the Baltic Sea, which can be blockaded by the Royal Navy. Germany therefore, according to Mahan's scheme, is naturally a land power rather than a sea power.

Kaiser Wilhelm II and Admiral von Tirpitz, the "father" of the German navy that the Kaiser insisted on building, chose to ignore this aspect of Mahan's thinking. Despite the Kaiser's lavish praise for Mahan's line of reasoning, he insisted on challenging the Royal Navy's dominance by embarking on a futile competition of battleship-building that cost both countries billions. Germany mounted a strong challenge to the Royal Navy's control of the sea, but it could not prevail. Mahan thought that the United States, unlike Germany, possessed the attributes to become a power on the sea.

A strong mobile navy in the age of steam necessitated overseas bases and coaling stations, and the seaborne commerce needed to sustain a country's wealth and strength required overseas markets and sources of raw material. Thus was Mahan led to the precept that has earned him more criticism than any other he proposed. A country that wished to become a sea power like Britain, he argued, must have colonies. Mahan's critics fault him for urging American leaders during the 1890s to join the headlong plunge into imperialism that the European powers were then making in Asia and Africa. Until he received his invitation from Luce to join the War College, Mahan was an outspoken anti-imperialist. After his reading and study between 1884 and 1886 transformed his thinking, he became an ardent expansionist. In his autobiography, published in 1907, he wrote, "I am frankly an imperialist." But he went on to explain what this meant: "I believe that no nation, certainly no great nation, should henceforth maintain the policy of isolation which fitted our early history; above all, should not on that outlived plea refuse to intervene in events obviously thrust upon its conscience." Theodore Roosevelt, who undoubtedly read the book when it appeared, must have said to himself, "hear, hear," when he read that passage. Franklin D. Roosevelt, if he had read it in 1941, probably would have said the same thing.

In Europe in 1890, the idea that a great power should acquire colonies was conventional wisdom. Britain was the most powerful country, and it had more colonies than any other. Obviously, if a country wanted to become a great power, it must have colonies. Germany under Bismarck mostly avoided the competition with Britain for colonies, because the canny Iron Chancellor understood that Germany would be at a disadvantage in such a competition. But Bismarck was ousted in 1890, the year Mahan's book appeared. Kaiser Wilhelm II enthusiastically embraced the idea of acquiring colonies, as he embraced the idea of Germany building a strong navy. In the United States, opinion was divided, and already by the early 1890s there existed a strong anti-imperialist movement.

Mahan in 1890, though an advocate of overseas expansion, thought the anti-imperialists would probably triumph and prevent the United

States from acquiring overseas colonies. With so much empty and unde-
veloped territory within their own borders, he reasoned, Americans
would never feel moved to acquire overseas possessions, despite his ad-
vocacy. But in 1890, the year his book was published, the frontier—
defined as the edge of settled land which contained more than two but
less than six people per square mile—was declared officially closed. The
western expansion that had been in progress for more than 350 years
had reached its end on the American continent. Continued westward
movement meant leaping across the Pacific to its islands and the lands
of Asia. Roosevelt, Lodge, and other young and restless expansionists,
watching the rapid expansion of European powers into Asia, thought
the United States must do the same. Mahan's argument for colonies
found a receptive audience among them.

Not surprisingly, Mahan has attracted plenty of critics since his death
who have tried to demonstrate that he was not as astute or farsighted as
so many of his contemporaries thought. They have charged that his
ideas about sea power and control of the sea were not original or even
fresh, because other people had already written about them in decades
and even centuries past. They have argued that he was not responsible
for the rebirth of the navy, because it had already begun when his first
sea power book appeared. They say that his books were not really influential in the sense of giving people new ideas or causing them to
change their minds. The books were admired and praised, critics say,
because they offered an elegant, scholarly rationale, based upon historical study, for ideas already popularly held.

Mahan himself denied that his ideas about sea power and control of
the sea were original with him. Early in his reading, around 1884, he
concluded that "control of the sea was an historic factor which had
never been systematically appreciated and expounded." However, looking back on his writings years later, he admitted that his role had been
"in popularizing, perhaps in making effective, an argument for which I
could by no means claim the rights of discovery." He cited predecessors
as early as Sir Francis Bacon and Sir Walter Raleigh. But it was also
true that when he hit upon the idea, their writings about sea power were
unknown to him, as, apparently, they were to a great many other people.

When Mahan reported to the War College in 1885, the rejuvenation
of the navy, in the form of construction of the ABCD ships, was already
underway. By 1890, when his first sea power book appeared, several

more modern steel ships had been launched or were under construction. They were all cruisers, however. In 1890, the fleet was still configured for the traditional defensive strategy of coastal defense and commerce raiding. Mahan, it is true, was not the only voice arguing for construction of battleships to create a strong offensive force. In 1889, an article by Stephen Luce published in the *North American Review* argued for battleships. "The battleship," Luce wrote, "is the very foundation of the Navy. The United States has no battleships, therefore she has no Navy." Just a few months later, in May, 1890, Mahan's book was published. Less than two months after it appeared, on June 30, Congress authorized construction of three battleships "to carry the heaviest armor and most powerful ordnance."

The publication of *The Influence of Sea Power upon History, 1660–1783* could not have occurred at a more propitious moment. In both Britain and the United States, it was that rare event all publishers seek, the appearance of a book just when its public is ready—indeed, eager—to read it, and there is nothing else like it available. If it had appeared twenty-five years earlier, at the end of the Civil War, it would have attracted scarcely any notice at all. Mahan probably could not have found a publisher for it. In its own sphere, its publication resembled the appearance of Darwin's *Origin of Species* a little more than thirty years earlier. Like Darwin's book, it explained many things that many people had sensed or even articulated, but that no one had ever explained so clearly and persuasively. The reaction of many readers to Mahan's sea power books, especially officers in the British Admiralty, recalled Alexander Pope's couplet about reaction to Sir Isaac Newton:

> Nature and Nature's laws lay hid in night:
> God said, Let Newton be! and all was light.

Perhaps for many of his most enthusiastic readers, Mahan was preaching to the converted, but his books changed a few minds, too. Hilary Herbert, the secretary of the navy who had only reluctantly approved his transfer from Newport to *Chicago*, was nevertheless still no fan of the Naval War College when he was appointed secretary. During his first summer as secretary—the first of Mahan's two triumphant summers in Europe—Herbert embarked on a trip from the Brooklyn Navy Yard to Newport (he travelled aboard that "mere pleasure craft," *Dolphin*). The visit was officially billed as a routine inspection, but his purpose, well-known in the navy department, was to announce at Newport that the War College would be closed down. When he boarded *Dolphin* for the leisurely cruise to Newport, the ship's captain, who was a friend of Luce and Mahan, gave him a book to while away the time on the voyage. It was Mahan's latest, *The Influence of Sea Power upon the French Revolution and Empire, 1793–1812.* By the time Herbert reached Newport, he had finished the book and had become an enthusiastic Mahanite. Rather than close the War College, he announced that it had his firm support. "If this institution has produced nothing more than this book," he declared, "it is worth all the expense incurred for it."

4

———

"THE DISASTROUS RISE OF
MISPLACED POWER"

"The only *good* things which Mr. Whitney has done," wrote William Chandler to Stephen Luce in September, 1887, "have been those which originated or were planned during my administration, and about the only original things which he has done have been the perpetration of the great outrage of destroying John Roach and the vain effort to damn the four Roach cruisers." Chandler was a senator from New Hampshire, and he had joined Nelson Aldrich as one of the congressional supporters of Luce and the Naval War College. He was not, of course, an objective or disinterested judge of his successor. Whitney's shabby treatment of Roach, his refusal to accept *Dolphin* despite its excellent performance, and his clashes with Luce and Mahan over the War College were not the sum total of Whitney's actions as navy secretary. His term of office should not judged solely by them. Although he was personally very different from William Chandler and came from a very different background, he continued the reform and rebuilding of the navy begun by Hunt and Chandler.

By the mid-1880s, rejuvenation of the navy was not a partisan political issue. There was disagreement in Congress and in the navy itself about the navy's proper mission in the event of war and, consequently, about the number, size, and kinds of new ships that should be built. But the disagreement did not divide along party lines. Opposition to naval expansion came mainly from isolationists in the midwest and prairie states, but they were a minority. Perhaps because of uneasiness prompted by the growing size of the navies of the European powers, or because increasing numbers of Americans felt that the prestige of the United States demanded a fleet of respectable size, or because Americans were feeling the first stirrings of imperialism—probably for all these and other reasons, too, there was growing agreement that the navy must be improved and expanded. Grover Cleveland and William Whitney were not bucking sentiment in their own party or among the people of the country at large as they sought to continue naval reform and expansion of the fleet.

Whitney effected reforms in the navy's personnel system and in its administrative structure by curtailing the virtual independence that each bureau had enjoyed, although bureau chiefs continued to wield considerable individual power. His administrative consolidation and reforms saved money by reducing waste and duplication in procurement, which had always been done independently by each bureau. He continued the attack on naval shipyard corruption and incompetence, although they were so entrenched and enjoyed so much tacit if not active approval in Congress that it would be years before real reform took hold.

He continued enlargement of the fleet. When he left office in 1889, more than ninety-three thousand tons of new steel warships had been added to the fleet or were under construction. However, all but three of those ships were protected cruisers or gunboats, no more formidable as warships than the ABCD *Chicago*. Two of the exceptions, *Texas* and *Maine,* were authorized by Congress in 1886. They were first designated armored cruisers but later called second-class battleships because of the large caliber guns in their main batteries. Their interior spaces were protected by armor both on the decks, like a protected cruiser, and along their waterlines, and they mounted guns larger than *Chicago*'s. They were still in the earliest stages of construction when Whitney left office, and the inexperience of American shipyards in building ships of their size and complexity caused long delays in their construction. They did not join the fleet until nine years after their authorization. The other exception, *New York,* authorized in 1888, was the United States' first true armored cruiser. At 8,400 tons, it was larger than either *Maine* or *Texas,* but it carried a main battery of eight-inch guns, smaller than the two battleships' main guns.

In the mid-1880s, if Congress had been able to agree that the navy should have first-class battleships and had sought to have them constructed, it would have been disappointed. Ever since the initial debates about the ABCD ships, everyone agreed that American warships should be built in the United States. But no one in the United States could build a ship equal to those being produced by Britain, France, and other

European countries. Even *Texas* and *Maine,* intended to be the most formidable warships ever built in the United States, were not designed to be the equal of the best British or French battleships. The main obstacle lay in American steel production. The largest ingots of gun steel that American plants could forge were large enough to manufacture only six-inch guns. European battleships carried main batteries of guns as large as thirteen-inch. Not one American steel plant could produce armor plate. Guns with bores eight-inch and larger, and armor plate, had to be obtained abroad. Accordingly, the eight-inch guns of the three ABCD cruisers and the armor for their decks were purchased in England.

Efforts to solve the steel problem began even before Whitney took office. The Gun Foundry Board appointed by William Chandler was charged by Congress to deal with a basic question. Who should manufacture the armor plate, the guns, and the ships of the new navy: the government or private enterprise? In Europe, armaments had always been manufactured by private companies such as Krupp in Germany and Whitworth in England. But Congress and the navy were wary of putting the responsibility completely in either the public or the private sector. They decided that government and private enterprise should cooperate in building the new navy.

The Foundry Board asked steel manufacturers what aid from the government they would require to enlarge their plants so as to be able to manufacture large-bore ordnance. Answers were uniformly disappointing. The response of the Cambria Iron Company of Philadelphia was typical. "Like all other steel manufactories in the United States," the company replied, "we have no apparatus capable of forging the large ingots required for modern guns." The president of the South Boston Iron Works replied that he would have to spend eight hundred thousand dollars to make his factory capable of producing what the navy wanted, and it would take two years to do so. A steel manufacturer would, in effect, have to build an entirely new plant to produce what the navy needed, but the only potential customer for armor plate and cannons was the government. Did the government want to buy enough of those products to justify such large capital investments by steelmakers? Whitney's task was to make government orders big enough to entice steel manufacturers to make such investments. He decided that private steel makers should forge the armor plate and the ingots for the

An assembled naval gun in the ordnance factory at the Washington Navy Yard.

Library of Congress photograph

guns, but the ordnance itself should be the responsibility of the government. A naval gun factory was established at the Washington Navy Yard. Construction of the ships themselves would be divided between government-operated and private shipyards.

On the day before the Cleveland administration took office in March, 1885, Congress authorized construction of four protected cruisers. In 1886, at Whitney's request, it authorized two armored cruisers which became the second-class battleships *Texas* and *Maine*. Displacing 6,500 tons each, they would be the largest warships yet built for the navy. Both would be built at the government's naval shipyards, *Texas* at Norfolk and *Maine* at Brooklyn. Whitney consolidated the orders for gun steel and armor for all six ships into one order large enough to entice a steel manufacturer to install the equipment necessary to produce it, and he allowed two and a half years for delivery.

Five companies submitted bids, but only Bethlehem Steel bid to provide both armor and gun steel. Its bid of $4.5 million was accepted, and a contract was signed in June, 1887, for delivery by the end of 1889.

Bethlehem began a search in Europe for a steel plant capable of producing gun and armor steel. The company planned to purchase it, dismantle it, and ship it to the United States, where it would be reassembled. Meanwhile, in May, alterations in the buildings at the Washington Navy Yard were begun to create a factory with equipment capable of turning rough steel ingots into gleaming, finished gun tubes with bores up to sixteen inches in diameter.

In 1887 and 1888, Congress authorized more cruisers, some of which became famous ships. One was *New York*, the first armored cruiser and the most powerful ship in the American battle fleet when it was commissioned in 1893. Another was the protected cruiser *Olympia*, Commodore George Dewey's flagship at the battle of Manila Bay in 1898. It turned out to be perhaps the best-designed of all the protected cruisers. Another cruiser, *Baltimore*, became notable for being involved in three wars. It was part of Dewey's squadron at Manila Bay, and it helped lay the mine barrage in the North Sea during World War I. By 1941, *Baltimore* had been decommissioned, but it was on hand at Pearl Harbor when the Japanese attacked.

The new navy was launched, but none of the ships afloat, under construction, or even authorized when Whitney left office in 1889 could yet equal the battleships of Britain, France, or Italy. It fell to Whitney's successor, Benjamin Franklin Tracy, to shift the drive to still bigger and more powerful warships. Tracy was a lawyer and politician from New York with no previous connection with naval matters or even with business. He was appointed by Benjamin Harrison to placate the Republican party's political boss in New York, Tom Platt. Thus, when he took office, Tracy appeared to be a throwback to such feckless politician-secretaries as Richard Thompson.

Tracy took up where Whitney left off, however, and went even further. A week after taking office, he told a newspaper reporter, "Within sixty days, we shall advertise for proposals for contracts for several new vessels." He appointed a Policy Board of naval officers to make recommendations for further enlarging and improving the fleet. While the board was deliberating, Tracy proposed in his first annual report a long-range goal: construction of twenty first-rate battleships.

He justified his proposal with a line of reasoning that would be echoed by military planners in Europe right up to the first thunder of the guns of August in 1914. Because of the prodigious advances that had occurred in technology, Tracy argued, future wars would be short and fought with existing forces. He wrote, "To strike the first blow will gain an advantage and inflict an injury from which [an enemy] can never recover." A country therefore needed a formidable navy already in existence when the guns began firing in any future war. Since it required years to build a battleship, the government would be guilty of the worst kind of folly if it waited until war was declared before starting to build a fleet. In a later message, he added a corollary to this axiom that revealed the influence of Alfred Mahan on Tracy's thinking: "A war, though defensive in principle, may be conducted most effectively by being offensive in its operations." Offensive naval operations demanded long-range, first-class battleships.

President Harrison in his first annual message to Congress backed his navy secretary by calling upon Congress to authorize immediate construction of eight battleships. With strong Republican majorities in both houses of Congress, prospects for obtaining what the president sought looked promising—until Tracy's Policy Board submitted its recommendations. They came as a shock to many people. The board reasoned that the United States needed two battle fleets—a "two-ocean navy" in later parlance—with one fleet on the east coast and one on the west coast. The board therefore recommended construction of ten long-range offensive battleships, twenty-five short-range coastal defense battleships, twenty-four armored cruisers, fifteen torpedo-cruisers, and more than one hundred torpedo boats. If all these ships were built, the United States would possess a navy second only to Britain and well ahead of France. Such a fleet would cost more than $280 million. Newspaper editors, even those who supported Harrison and Tracy, attacked the board's plan as "naval fanaticism." Perhaps the United States ought to possess a bigger navy, and maybe two battle fleets were needed. But with no discernible threat to the country's security on the horizon on either coast, few people could bring themselves to support such a gargantuan financial outlay for warships.

In the midst of the outcry raised against the Policy Board's proposals, Harrison's more modest program of eight battleships was placed in jeopardy. Navy opponents in Congress quite properly questioned not just the initial cost of building so many first-class battleships but also the annual cost of maintaining and operating them. Building Harrison's fleet would commit the country to massive expenditures for years in the future, long after the ships themselves were completed.

The Republican-controlled Congress finally reached a compromise of sorts by authorizing in June, 1890, construction of three first-class battleships possessing ordnance and armor equal to any in the world. They became *Indiana, Oregon,* and *Massachuetts.* Their authorization was probably helped along by the publication of Mahan's first sea power book less than two months earlier. All three ships would be built in private shipyards, *Indiana* and *Massachusetts* at William Cramp and Sons in Philadelphia (which had been one of John Roach's principal rivals before he went bankrupt), and *Oregon* at Union Iron Works in San Francisco. Before Tracy left office, Congress authorized one more battleship, *Iowa,* in July of 1892. It completed the lineup of ships that defeated two Spanish fleets in 1898.

Authorizing construction of battleships was one thing, however, and actually building them was something else. By 1890, a backlog of warships under construction was becoming a logjam because of the maddening problems associated with the manufacture of armor. The thirty-month deadline given by William Whitney to Bethlehem Steel to produce armor plate passed, but the company could not deliver and asked for an extension. Moreover, a debate developed over what kind of armor plate should be manufactured. Whitney and Tracy had opted for a homogeneous steel plate, but the Royal Navy in Britain used a sort of sandwich of hardened steel backed by softer iron which, the British Admiralty claimed, was less likely to shatter. In the midst of this debate, Tracy heard reports that a French steel maker was experimenting with a new, even stronger armor plate made of an alloy of steel and nickel. The stronger alloy was further strengthened by a new hardening process invented by a man named August Harvey, and it came to be called "Harveyized" steel.

Tracy decreed that the issue of which armor was superior would be decided by a test of all three types. To the steelmen's surprise and dismay, he insisted that the tests must be conducted using an eight-inch gun firing at point-blank range. All earlier tests of armor had been done with six-inch guns. The results were conclusive. The British compound armor was completely demolished, and the homogeneous steel plate cracked badly. Only the nickel-steel Harveyized armor successfully

The results of armor-plate tests made in 1890 in which four six-inch shells and one eight-inch shell were fired at each plate at point-blank range. The newest kind of armor made of nickel alloy (center) proved to be the strongest

U.S. Naval Historical Center photograph

withstood the eight-inch shells. The test results touched off alarm bells in the British Admiralty, warning that Britain's vaunted fleet of battle-ships was vulnerable.

Knowing which armor was best did not, however, break the armor production bottleneck. By May, 1890, Bethlehem Steel was reportedly still eighteen months away from delivery of the first shipment of armor. Construction of all armored vessels slowed. It was obvious that even when Bethlehem began delivery, it could not supply enough steel to cover its original contract and three additional battleships, too. Tracy urgently needed armor plate. The man who solved his problem was the steel magnate, Andrew Carnegie. He controlled the largest steel-making complex in the country, but as savior of the navy, the Scottish-born multimillionaire played a role that was somewhat surprising.

When William Whitney was searching for an American company to produce armor in 1886, he had approached Carnegie. The industrialist responded with a series of rather strange communications. Carnegie assured Whitney that his steel works in Pittsburgh were "the largest and best" in the United States and could soon produce armor superior to anything produced elsewhere. But he also wrote to Whitney, "to tell the truth, I am more and ever opposed to every dollar spent by our Republic upon instruments of any kind for destructive purposes." He scolded the secretary. "You are fast transforming a peaceful republic into a warlike power," Carnegie wrote, "degrading it to the level of monarchs of the old world." Nevertheless, only a short time later he told Whitney, "You need not be afraid that you will have to go abroad for armour plate. I am now fully satisfied that the mill we are building will roll the heaviest sizes you require, with the greatest ease."

In the end, though, Carnegie did not submit a bid to Whitney, because he objected to the rigid standards the navy insisted on maintaining for the armor plate and everything else it bought from private contractors. No one could guarantee that every batch of armor-plate steel would be exactly uniform, and several batches might have to be made to produce one acceptable order. Carnegie feared, he said, that meeting the navy's impossibly exact standards would produce for his company excessive costs, many headaches, and little or no profit.

In the spring of 1890, with Bethlehem Steel unable to deliver its promised armor, Tracy approached Carnegie and thereby initiated a long, complicated minuet of negotiations with the canny Scot. Carnegie pointed to Bethlehem Steel's failure to meet its delivery deadline to underscore the technical challenge Tracy was asking his company to take on. At one point, while vacationing in Scotland, he cabled Tracy, "armour-making no child's play." He told Tracy that his company had plenty of business, so "it will not disappoint us very much if you decide to drop us as to Armour." But he followed up that affectation of indifference with a boast that probably more accurately reflected his desire to land a contract: "We could no doubt deliver finished plates a year before any other party in the United States. Any one else who tries to deliver in a year will land just where Bethlehem is." Price was one stumbling block that delayed agreement. Another was the question of nickel alloy. Carnegie was not convinced of its superiority, despite the results of Tracy's tests, and he reminded the secretary that he and his company were experts in steel-making. When Tracy's test results were made public, the price of nickel skyrocketed, and it appeared for a while that the metal would be just too expensive to permit its use in the quantities needed for tons of armor. The main source of the metal was Canada, and the high protective tariff passed in 1890 threatened to drive its price in the United States still higher. Tracy had to appeal to Congress to grant a tariff exemption for nickel on the basis of national security. The price stabilized, and Harveyized nickel-alloy armor became the standard for American warships.

After months of negotiation, a deal was finally struck with Carnegie, and by 1891, both Bethlehem and Carnegie had contracted to provide armor. However, the continuing difficulties of constructing whole new plants to manufacture it and the need for further tests of nickel alloy meant that it could not be delivered before 1892.

Even after deliveries began, the problem of obtaining armor continued to plague the navy for more than a decade. Bethlehem Steel and Carnegie were the only steel makers capable of producing armor, and rumors of collusion between them to fix prices began to circulate. Congress decided that the price of armor was too high, and it set a ceiling price of three hundred dollars per ton. When three new battleships were authorized in the mid-1890s, and bids for the armor were solicited, both firms declined even to submit bids. They claimed that the new price set by law was too low to produce a profit.

Congress ordered a study to investigate the possibility of the government building a steel plant to produce armor. It learned that a plant would cost four million dollars to build, that it would require several years to construct, and that the armor it would produce almost certainly would be more expensive than armor produced in privately owned plants. Congress relented and raised the price to four hundred dollars per ton, and construction of the new battleships proceeded.

Two years later, the price was again reduced to three hundred dollars. When the next round of bids for new ships were solicited, the only bid below the legally fixed limit was submitted by a company that admitted it had never produced armor, would have to build a new plant, and would require five years to make delivery. Congress threw in the sponge, and in 1900, it gave the secretary of the navy authority to negotiate the price of armor with steel manufacturers.

The struggle waged by William Whitney and Benjamin Tracy to create a domestic American capacity to manufacture armor plate and large-bore naval ordnance, and the warships to carry them, posed ramifications that extended beyond the life of any warships they added to the fleet. The contracts they signed with American steelmakers and private shipyards to build warships marked the beginning of something new in American life, something with a dangerous potential that President Dwight Eisenhower warned against seventy years later in his farewell address: "We must guard against the acquisition of unwarranted influence, whether sought or unsought, by the military-industrial complex. The potential for the disastrous rise of misplaced power exists and will persist." By 1891, a large portion of key American industries and large numbers of American workers—among them some of the most highly skilled technicians in the country—were committed to manufacture something only the government wanted or could buy: armored warships. Would the government continue to buy them? What would happen when the warships contracted by Whitney and Tracy were completed? Would the steel plants and the shipyards, and their swarms of workmen, be idled? Or would the government continue to build warships that needed armor and cannons? How many warships did the navy need? These were questions of intense interest not only to the affected businessmen and workers, but also to the members of Congress who sought their votes.

Battleships with their huge guns, heavy armor, and expensive price tags became the navy's glamor ships that attracted the most attention, but other kinds of ships were important and had to be built, too. Cruisers could be built more quickly and cheaply than battleships, and they remained the backbone of the fleet until the first battleships began to arrive in the mid-1890s. Battleships were built to mete out and absorb punishment. The raison d'être for a cruiser was range and speed. One of William Whitney's principal criticisms of the ABCD cruisers focussed on their obsolete power plants. It became conventional wisdom to say that they were "too weak to fight and too slow to run." Whitney wanted the cruisers authorized during his term of office to be *fast*, and there developed a "craze for speed" in designing cruisers.

It reached its height with the manufacture of *Columbia* and *Minneapolis*, which joined the fleet in 1893 and 1894 respectively. They were huge, displacing 7,375 tons, and at 412 feet, they were the longest warships in the navy. At its sea trials, *Columbia* clocked 22.8 knots, which made it the fastest ship of its class afloat—until *Minneapolis* exceeded 23 knots a year later. In July, 1895, in a well-publicized race from Southampton to New York, *Columbia* easily bested a fast Hamburg-America Line steamer, sustaining an average speed of eighteen knots, even without using forced draft. But *Columbia* and its sister ship were like their speedy Civil War ancestor, *Wampanoag*. Practicality as a warship had been sacrificed for speed. They were thinly armored, undergunned, and expensive to man and operate. Three years after being commissioned, they were laid up in reserve.

When Grover Cleveland took office for his second term as president in 1893, the man he chose for secretary of the navy was Hilary Herbert, who had served as chairman of the House naval affairs committee. Herbert was well versed in naval affairs and in favor of a large fleet. He might have immediately pressed for continued construction of still more battleships and cruisers, except for a seriously inhibiting consideration. Within a few months of the Cleveland administration taking office, the financial panic of 1893 sent the American economy into a tailspin that created the long economic depression of the mid-1890s. In such uncertain, straitened financial circumstances, Congress was reluctant to authorize large expenditures for more battleships.

Fortunately for the industrialists and the workmen dedicated to the construction of warships, as well as the politicians who sought their votes, Congress did not have to make any such authorizations. American shipyards and steel mills were fully occupied with the construction of ships authorized during the Whitney and Tracy eras, including even *Texas* and *Maine*, authorized way back in 1886 but still unfinished. There was no immediate need for Congress or the Cleveland administration to arrange large authorizations to keep the warship-building industry humming. In 1893 and 1894, only three light gunboats, three torpedo boats, and one experimental submarine were authorized. In August, 1894, Theodore Roosevelt wrote to his sister, Anna Cowles, that Cleveland should get on with building up the navy and should in addition order the digging of an inter-oceanic canal across Central America. Roosevelt's brother-in-law, William Sheffield Cowles, was a lieutenant commander in the navy.

By the end of 1894, the backlog of warships under construction was almost cleared away. The depression was continuing, and Congress was forced to weigh a desire to avoid large expenditures for more battleships against a need to keep the steel mills and shipyards busy. Capital and labor were locked in increasingly bitter disputes punctuated by strikes that produced violence, but they could agree on one issue. Industry devoted to national defense, which was almost entirely devoted to building warships, had become important to the national economy. The steel mills and shipyards must not be permitted to close and further shrink profits already shrunk by the depression, thereby forcing more bankruptcies and sending swarms of idled workmen to swell the already swollen ranks of the unemployed. There was no discernible threat to the nation's security that might demand more battleships, but in his annual message to Congress in December, 1894, Cleveland pointed out: "The manufacture of armor requires expensive plants and the aggregation of many skilled workmen. All the armor necessary to complete the vessels now building will be delivered before the 1st of June next. If no new contracts are given out, contractors must disband their workmen and their plants must lie idle." Congress was persuaded. Those members of Congress principally concerned about the depression but indifferent or even hostile to the navy made common cause with the big-navy advocates. Despite reduced revenues, in March of 1895, Congress authorized construction of two battleships, both to be built at the privately owned Newport News Shipbuilding Company. They became *Kearsarge* and *Kentucky,* the two oldest battleships of Roosevelt's Great White Fleet. In June of the following year, three more first-class capital ships were authorized. Construction of five battleships and a number of smaller vessels ensured that the steel mills and shipyards would be kept busy until the turn of the century, and after. It also meant that the vision long held by Roosevelt, Mahan, Luce, Lodge, and others of a muscular American navy capable of taking on the navy of just about any other power (except, perhaps, Britain) was becoming reality.

The first true American battleship to join the fleet was *Indiana,* the first of the three ships authorized by Congress in 1890 to be completed. It was commissioned on November 20, 1895. In the system later adopted by the navy to identify warships by type, *Indiana* was designated BB1. It was regarded as perhaps the most powerful warship in the world when it joined the fleet. It was 350 feet long, displaced 10,200 tons, and had a designated speed of fifteen knots. It carried four thirteen-inch guns in two turrets as its main battery, eight eight-inch guns and four six-inch guns in the secondary battery, and six torpedo tubes. It was protected by eighteen-inch Harveyized nickel-alloy armor. The officer chosen for the plum assignment to command America's first battleship was Captain Robley D. "Fighting Bob" Evans.

Evans was born in Virginia in 1846, the son of a country physician. He entered the Naval Academy in the autumn of 1860, on the eve of the Civil War. His family in Virginia wanted him to join the Confeder-

U.S.S. *Indiana* (BB1), America's first battleship

Library of Congress photograph

ate forces, but he resisted their pleas and stayed in the Union navy. His younger brother became an officer in the Confederate army. Evans's studies at the Naval Academy were cut short by the war, and he was commissioned an ensign in October, 1863. He served mostly on block-ade duty until almost the end of the war.

In January, 1865, when he was still only eighteen years old, his naval career nearly ended before it had well begun. He was commanding a company of marines in an attack at Fort Fischer in South Carolina. As he led the charge, he was wounded by a bullet that grazed his chest. He continued to lead the attack until he was knocked down by a second bullet that hit his left leg below the knee. He dragged himself forward, urging his men on, until a third bullet brought him down for good by smashing his right knee. While he was lying on the ground, a fourth bullet took away part of one toe. Badly wounded, he nevertheless was able to use his revolver to finish off the Confederate sniper who was trying to kill him.

Evans was evacuated to the naval hospital at Norfolk. By the time he arrived and was deposited in a bed, his legs were numb and hanging useless. He was immediately examined by a team of physicians, who withdrew to one end of the room for a conference. The patient heard one of them say, "take off both legs in the morning."

When a surgeon's assistant arrived the next morning to prepare him for surgery, Evans confronted the surprised orderly with his revolver, which he had hidden under his pillow when he was brought into the hospital.

> I told him that there were six loads in it, and that if he or any one else entered my door with anything that looked like a case of instruments, I meant to begin shooting, and that he might rest perfectly sure I would kill six before they cut off my legs. This brought matters to a crisis at once, and in a few minutes the surgeon in charge came in very angry and full of threats. But the result was that they left my legs on.

He had a long, painful recovery. He wasted away until he resembled a skeleton. He was invalided out of the service. But he slowly regained the use of his legs, and in 1866, he was able to regain his naval commission when he petitioned Congress for reinstatement back into the service. His legs remained scarred and misshapen, and until the end of his life they often caused him to suffer excruciating pain. He walked with a noticeable limp, and he came to be known affectionately in the service as "Old Gimpy."

Evans might well have received his nickname, "Fighting Bob," as a result of his wartime exploit or his long struggle to recover from his wounds, but he did not. He was given the name years later by newspapermen writing about him in connection with an incident in which, ironically, there was no fighting at all. In 1891, Evans was given command of a small gunboat, *Yorktown*. Soon after taking command, he received urgent orders to proceed to Valparaiso, Chile. A revolution—or a civil war, according to some participants—had occurred in Chile, and the American Legation had become involved by giving asylum to certain Chileans. Resentment and hard feelings toward the United States ran high, because it had interfered in what Chileans regarded as a domestic matter. The American cruiser *Baltimore*—one of William Whitney's ships—was in the harbor at Valparaiso to protect American interests. *Yorktown* was dispatched to reinforce *Baltimore* in case overt hostilities broke out.

Evans and *Yorktown* arrived at Valparaiso in December, 1891, after a passage of fifty-one days around South America and through the Strait of Magellan, to find *Baltimore* anchored in the harbor, facing several Chilean warships. After the uproar of the revolution subsided but before *Yorktown* arrived, a liberty party of sailors from *Baltimore* had gone ashore and been attacked by a mob of Chileans. Two Americans were killed and eighteen suffered serious stab wounds. Not only had the police stood by and allowed the attack on the unarmed Americans to continue, but one of the dead Americans had been shot by a policeman. The United States demanded an apology. Chile refused, and relations between the two countries deteriorated. In Valparaiso, feelings ran high and were mounting.

Immediately after arrival, Evans called on the captain of the *Baltimore*. He was Winfield Scott Schley, a highly-regarded officer who would become a controversial figure in the battle of Santiago in 1898. He was a rather different personality from the bluntly direct Evans, who did not much like him. Evans found Captain Schley in his cabin writing a letter, and Evans's account of his reaction to the scene reveals much about himself and why he came to be so fondly regarded by Theodore Roosevelt:

> [Schley] was in the midst of a correspondence with the intendente, conducted in the most perfect Castilian, to show, or prove, that his men were all perfectly sober when they were assaulted on shore. I did not agree with him in this, for in the first place, I doubted the fact, and in the second it was not an issue worth discussing. His men were probably drunk on shore, properly drunk; they went ashore many of them, for the purpose of getting drunk on Chilean rum paid for with good United States money. When in this condition, they were more entitled to protection than if they had been sober. This was my view of it, at least, and the one I always held about men whom I commanded.

Schley's correspondence with the intendente apparently did nothing to reduce the tension. He had received orders to proceed to California, and soon after Evans's arrival, *Baltimore* departed. The tiny *Yorktown*, which carried only a few six-inch guns in open mounts, was left alone to face nine Chilean warships in the midst of a growing international crisis. By early January, there was talk of war in both countries, and reports published in Britain confidently predicted that war would break out any day. The cruiser *Boston* was ordered to Valparaiso, but for several weeks, *Yorktown* was the lone American warship in the harbor.

The Chileans engaged in provocative acts towards the Americans, and the fiery Evans held himself and his men in check with difficulty. Chilean torpedo boats made speed runs at *Yorktown* as though using her for target practice, swerving aside at the last minute. One boat missed hitting the American ship's stern by less than six feet. Evans informed the Chilean officer in command of the torpedo boats that "if one of them struck me, I would blow her bottom out." He had his crew stand prominently to their guns to show they were ready to fight if necessary, even against such odds, and he issued orders to his gunners that if any Chilean vessel "even scratched the paint on the *Yorktown*, to blow the boat out of the water and kill every man on her."

By late January, the crisis subsided when the government of Chile offered an apology for the *Baltimore* affair and agreed to pay an indemnity. Evans received orders to leave Valparaiso. On February 6, at Callao, Peru, he wrote in his journal:

> A mail is in, and I have nice letters from friends commending my course at Valparaiso; very satisfactory, but I wish the newspapers would let me alone. Why should they call me "Fighting Bob?" . . . Some of the letters say, "we are waiting for you to stir up the war," and the writers will never know how near I came to doing it. . . . In the discharge of my duty I gave the Chileans a fine chance to fight if they wanted to, and the odds were enough in their favour—nine ships to one. But they backed water every time. . . . Of course, if they had provoked it, I should have engaged their nine ships without hesitation, and the chances would not have favoured my getting the *Yorktown* out of their harbor.

Ever after, he was known in the press as "Fighting Bob" Evans, a sobriquet which the newsmen knew perfectly fitted his personality, but in the navy he was still "Old Gimpy."

When Evans received orders to take command of *Indiana* in 1895, he was in command of *New York*, the armored cruiser that was the most powerful American warship until *Indiana* joined the fleet. Evans took over the new battleship in October even before it was placed in commission, and he was slightly bewildered by it: "The *New York* seemed to me a complicated mass of machinery, but this new thing was a real machine shop from top to bottom. It required several weeks of hard work and study after I joined her before I felt reasonably sure that I would not get lost if I attempted to inspect her throughout." Like all warships, *Indiana* was a product of compromises among size, range, speed, armament, and armor. Its secondary batteries were greater than those of existing battleships, and combined with the main battery, they gave the ship a broadside of greater firepower than any other warship. The sixty-ton, thirteen-inch rifles of the main battery could throw a 1,100-pound projectile up to four miles with fair accuracy. American battleships became known for their unusually powerful armament, but engine and fuel capacity, and berthing space, were sacrificed to accommodate the weight of guns, ammunition, and armor. With a top speed of sixteen knots, the *Indiana*-class battleships were slow compared to existing British capital ships and even to *Texas* and *Maine*. Their normal bunker capacity of only four hundred tons of coal limited their range so as to make them suitable only as coastal defense ships, as their congressional authorization had specified. The influence of the Civil War monitor could be detected in their low freeboard—only ten feet—which made the three ships very wet at sea, especially in heavy weather.

Life aboard an American warship in the 1890s had not changed nearly as much as the ships themselves over the past fifty or seventy-five years. The crew still slung their hammocks on the gun deck at night, as sailors aboard the frigates of Stephen Decatur and Thomas Truxton had done. Each sailor still received a monthly allotment to buy food, which he pooled with several other sailors to form a "mess." One member of each mess was designated the "mess cook," who was responsible for drawing his mess's rations and cooking them under the supervision of the ship's cook. They ate from bare wooden tables lowered at meal time from overhead racks in the same space where they slept. They enjoyed such traditional sailor's delights as "plum duff," "dunderfunk," "rope-yarn stew," and "slush." Hard liquor was not permitted aboard navy ships, but unlike today's navy which bans all alcoholic beverages aboard ship, beer was permitted. Officers were permitted to maintain a wine-mess.

The captain and his officers still had their quarters aft in the stern, as had been the case for centuries in sailing ships. The stern was roomy, but a more important reason for placing the captain aft in sailing days was that his place of command was the quarterdeck, aft and just over his cabin. The place of command on steamships was the bridge, closer to the bow than the stern. Nevertheless, naval architects would not move the officers' quarters forward to the amidships section, nearer the bridge, and the crew's quarters aft, until after the turn of the century. Wardrooms and officers' cabins were often panelled in richly finished wood and beautifuly appointed.

As late as the 1880s, American bluejackets were a polyglot bunch recruited from all over the world. Admiral David Dixon Porter once described them as "as fine a body of Germans, Huns, Norsemen, Gauls, Chinese and other outside barbarians as one could wish to see, softened by time and civilization." Even by 1899, only about three quarters of American bluejackets were American citizens. In that year, a law was passed which for the first time granted retirement pay after thirty years of service. In 1901, the navy announced that as a policy, it would recruit only American citizens.

Between 1890 and 1910, immigration into the United States crested at the highest levels in the nation's history. Life for a navy bluejacket was no bowl of cherries, but compared with life for the average immigrant in the slums of a large American city, it did not look bad to a prospective young recruit. By 1901, desertion from the navy still occurred at a rate of fourteen percent a year, but the expanding navy never had trouble recruiting men to man its ships. Ashore, sailors were welcomed in the dives of San Francisco's Barbary Coast or New York's Tenderloin, but signs reading "Sailors and Dogs Not Allowed" were common in more respectable hotels and restaurants. In 1906, Theodore Roosevelt gave his strong personal support to a navy sailor who sued a Newport, Rhode Island, dance hall where he had been denied admittance. Roosevelt's support called attention to the case and prompted passage of local laws prohibiting discrimination against sailors and soldiers in uniform. Bob Evans was once quoted as saying, with pardonable hyperbole, "You don't need armor when you have men like mine."

In early May, 1896, Evans gave Theodore Roosevelt a tour of *Indiana* when it was tied up in New York for some refitting. Roosevelt was serving as a police commissioner in New York, having resigned his position as civil service commissioner in Washington the previous year. His job had nothing to do with the navy, but his intense interest in naval matters had not faded. The previous February, he had dined with Alfred Mahan, and during the weeks of early spring, he had read several books on naval subjects. He was no doubt eager to inspect the first American battleship. He went over *Indiana* "from top to bottom," and he pronounced it "a splendid ship." Whether this was his first meeting with Robley Evans is uncertain, but Roosevelt apparently was not yet well acquainted with Evans. In a letter to a friend a few weeks later, Roosevelt referred to the visit and to "Captain Robert Evans."

In the summer of 1896, *Indiana*'s sister ships, *Massachusetts* and *Oregon*, joined the fleet. *Indiana*'s shakedown was complete, so Bob Evans was detached and rotated to shore duty. His assignment was lighthouse inspector, an unchallenging but pleasant billet he had filled in the 1880s, which allowed him to travel extensively up and down the country's coasts. In New York, Police Commissioner Theodore Roosevelt was preoccupied that summer with thinking about the presidential election to be held in November and about his prospects for appointment to a particular position he coveted in the new administration if the Republican candidate, William McKinley, was elected.

5

"I Have the Navy in Good Shape"

In late July or early August of 1896, the Roosevelt family entertained two houseguests at Sagamore Hill. They were Bellamy Storer and his wife, Maria. Storer was a wealthy congressman from Cincinnati, as well as a friend and political supporter of his fellow Ohioan, William McKinley. He was one of a group of wealthy Republicans who had contributed money to a fund to save William McKinley from bankruptcy in 1893 and consequently from political ruin. If McKinley won in November, Storer was widely thought to be in line for a high level position, perhaps even a cabinet post. He was Maria's second husband. She was politically influential and wealthy in her own right, a grande dame of society in Cincinnati and Washington. She also happened to be the aunt of Nicholas Longworth, a future congressman, speaker of the house, and son-in-law of Theodore Roosevelt. She considered the Roosevelts "very dear friends," and she later wrote that "Theodore seemed to us at that time like a younger brother."

One warm afternoon, Roosevelt invited Mrs. Storer to accompany him for a row on Oyster Bay. As he pulled on the oars in the hot afternoon sunshine, he ruminated about his future, and he appeared to Mrs. Storer to feel depressed. "I have done all I can on the Police Board in New York," he told her. "I can't stay much longer there. I don't know what I shall do next. I have no future." As they walked home, he finally blurted out what probably was really on his mind when he invited his guest for the little outing. "There is one thing I *would* like to have, but there is no chance of my getting it—McKinley will never give it to me. I should like to be assistant secretary of the navy." Mrs. Storer promised that she and her husband would speak to McKinley on Roosevelt's behalf. She left unsaid what Roosevelt suspected and she knew to be true: the placid McKinley did not like the headstrong, combative Roosevelt.

Soon after the Republicans nominated McKinley, Roosevelt made a point of becoming acquainted with Mark Hanna, McKinley's political manager and financial angel. He offered to campaign for the Republican ticket and was assigned to follow the Democratic candidate, William Jennings Bryan, around the Middle West to rebut Bryan's campaign speeches. He followed hard on Bryan's heels for weeks, speaking to the same audiences that Bryan had addressed only days or even hours earlier. When McKinley was elected in a landslide, Roosevelt's campaigning had earned him consideration for an appointment in the new administration. His friend, Henry Cabot Lodge, now a senator and rising figure in the Republican party, lunched with McKinley at his home in Canton, Ohio, on November 29 and put in a word for Roosevelt. He reported that McKinley had responded with some positive comments about Roosevelt but had added, "I hope he has no preconceived plans that he would wish to drive through the moment he got in." Lodge reported that he told McKinley that "he need not give himself the slightest uneasiness on that score."

The Storers had dinner with McKinley a few days later. True to her promise, Mrs. Storer drew the president-elect aside after dinner to plead Roosevelt's case. McKinley looked at her quizzically. "I want peace," he said, "and I am told your friend Theodore—whom I know only slightly—is always getting into rows with everybody. I am afraid he is too pugnacious." "Give him a chance to prove he can be peaceful," Mrs. Storer pleaded. "I shall have to think it over," McKinley said as they parted. "If I can, I will make that appointment."

Roosevelt's prospects looked dim, not only because of McKinley's reluctance, but also because of a political problem. The Republican boss in New York, Tom Platt, was expected to be elected to the Senate in January. Platt and Roosevelt were political enemies, dating back to Roosevelt's service in the New York state legislature. In the Senate, Platt could be expected to oppose the nomination of Roosevelt to any post in the new administration, and with that expectation looming, McKinley could be expected to decide against submitting a nomination for Senate confirmation. Roosevelt swallowed his pride and set about ingratiating himself with Platt. The powerful political boss was elected, and he let it be known that while he did not support a nomination of Roosevelt, he would not oppose it. Actually, he was delighted to see the troublesome Roosevelt leave New York for Washington. In private, Platt said that

Roosevelt would "do less harm to the organization as assistant secretary of the navy than in any other office that could be named." Roosevelt's nomination was supported by a galaxy of influential friends, including Lodge, Judge William Howard Taft, John Hay (another contributor to the fund that saved McKinley from bankruptcy), and the speaker of the house, Thomas Reed.

The months of uncertainty ended when he was nominated on April 6. Two days later, he was confirmed by the Senate. McKinley's fears may have been revived when he read what the *Washington Post* had to say that day. Roosevelt, the newspaper predicted, "will bring with him to Washington all that machinery of disturbance and upheaval which is as much a part of his entourage as the very air he breathes." Roosevelt took up his duties on April 19, and within a week, he sent two long letters to McKinley about fleet dispositions to Hawaii in the Pacific and to the Mediterranean. They bristled with technical details and were amazing products for someone who had been in his job only a matter of days before they were written.

Roosevelt's boss as secretary of the navy was John Davis Long. He had served as governor of Massachusetts and three terms in Congress. He and Roosevelt were both politicians, but any similarity between them ended there. Long was Roosevelt's senior by twenty years, but he looked and acted even older. He was short, soft, and plump, in contrast to the robust Roosevelt with his muscular, barrel-chested body and thick, bull neck. Long had no background in naval affairs, and in contrast to Roosevelt, who had a voracious appetite for all the nuts and bolts of operating a navy, he had no desire to acquire any more information. "My plan," he wrote in his journal, "is to leave all such [technical] matters to the bureau chiefs . . . limiting myself to the general direction of affairs." He wrote poetry which was collected in books with such titles as *By the Fireside* and *Bites of a Cherry,* and he liked to spend time puttering about his farm at Buckfield, Maine. He was genial, kindly, and easy-going, in contrast to his hyperactive, combative assistant secretary.

For all their differences, Roosevelt liked his chief. He thought Long was "a perfect dear" and "one of the most high-minded, honorable and upright gentlemen I have ever had the good fortune to serve under." By contrast, a very influential senator's wife, who happened to be the niece of the new secretary of state, John Sherman, wrote to a friend, "Rightly or wrongly, Uncle John and Long are considered and treated as senile." After his first formal meeting with Roosevelt, Long wrote in his diary that his subordinate was the "best man for the job."

Several years later, while Roosevelt was serving as president, Long described Roosevelt as he appeared in 1897 in the Navy Department. Roosevelt was, Long wrote, "an interesting personality" whom he, Long, had been responsible for selecting to be assistant secretary. He recalled that Roosevelt was "heart and soul in his work," so much so that "his typewriter had no rest. He, like most of us, lacks the rare knack of brevity." When war with Spain loomed, Long found on his desk every morning a memorandum from Roosevelt offering detailed recommendations about preparing the navy for the coming conflict. Long pointed out that the individual bureaus were capable of foreseeing much of what Roosevelt suggested. Roosevelt accepted the gentle criticism "with the generous good nature which is so marked in him." Long recalled that "nothing could be pleasanter than our relations."

In early May, Roosevelt received a letter from Alfred Mahan marked "Personal & Private." Mahan had retired from the navy the previous autumn to continue his writing career. At a gala retirement banquet in early December, his old enemy, William Whitney, had made some very graceful remarks praising the famous naval philosopher, and Mahan had graciously replied in kind. In his letter to the new asistant secretary of the navy, Mahan wrote, "You will, I hope, allow me at times to write to you on service matters, without thinking that I am doing more than throw out ideas for consideration." He immediately made it clear that by "service matters" he did not mean the professional minutiae of warships or naval administration, in which Roosevelt was immersing himself with such delight, but which had always bored Mahan even when he was on active duty. Mahan wanted to write about geopolitics, specifically about Japan and Hawaii.

By virtue of its triumph over China in the Sino-Japanese War of 1894–95, Japan had emerged as one of the powers in Asia and was busy further expanding its navy. Two Japanese battleships were under construction in Britain. In March of 1897, the American-run government of the Republic of Hawaii, fearing that an avalanche of Japanese immigrants seeking work in the islands might tilt the balance of political power away from the ruling Americans, returned to Japan more than a thousand immigrants. In protest, Japan sent a cruiser to the islands and demanded an indemnity. This vaguely threatening cruiser remained at Honolulu all summer. Mahan thought the Japanese had designs on Hawaii, so the United States should immediately annex the islands. If there were "political problems" preventing annexation, he wrote to Roosevelt, "take them first and solve afterward."

Roosevelt sent Mahan an immediate response which said, "as regards Hawaii, I take your views absolutely, as indeed I do on foreign policy generally. If I had my way, we would annex those islands tomorrow." Moreover, he wrote, Secretary Long shared the same views. Roosevelt went on to discuss another foreign policy problem that Mahan had not raised, which was being reported much more widely and vehemently in the press than Japan or Hawaii: "There are big problems in the West Indies also. Until we definitely turn Spain out of those islands (and if I had my way, that would be done tomorrow), we will always be menaced there." Roosevelt also marked his letter "Personal and Private," cautioning Mahan that "this letter must, of course, be considered as entirely confidential . . . to no one else excepting Lodge do I talk like this." He was, after all, only an assistant secretary without cabinet rank.

Unlike Hawaii, Cuba was a front-page story in American newspapers in the spring of 1897. The Cubans had been in open revolt against Spain since 1895, and Spanish efforts to suppress them were growing ever more repressive. Hardly anyone advocated annexation of Cuba by the United States, but there was growing sentiment that the United States ought to help the Cubans gain independence from Spain. Roosevelt expressed sympathy for the downtrodden Cubans, but his real concern was to prod the United States to take vigorous action to see that *all* remaining European political presence in the western hemisphere ended. If the United States built an isthmian canal, and the Caribbean became the highway of commerce that Mahan foresaw, he and Roosevelt feared that Spanish power based in Cuba could threaten that commerce flowing past America's southern doorstep, much of it probably American.

Roosevelt and Mahan continued to exchange letters throughout 1897 and early 1898, right up to the eve of the declaration of war against Spain. They continued to discuss Hawaii and the Spanish colonies in the Caribbean, and they assured each other of their complete agreement that the United States should annex Hawaii and should drive Spain from Cuba and Puerto Rico. Roosevelt on several occasions urged Mahan to bring his influence and prestige to bear on members of Congress and others, and he reported that he used his famous correspondent's letters to urge his superiors in government to take action. He did not forget that his responsibilities were to the navy. He told Mahan that Long "is only luke-warm about building up our Navy," and suggested that Mahan write to the secretary. On June 9, he reported, "Yesterday I urged immediate action by the President as regards Hawaii. Entirely between ourselves, I believe he will act very shortly."

McKinley did not have to persuaded of the wisdom of annexing Hawaii. He was already convinced that the islands were important to the United States, both commercially and strategically. In June, the United States signed a treaty of annexation with the government in Honolulu. However, the annexationists did not have enough votes in the Senate for the two-thirds majority needed to ratify a treaty, especially after Japan learned of the treaty and protested American annexation of the islands. The treaty failed to gain ratification, and Hawaii continued to be an independent country, although it maintained very close ties to the United States. A year later, the annexationists were successful. In the midst of the outpouring of patriotic fervor attending the war with Spain, Hawaii was annexed by passage of legislation, which required a simple majority in Congress, rather than by treaty.

On June 2, Roosevelt gave his first public speech as assistant secretary. The venue he chose was the Naval War College. According to one of his recent biographers, it was "the first great speech of his career." He delivered a stirring, flag-waving oration guaranteed to set the pulses of his audience of naval officers racing. His theme was taken from George Washington: "to be prepared for war is the most effectual means to promote peace." For Roosevelt, that meant immediate further expansion of the navy. If war nevertheless came, he argued, it would stimulate and enhance the manly, martial virtues that in Roosevelt's judgement made a country great. "All the great masterful races have been fighting races," he thundered. "Cowardice in a race, as in an individual, is the unpardonable sin. . . . No triumph of peace is quite so great as the supreme triumphs of war." Although his declared subject was peace, he had uttered the word "war" sixty-two times by the time he reached his stem-winding conclusion:

> There are higher things in this life than the soft and easy enjoyment of material comfort. It is through strife, or the readiness for strife, that a nation must win greatness. We ask for a great navy, partly because we

Assistant Secretary of the Navy Roosevelt at the Naval War College in June 1897, when he delivered the first great speech of his public career.

U.S. Naval Historical Center photograph

feel that no national life is worth having if the nation is not willing, when the need shall arise, to stake everything on the supreme arbitrament of war, and to pour out its blood, its treasure, and its tears like water, rather than submit to the loss of honor and renown.

The massive outpouring of blood and treasure in the Civil War was more than thirty years in the past, and Roosevelt was a member of the generation, just coming into positions of power and responsibility, which had no personal memories of that great bloodletting. None of the middle-grade naval officers in his audience had any such memories. They had to sit quietly and listen to their elders spin stirring tales of their experiences in the great national epic of the nineteenth century, as Roosevelt had listened to the stories of his uncles Bulloch about *Alabama*. The growing crisis with Spain offered the possibility that this new generation might experience its own epic struggle. Few people stopped to consider how the headlong rush of the technology of war since 1865 had increased the potential for carnage many times over, especially in naval warfare. No one really knew what a salvo of explosive shells, each weighing a half ton, fired from a battery of thirteen-inch naval rifles, might do to a fleet of ships and the crews aboard them or targets on shore. There had been nothing like it in the Civil War.

Roosevelt's speech struck a resounding chord, not just among his immediate audience in Newport, but among the general American public of 1897, with its fading memories of the horrors of Antietam, Shiloh, and the Wilderness. It was widely reported, and widely praised, in the press. Many newspapers printed the entire text. "Well-done, nobly spoken," rhapsodized the *Washington Post.* "Theodore Roosevelt, you have found your place at last!" The *New York Sun* described it as "manly, patriotic, intelligent, and convincing." John Davis Long, by contrast, did not like the speech, but McKinley—known privately as "The Majah" for his service in the Civil War—admitted to a friend, "I suspect Roosevelt is right."

The warm reception given his Naval War College speech encouraged him to redouble his campaign to persuade McKinley and his administration to accelerate the build-up of the navy, annex Hawaii, and drive Spain from the western hemisphere. In July, he made a tour of naval militia stations around the Great Lakes. At Sandusky, Ohio, on July 23, he delivered another thundering speech about military preparedness and overseas expansion. "The United States is not in a position which requires her to ask Japan, or any other foreign Power, what territory it shall or shall not acquire," he declared. This speech sparked headlines, too. The New York *Tribune* commented that Roosevelt should "leave to the Department of State the declaration of the foreign policy of this government." John D. Long, still unsettled by the Naval War College speech, read the news reports. "The headlines . . . nearly threw the Secretary into a fit," wrote Roosevelt to Lodge, "and he gave me as heavy a wigging as his invariable courtesy and kindness would permit."

Whatever fears Long might have entertained about his rambunctious subordinate did not prevent him from departing Washington on August 2 to spend the hot months of August and September at his Maine farm, leaving Roosevelt in charge of the department as acting secretary. His kindly "wigging" did not deter Roosevelt from grabbing the reins of responsibility and generating a whirlwind of activity throughout the Navy Department, nor from continuing his publicity campaign. In the middle of August he wrote to Paul Dana, the publisher of the *New York Sun:* "I am rather afraid that there is a very foolish feeling growing that we now have enough of a Navy. . . . It would be horrible folly to stop building up our Navy now." He issued a blizzard of memos and orders on a multitude of subjects. He wrote letters to Long to report what he was doing, and he assured the absent secretary that everything was going along smoothly. "I shan't send you anything unless it is really important," he told his boss. Long need not even answer his letters, he

wrote, because "I don't want you bothered at all." "You must be tired,"
he wrote soothingly, "and you ought to have an entire rest." On August
19, he wrote to Bellamy Storer, "I am having immense fun running the
Navy." On August 23, the *New York Sun* reported: "The liveliest spot in
Washington at present is the Navy Department. The decks are cleared
for action. Acting Secretary Roosevelt, in the absence of Governor
Long, has the whole Navy bordering on a war footing. It remains only
to sand down the decks and pipe to quarters for action." Meanwhile,
Roosevelt in his letters to Long in Maine was urging his chief to "stay
there just exactly as long as you want to."

In early September, Roosevelt spent three days with the North Atlantic Squadron as it went through maneuvers in the Atlantic off Hampton
Roads. He sailed aboard *Dolphin,* and he brought along the western artist Frederick Remington as a guest. The squadron flagship was *New York,*
and included in the little fleet was an even newer armored cruiser, *Brooklyn.* Also on hand was *Iowa,* the newest and most powerful American
battleship, which had been in commission only since June. Most of its
crew had never even heard the main battery guns fired. They were
twelve-inch guns, with a smaller bore than those on the three battleships
built earlier, which fired a lighter projectile. But their higher muzzle velocity gave them greater range and more hitting power.

The assistant secretary was invited aboard *Iowa* to witness the battleship's first target practice. He was handed earplugs and advised to
"open your mouth, stand on your toes, and let your frame hang loosely"
when the huge cannons were about to fire. The concussion from the
secondary battery's eight-inch guns shook the ship from stem to stern.
The first salvo by the main battery stove in a lifeboat and burst several
locked steel doors. Roosevelt reported in a letter to Rudyard Kipling
that when the main battery guns opened fire, Frederick Remington
"was very nearly blown up through incautiously getting too near the
blast line of one of the 13-inch [*sic*] guns." Roosevelt squinted at the
destroyed target through spectacles dimmed by the grime of powder
smoke. He had looked forward for weeks to going aboard the warships
and observing their evolutions, and he was not disappointed. The boy-
ish glee it aroused in him was reported to Lodge:

> I have never enjoyed three days more than my three days with the fleet.
> . . . Think of it, on the Atlantic Ocean, out of sight of land, going out to
> dinner to a battleship in evening dress without an overcoat! I saw for
> myself the working of the different gear for turning turrets—electric,

hydraulic, steam, and pneumatic. I was aboard *Iowa* . . . and was able to satisfy myself definitely of the great superiority of the battleship as a gun platform. I was on *New York* during the practice at night with searchlights and rapid fire guns at a drifting target, the location of which was unknown. I saw the maneuvers of the squadron as a whole, and met every captain and went over with him, on the ground, what was needed.

In the middle of September, the president returned to Washington from his home in Canton, Ohio, where he had spent the hot weeks of August and early September. Roosevelt and McKinley had first met as long before as the 1884 Republican Convention, where they had been political opponents. McKinley had been a key supporter of James G. Blaine, who received the presidential nomination, while Roosevelt vehemently opposed Blaine. Though both were Republicans, they remained political opponents, and Roosevelt had privately opposed McKinley's nomination for president.

Soon after McKinley's return to Washington, Roosevelt—to his surprise, no doubt—was given several opportunities to present his views about the navy, Hawaii, and Cuba to the president personally. McKinley invited him out for an afternoon drive in the presidential carriage and followed that up with a dinner invitation and then another carriage drive. Roosevelt pressed home his ideas about the navy and foreign policy. He told the president that if war broke out with Spain, he wanted to see action. McKinley, somewhat amused, assured him that his wish could probably be granted. McKinley surprised him by saying that his views about Cuba expressed in his Sandusky speech were correct.

As the chairman of a personnel board that met in the early autumn, Roosevelt made what was probably his most lasting contribution to the navy as assistant secretary. Among the questions the board considered was a proposal to combine the deck and engineering officer groups into a single officer corps. Ever since the introduction of steam propulsion, the engineers of the "black gang" in their filthy dens below decks had been treated as second-class citizens aboard American ships. The grimy engineers with their dirty fingernails were regarded as inferior to deck officers in the navy's hierarchy. During the post–Civil War years, as ships became more and more complicated, with increasingly intricate machinery, the engineers sought without success to gain equality with their colleagues on the bridge. Most of the older, more senior deck officers resisted allowing the mechanical tinkerers from below deck into their command circle. Alfred Mahan, for example, expressed only mildly disguised contempt for any naval officer concerned with machinery rather than the art of war. Roosevelt was sympathetic to the plight of the engineers, who he believed had long since earned their right to equal status, and his board recommended that it be granted by merging the deck and engineering officer groups.

Long returned to Washington at the end of September, despite Roosevelt's urging him to remain at his farm through October. He found that two very senior officers, the commanders of the European and the Asiatic squadrons, were due for transfer, and actions had begun during his absence to name their replacements. He also found that politics, in the person of William Chandler, a member of the Senate Committee on Naval Affairs, was playing a hand—as was his assistant secretary.

Three officers were candidates for the two assignments. One of them, John A. Howell, was a friend of Chandler, who was pushing his appointment. Howell had been rejected for command of a squadron once before, and Roosevelt considered him indecisive and afraid of responsibility. Command of the European Squadron was the senior of the two positions, but Roosevelt regarded the appointment of a new commander of the Asiatic Squadron as much more important. In the event of war with Spain, which appeared increasingly possible, if not inevitable, this commander would engage the Spanish forces in the Philippines. He would be operating far from home with little chance of receiving orders or support from Washington. Roosevelt wanted to be certain that a decisive, self-reliant, aggressive officer was given the billet. The man he had in mind was Captain George E. Dewey.

Dewey was born in Vermont in 1837 and graduated from Annapolis in 1858. He served under David Farragut in the early years of the Civil War at New Orleans and on the lower Mississippi. He wrote in his autobiography that "valuable as the training at Annapolis was, it was poor schooling beside that of serving under Farragut in time of war." In 1865, he commanded a steam frigate in the attack on Fort Fischer in South Carolina, the attack in which Bob Evans was so severely wounded. During the postwar years, Dewey gained a reputation as an energetic, bold officer, eager to take initiatives.

In 1895, Dewey was fifty-eight years old and held the rank of captain. He was short and wiry and known as one the navy's snappiest dressers. He was always immaculately turned out in a faultlessly tailored uniform and highly polished boots. He welcomed responsibility, and he was hoping against hope for one more chance to command in combat before he retired. Late in the year, he was appointed president of the Board of Inspection and Survey. The position was important at the time, as he later wrote, because the incumbent was responsible for supervising the sea trials of all the new ships being completed and approving their fitness to be commissioned. During the year and a half he spent in the position, he presided at the sea trials of *Maine, Texas, Indiana, Massachusetts,* and *Iowa*—all the battleships except *Oregon,* which was built and given sea trials on the west coast. When he learned that a new commander of the Asiatic Squadron was to be named, he immediately applied for the assignment. He was due for a command at sea, and he knew that the Asiatic Squadron commander, on the other side of the world from Washington, was free to operate with a large degree of independence, far from the red tape of headquarters. He also knew that in the event of war with Spain, the Asiatic Squadron would see action in the Philippines.

The exact circumstances of Dewey's appointment to command the Asiatic Squadron are a bit uncertain. John Davis Long later wrote that he simply examined the records of the candidates, decided that Dewey should go to the Pacific and Howell to Europe, and made those recommendations to McKinley, who approved them. Dewey in his autobiography credits Roosevelt with engineering his appointment, and other accounts support him. Roosevelt had first met Dewey the previous June, and he was impressed by the dapper little officer. Both men lived and worked in Washington, and after their first meeting, they were often seen on pleasant afternoons riding together in Rock Creek Park. The stories Roosevelt heard in the Navy Department about the independent-minded Dewey confirmed his favorable opinion.

On September 27, the day before Long was scheduled to return to the Department, Roosevelt intercepted a letter from Senator Chandler, addressed to Long, recommending Howell for a squadron command. Roosevelt quickly sent a note to Chandler asking him to withhold his recommendation until Roosevelt could speak to him about it. Apparently, Roosevelt's plea was ignored, because Chandler did not withdraw his letter.

Roosevelt summoned Dewey urgently to his office and told him about the letter. Chandler did not specify which command Howell should be given, but Roosevelt feared that McKinley might give him the all-important Asia command. "I want you to go," he told Dewey. "You are the man who will be equal to the emergency if one arises. Do you know any senators?" Dewey replied that Senator Proctor from his home state of Vermont was a family friend. Proctor supported an expansionist foreign policy and could be expected to be sympathetic to a recommendation by Roosevelt. "You could not have a better sponsor," Roosevelt replied, and told Dewey to talk to Proctor without delay. "I went immediately to see Senator Proctor, who was delighted that I had mentioned the matter to him," Dewey later recounted. "That very day, he called on President McKinley and received the promise of the appointment before he left the White House." Long returned from Maine to find a memo from the president ordering Dewey's appointment. He expressed annoyance that an officer would employ "political pull" to gain an assignment, until he discovered Chandler's letter supporting Howell's candidacy.

Dewey's orders were signed on October 21, and he sailed by steamer from San Francisco on December 7 to join his flagship, *Olympia,* in Japan. In San Francisco, he made arrangements for a shipment of ammunition to his squadron, because he heard it needed to be resupplied. On January 3, 1898, he hoisted his commodore's pennant aboard *Olympia* at Nagasaki.

Roosevelt and Dewey were practically alone in their concern about preparations for possible action in the Philippines. Hardly anyone else in Washington was thinking about little-known islands halfway around the world. McKinley later admitted to a friend that he "could not have placed those darned islands within two thousand miles." Virtually no one in the United States was aware that an insurrection against Spanish rule was in progress, and being savagely suppressed, in the Philippines. What dominated American headlines and thinking in the autumn and winter of 1897 was the savagely suppressed insurrection in Cuba.

The Cubans had been in armed revolt since 1895, although active resistance to Spanish rule had been going on for decades. In February, 1896, the government in Madrid somewhat reluctantly sent General Valeriano Weyler as governor-general to quell the revolt. An admirer of General William Tecumseh Sherman, Weyler was expected to take drastic measures against the revolutionaries, and he fulfilled those expectations. To deny the insurrectionists aid and support by the general population, he herded Cubans into concentration camps where they died by the thousands from disease, starvation, and torture. American newspapers, especially those published by William Randolph Hearst and Joseph Pulitzer, vied to boost circulation by publishing in sickening detail accounts of Spanish atrocities in Cuba. The governor-general became known as "Butcher" Weyler to Americans.

If there had been public opinion polls in 1897, they would no doubt have revealed that increasing numbers of Americans favored taking strong action against Spain over Cuba. Many of the stories of atrocities were highly exaggerated or even pure fiction, but there was more than a grain of truth in the overall tone of the reporting. By mid-1897, the Spanish themselves estimated that fully a third of the rural population—more than four hundred thousand people—had died in the concentration camps. Soon after his inauguration, McKinley sent a representative to Cuba to investigate the situation. His report confirmed many of the accounts of atrocities. "Cuba," he wrote, "is wrapped in the stillness of death." Weyler's draconian policies were achieving success in his assigned mission: they were reducing revolutionary activity. But they were also stoking the fire of the American public's indignation and revulsion which, in turn, encouraged the revolutionaries to continue their fight, in the hope that the United States would soon actively intervene.

By the autumn of 1897, the governments in both Madrid and Washington were trying to avoid a clash between the two countries over Cuba. In October, Spain recalled "Butcher" Weyler and replaced him with an official who arrived in Havana with orders to pursue a less severe poicy. McKinley had his minister in Madrid sound out the Spanish government about the possibility of the United States buying Cuba outright, in order to grant it independence, but the Spanish refused even to discuss the idea. American ships patrolled around Cuba to intercept possible American filibusters intending to land in Cuba to assist the revolutionaries and perhaps exacerbate tension with Spain in order to force official American intervention.

American warships had not visited Cuban ports since President Cleveland ordered visits suspended to protest Spanish policies and to avoid any possible incidents that might further strain relations. In October, the American consul in Havana, a former general in the Confederate army named Fitzhugh Lee, requested that an American warship be placed on stand-by orders for a possible visit to Havana. Lee feared that rising resentment against the United States on the part of the Spanish authorities and their Cuban supporters in Havana might spark violence against Americans. He wanted an American warship nearby, ready to respond quickly if needed. The navy ordered a ship to sail south from Hampton Roads and stand ready at Key West to respond to any call for help from Havana. The ship chosen for the assignment was *Maine*.

Maine had been in commission only two months longer than *Indiana*, but it represented an older generation of capital ship. Nine years had elapsed between its authorization and commissioning. Its design, dating from the mid-1880s, was already obsolete when the ship joined the fleet in 1895. The original plans had even called for full sail power. As a main battery, *Maine* carried four ten-inch guns. Its main battery guns therefore were larger than a cruiser's but smaller than a first-class battleship's. The only other American ships that carried ten-inch guns were obsolete monitors.

The guns were mounted in two *en echelon* turrets—that is, in turrets sited off the centerline, diagonally and overhanging the ship's sides on sponsons. This was one of the experimental designs of the 1870s and early 1880s which permitted all the guns of a main battery to fire past the ship's central superstructure dead ahead or astern as well as broadside. The barbettes holding the main battery guns of the ABCD cruisers were sited *en echelon*. This arrangement was soon abandoned by naval architects, because a warship would seldom, if ever, need to fire a full salvo either straight ahead or astern, and navies found that the muzzle blast of big guns firing close alongside the superstructure could damage the ship. Turrets mounted on the ship's centerline forward and abaft the superstructure became standard for main battery guns.

Maine was called a second-class battleship, but everyone knew it was something of an anomaly in the American fleet, a ship that was neither battleship nor cruiser and built to an experimental, obsolete design. While it was still under construction, Secretary of the Navy Benjamin Tracy told the Senate Naval Affairs Committee that the navy would never again build a ship like *Maine*, which "has neither the speed of a cruiser nor the fighting or resisting force of a battleship." Nevertheless, it was regarded as a powerful warship. On December 15, *Maine* arrived at Key West to await developments.

On January 12, Fitzhugh Lee reported from Havana that riots had occurred in the city when mobs, led by Spanish officers, attacked the offices of newspapers that advocated independence. The official asked that American ships be ready to move to Havana immediately if needed, but he did not think the situation demanded them as yet. McKinley decided that the time had arrived for an American warship to make an appearance at Havana, and on January 24, the assistant secretary of state discussed a possible visit with the Spanish minister in Washington. He stressed that the visit was not intended to be a threat, and the two diplomats even agreed that a Spanish ship should make a reciprocal visit to New York to underscore the friendly nature of the port call at Havana. Orders were issued for *Maine* to proceed to Havana, despite Fitzhugh Lee's opposition. He wanted a ship available, but he feared that the appearance of an American warship just then might trigger an incident. He was wrong. *Maine* arrived in Havana harbor on January 25 to a polite, if not warmly cordial, official welcome.

By the middle of February, *Maine* had swung peacefully around its mooring buoy in Havana harbor for three weeks. Its visit had not been marred by a single incident. The city was calm and quiet. Its presence was no longer needed, and the ship was being readied to depart Havana for New Orleans to make an appearance at the Mardi Gras. At 9:40 P.M. on February 15, a calm tropical evening, a tremendous blast blew apart the entire forward third of the battleship. The forward part of the hull was lifted out of the water before it settled back into the mud of the harbor's bottom, leaving a forest of twisted steel wreckage protruding above the surface. Two hundred and sixty officers and men, fully three-fourths of the entire personnel complement, were killed in the explosion or drowned.

The destruction of *Maine* sent shock waves through Cuba, Spain, and the United States. McKinley was awakened a few minutes before 2:00 A.M. to hear the news from Secretary Long over the telephone. After he hung up the phone, he paced back and forth, mumbling repeatedly, "The *Maine* blown up! The *Maine* blown up!" When the news was announced to the public in the morning, flags were lowered to half-mast, and crowds gathered quietly at the White House and the Navy Department to learn the details. The subdued, funereal atmosphere in the city reminded people of the day President James Garfield was shot in the city's railroad station in 1881. A board of inquiry to investigate the cause of the explosion was immediately convened by the navy and sent to Ha-

Wreckage of *Maine* protruding above the surface after the ship blew up in Havana harbor on February 15, 1898.

U.S. Naval Historical Center photograph

vana. It met behind closed doors and spent several weeks taking testimony from numerous witnesses, both American and non-American. They included survivors among the crew and divers who had examined the wreckage on the harbor bottom.

As the country awaited the findings of the *Maine* Board of Inquiry, the initial subdued reaction of the public was replaced by increasingly strident calls for action against Spain. McKinley was torn between finding a peaceful solution to the Cuban problem and making preparations for a war that looked increasingly inevitable. He astounded everyone by asking Congress to pass a special authorization of fifty million dollars, saying, "I must have money to get ready for war." Congress obliged by passing a "Fifty Million Bill" on March 8. Most of it was allotted to a crash program for expansion of the navy. Construction of three 12,500-ton battleships was approved. The Congressional action was, at best, a gesture that could have no effect on an imminent war with Spain, because the ships could not possibly be completed in less than three or four years. Sixteen destroyers and fourteen torpedo boats were also authorized.

The navy was also granted permission to buy warships abroad to beef up the fleet immediately. Two protected cruisers were purchased from Brazil, although one was still under construction in Britain and did not join the fleet until 1900. They became *New Orleans* and *Albany.* Several smaller craft were obtained from different countries. A motley fleet of yachts and other smaller vessels was rounded up in the United States and fitted out as auxiliary vessels and gunboats. Roosevelt was given responsibility for arranging the purchases, which he pushed through with his customary speed. The Spanish were astonished that any country could, like an individual snapping his fingers, suddenly and without warning spend so much money on armaments.

On March 24, the report of the *Maine* Board of Inquiry was received at the Navy Department. The board concluded that *Maine* had been destroyed by the explosion of its forward magazines of eight-inch and six-inch ammunition. It had been triggered by a smaller explosion that originated outside and under the ship, presumably from some kind of underwater mine detonated by a person or persons unknown. The captain and ship's officers were exonerated of any fault or negligence.

The precise cause of the explosion that destroyed *Maine* has remained a matter of controversy and dispute for almost a century despite the availability of copious evidence and repeated, exhaustive attempts to pinpoint its origin. If a mine had been planted under the ship, no one was ever identified as the person responsible, nor has a convincing explanation ever been offered as to how it could have been planted without detection. The Spanish authorities in Cuba would have been absolutely mad to destroy the American battleship while it lay moored in their own harbor amid growing tension with the United States. Logic would support the likelihood of its having been done by Cuban revolutionaries hoping to bring about a war between Spain and the United States. In view of the stringent security precautions taken by both the Americans and the Spanish authorities in Havana, revolutionaries would have had a very difficult time planting a mine undetected.

Even before the board of inquiry submitted its findings, some experts argued that the cause of the explosion must have been internal—perhaps spontaneous combustion in a coal bunker or the deterioration of powder in the ammunition. Some of the board's witnesses testified that they heard two explosions, the first much weaker than the second, suggesting an initial mine explosion under the ship. Others reported hearing only one tremendous blast. The configuration of the wreckage, as reported by divers, was interpreted by some engineering experts as indicating an external cause; others read the evidence as pointing to an internal one. Throughout the navy's era of coal and steam, no other American warship was ever destroyed by spontaneous combustion of coal or deterioration of powder.

In 1911, the wreck was raised from the bottom of Havana harbor by the Army Corps of Engineers. President William Howard Taft took advantage of the raising to appoint another board of inquiry to investigate again. The board convened in Havana and examined a mountain of evidence. The members had an opportunity, which the first board had not had, to examine the complete wreck raised dry from the water. After they finished their examination, what was left of *Maine* was towed out to sea and given a solemn burial. The second board decided that an external explosion had not occurred at the point on the ship's keel fixed by the first board. The damage there had been caused by the explosion of the ship's magazines, it decided. However, it did conclude that an external explosion had occurred along the keel, somewhat further astern, which triggered the magazine explosion. *Scientific American* magazine published a report entitled "*Maine* Explosion No Longer A Mystery." A mine of low-level intensity, planted under the ship, had caused the tragedy, the magazine said. But it did not explain who had planted the mine or how they had done it.

In 1974, Admiral Hyman Rickover, the "Father of the Nuclear Navy" and one of the navy's most brilliant engineers, became intrigued by the *Maine* mystery and undertook an investigation. He and a team of experts examined all available evidence. Rickover concluded that heat from a fire in a coal bunker, which was ignited by spontaneous combustion, caused ammunition in an adjacent magazine to explode. In other words, Rickover argued that no external agency was involved.

A book published in 1992 entitled *A Ship To Remember*, by Michael Blow, reviewed in detail the entire *Maine* story, including the findings of the two boards of inquiry and Admiral Rickover. Blow had long been fascinated by the *Maine* because his grandfather had been a ship's officer who died in the explosion. Blow's exhaustive review of the evidence makes clear why so many people became convinced that the ship was destroyed by an external mine. He himself, however, refused to argue in favor of any single explanation. Blow concluded:

> It may have been a mine; it may have been powder decomposition or spontaneous combustion in a coal bunker. It may have been treachery, an accident, or an act of God. But like the identity of Jack the Ripper in London, the killing of John F. Kennedy in Dallas, and the Tonkin Gulf "incident" of August, 1964, the mystery of the *Maine*—the "crime" of the nineteenth century—will forever remain unsolved.

For many Americans in the late winter of 1898, including Theodore Roosevelt, there was no mystery about who had destroyed *Maine*, even before the report of the board of inquiry was received. "The *Maine* was sunk by an act of dirty treachery on the part of the Spaniards, *I* believe," Roosevelt wrote in a letter. If feelings against Spain and its activities in Cuba had been running high before, the *Maine* disaster, followed by the board of inquiry's conclusion that it was not an accident, raised them to white-hot heat. Calls for a declaration of war were heard on all sides. The Navy Department had been busy for months, but after news of the destruction of *Maine* arrived, it became a madhouse as efforts to ready the fleet for war accelerated.

John Davis Long was feeling the strain. "These are trying times," he wrote in his journal ten days after the *Maine* disaster. He suffered from insomnia, and feeling exhausted, he took the afternoon of February 25 off, leaving Roosevelt in charge. Roosevelt's wife was seriously ill, and one of his children was just beginning to recover from an illness, but his attention was not deflected from the opportunity that Long's absence from the office presented. The acting secretary immediately dispatched a stream of cables and memoranda to put the navy on a war footing. Orders flew off to the North Atlantic Squadron to stand ready for action, and naval coal agents were instructed to make maximum purchases.

In the midst of all the furor over *Maine* and Cuba, Roosevelt had not forgotten Dewey, off in the far reaches of Asia. He shot off a cable to the Asiatic Squadron commander: "Order the Squadron except *Monocacy* to Hong Kong. Keep full of coal. In the event of declaration of war Spain, your duty will be to see that the Spanish squadron does not leave the Asiatic coast and then offensive operations in the Philippine islands. Keep *Olympia* until further orders." Dewey and his tiny squadron were already in Hong Kong. *Monocacy* was an obsolete, Civil War–era paddle-wheel steamer that Dewey knew would be a hindrance rather than an asset in a battle. He had no intention of taking it along if he sailed off to do battle with the Spanish in the Philippines. The last sentence of Roosevelt's cable was probably the most important and welcome to Dewey. *Olympia,* the squadron flagship, was due to be rotated back to the United States. It was the best of the navy's protected cruisers and by far the most formidable ship Dewey had under his command. He was no doubt delighted to receive authority to keep it until the crisis passed. He was probably also happy to receive explicit orders to take offensive action in the event war was declared.

When Long, refreshed from having enjoyed "a splendid night," returned to his office in the morning after his brief afternoon vacation, he was astounded to learn what Roosevelt had done during his few hours of absence. That evening he wrote in his journal: "During my short absence, I find that Roosevelt, in his precipitate way, has come very near causing more of an explosion than happened to the *Maine.* . . . I really think he is hardly fit to be entrusted with the responsibility of the Department at this critical time." However, Long did not rescind any of the orders Roosevelt had issued.

If the navy was to be readied for a possible war with Spain, one perplexing problem to be resolved was the disposition of *Oregon.* As a sister ship of *Indiana* and *Massachusetts,* it was one of the country's five remaining battleships after the destruction of *Maine.* It had been built at Union Iron Works in San Francisco, where *Olympia* was built, and after its commissioning in the summer of 1896, it remained on the west coast. It was the fastest of the three 1890 battleships, having achieved eighteen knots during sea trials. If there were any battles to be fought with the Spanish navy, *Oregon* was needed, urgently and critically. But in March, 1898, it was about as far from any likely battle site as it could conceivably get. It was at the naval shipyard at Bremerton, Washington, where it had just emerged from dry dock. It was therefore about seven thousand miles from Dewey and his squadron at Hong Kong and, in the absence of an isthmian canal across Central America, more than twice that distance—about fifteen thousand miles—from Cuba. Moreover, the *Oregon*'s ammunition was at San Francisco where it had been off-loaded in preparation for dry-docking. Should *Oregon* be sent across the

Pacific to reinforce Dewey, or should it steam all the way around South America to join the Atlantic Fleet in Cuban waters? Or might the best course of action be simply to leave it on the west coast?

From what was known of the Spanish forces in the Philippines, the navy thought that Dewey's small squadron, with a bit of reinforcement, could probably deal with them successfully. *Oregon* would be much more useful in Cuban waters, because Spain could conceivably mass a strong fleet there on short notice. But to steam all the way around South America would be a formidable undertaking. No battleship of any country had ever made such a voyage. It would take weeks, maybe months, and no one could be sure what the ship's condition would be when it arrived—if it did arrive. *Oregon* was a "coastal defense battleship" that sat low in the water with only ten feet of freeboard. It had not been designed to make long voyages on the open sea, particularly in the stormy latitudes of Cape Horn. John Davis Long finally ordered the ship to proceed to San Francisco to reclaim its ammunition and await further orders.

On March 12 at San Francisco, telegraphed orders arrived from Long for *Oregon* to proceed to Callao, Peru, where the ship would coal and await further orders. From Callao, it could steam off into the Pacific to help Dewey, or continue south to the Straits of Magellan. But when the battleship was on the point of departing San Francisco, the captain suddenly fell ill and had to be taken ashore. His hurriedly appointed replacement, Captain Charles E. Clark, had been a member of the board that had tested the ship on its sea trials. He liked the ship immensely, and he was delighted with the sudden opportunity to command it, perhaps even in battle. On March 19, only a week after taking command, he stood on the bridge as *Oregon* steamed through the Golden Gate and headed south at top speed for Callao.

Long and Roosevelt continued to put the fleet in a state of readiness. There was growing apprehension along the eastern seaboard that in the event of war, Spain might send a flotilla of fast cruisers to bombard and raid cities up and down the east coast. Every city demanded a protective naval force. Roosevelt urged Long and the president to "pay absolutely no heed" to such "outcries for protection." Even if New York were bombarded, he wrote to Mahan, "It would amount to absolutely nothing, as affecting the course of the war, or damaging permanently the prosperity of the country." He did, however, think that the two battleships under construction at Newport News, *Kentucky* and *Kearsarge,* should be given protection from a possible Spanish bombardment.

Bowing to political pressure from Congress and popular pressure from the populations of east coast cities, Long violated basic Mahanian doctrine and divided the available ships in the Atlantic into three groups to provide protection for the cities. A Northern Patrol Squadron, composed of old monitors and gunboats, cruised the coast from Delaware to Maine to deal with the unlikely possibility that a Spanish force might appear so far north. If one had, the small, slow, obsolete ships assigned to the duty would have been no match for a force of armored cruisers. A much stronger Flying Squadron, with the new armored cruiser *Brooklyn* as flagship and including *Massachusetts* and *Texas,* was based at Hampton Roads, ready to move toward any spot where a Spanish fleet was sighted. The two super-fast cruisers, *Columbia* and *Minneapolis,* were hurriedly put back into commission and added to the Flying Squadron. The main body of the North Atlantic Squadron was the strongest of the three groups, with *New York* as flagship and including *Indiana* and *Iowa,* and was based at Key West and responsible for the blockade of Cuba.

The officer chosen by Secretary Long to command the Flying Squadron was Commodore Winfield Scott Schley, who had commanded *Baltimore* at Valparaiso when Robley Evans arrived there during the crisis with Chile in 1891. A native of Maryland, Schley graduated from the Naval Academy in 1859 and served in several combat commands during the Civil War. He became famous in 1884 when he commanded a relief expedition sent to the arctic to rescue survivors of a party of explorers commanded by Lieutenant A. W. Greely that had become stranded on the ice pack. The exploit attracted widespread admiration for Schley. He succeeded Evans in command of *New York* in 1895 and was promoted to the rank of commodore in February, 1898. Schley was a charismatic, flamboyant figure, more popular with the general public, thanks in large measure to the publicity from the Greely rescue mission, than among his fellow naval officers.

The North Atlantic Squadron at Key West was commanded by one of the navy's most senior officers, Rear Admiral Montgomery Sicard. He had almost reached retirement age and was in precarious health from a recurrence of malaria. On March 14, Long issued an order assigning Captain William T. Sampson, who was serving as captain of *Iowa,* to replace him, with the temporary rank of rear admiral. Born in

Palmyra, New York, Sampson graduated from Annapolis in 1861, ranked first in his class. By coincidence, Sampson, Mahan, Dewey, and Schley all were together as midshipmen at Annapolis just before the Civil War, though not all in the same class. Sampson saw combat service in the war and the usual assignments during the postwar years. He became known and respected in the navy for his scientific knowledge in physics, chemistry, and metallurgy, and for the clarity and painstaking attention to detail in his lectures on those subjects as an instructor at Annapolis.

Theodore Roosevelt undoubtedly had much to do with Sampson's appointment to command the North Atlantic Squadron. Sampson was the first commanding officer of *Iowa,* and he had made a favorable impression on Roosevelt when the assistant secretary observed fleet maneuvers aboard the ship in September. Roosevelt chose him to be the senior line officer in his personnel committee that merged the deck and engineering officer groups, and Sampson was chosen to head the *Maine* Board of Inquiry. He was advanced over several more senior officers, including Schley, to command the North Atlantic Squadron. Sampson's reticent, austere manner sharply contrasted with Schley's charismatic personality and was often interpreted as coldness. He was not a favorite with newsmen as Schley was. As a two-star admiral, he was senior to Schley, who rated only one star as a commodore, but the two officers held independent commands.

When Long issued his order for Sampson to replace Sicard at Key West, Robley Evans happened to be standing in the secretary's office. Evans was still a lighthouse inspector and had been on an inspection tour along the gulf coast when the *Maine* disaster occurred. He had visited the North Atlantic Squadron at Key West and had hurried back to Washington to alert Long and Roosevelt to the squadron's alarming weakness in torpedo boats and torpedo boat destroyers. After Long issued his order about Sampson, he turned to Evans and said, "Now, captain, I have a surprise for you. I am going to order you to relieve Sampson on the *Iowa.* How soon can you start?" During the previous year, Evans had become Roosevelt's "right-hand man," an invaluable source of information and advice for the assistant secretary, who no doubt influenced Long's selection of him to command *Iowa.* It was the navy's newest, biggest, most powerful warship, and to be given command of it on the eve of a war that offered the prospect of major naval engagements was a plum assignment. The delighted Evans departed Washington for Key West on the same day he received his surprising assignment. That day, March 24, was especially notable for the navy. In the morning, both *Kentucky* and *Kearsarge* were launched with suitable ceremony and oratory at Newport News, and in the evening the report of the *Maine* Board of Inquiry was delivered to the secretary of the navy.

In contrast to Sampson at Key West and Schley at Hampton Roads, Dewey in Hong Kong commanded a pitifully weak force. He had the excellent *Olympia* but little else. There was the 3,000-ton ABCD *Boston*, a 900-ton gunboat, *Petrel*, and the ancient *Monocacy*, which he sent off to Shanghai to get it out of the way. In March, reinforcements were sent. *Olympia's* scheduled replacement as flagship was 4,600-ton *Baltimore*, cruising in Hawaiian waters. *Baltimore* was ordered to join Dewey immediately after taking on a load of ammunition sent urgently from California. A smaller cruiser, the three-thousand-ton *Raleigh*, was dispatched from the Mediterranean through the Suez Canal. A 1,700-ton gunboat, *Concord*, was ordered to sail from Mare Island at San Francisco carrying a load of ammunition, and a tiny revenue cutter, *McCulloch*, was ordered north from Singapore to serve as a dispatch boat.

McKinley for months had worked and hoped for a peaceful negotiated settlement of the dispute with Spain over Cuba, as the war drums of Hearst and Pulitzer beat ever louder. When the *Maine* Board of Inquiry report was made public on March 28, calls for war echoed in Congress: "Remember the *Maine*! To hell with Spain!" As McKinley continued to vacillate in the hope of reaching a last-minute accommodation with Madrid, Roosevelt exploded with one of his often-quoted lines. "McKinley," he fumed to a friend, "has no more backbone than a chocolate eclair." Into April, the president continued to resist growing congressional pressure. He held off the war advocates with pleas to give his last-minute diplomatic initiatives a chance to produce agreement.

For several months, Madrid had sought to end the insurrection by offering a string of concessions to the Cuban revolutionaries. All fell short of granting independence, and the Cubans, scenting complete victory, rejected all of them. Spanish pride had been pushed to its limit. Madrid refused to grant independence, especially as it would appear to be doing so in response to dictation by the United States. All American diplomatic efforts to reach an agreement that would include Cuban independence proved fruitless. In mid-April, Congress spent several days debating the wording of an ultimatum and war declaration to be delivered immediately to Spain. It included recognition of Cuba as an independent country. It was passed overwhelmingly on April 19, was signed by the president on April 20, and was delivered to the Spanish minister the same day. On April 22, the White House proclaimed a blockade of Cuban ports, and the next day it issued a call for 125,000 volunteers. The United States and Spain were at war.

The war was a matter of intense interest among naval experts all over the world. It was bound to be a naval war and would therefore constitute a test under combat conditions of steam-powered steel warships. During the evolution of modern warships in the three decades since the battle of Lissa, only one significant naval battle had occurred. On September 17, 1894, Chinese and Japanese fleets clashed in the battle of the Yalu in the Yellow Sea during the Sino-Japanese War. The ships on both sides were modern battleships and cruisers built in Germany or Britain. The Chinese ships were large with heavier armament, while the Japanese had deliberately built a navy of smaller but faster ships. The Japanese won a resounding victory, sinking five Chinese capital ships while losing none themselves. Personnel losses were equally one-sided.

Superior Japanese leadership and training contributed to the victory. Many Japanese officers had studied at Annapolis. Naval experts noted that the battle was decided by gunfire, not torpedoes, mines, or ramming. The deadly accurate fire of Japanese rapid-fire small caliber guns was especially noted. Reports written immediately after the battle by foreign naval observers attested to the havoc wrought by modern naval armament. An American naval captain wrote:

> I saw something of the effect of modern shell fire. The Japanese fire was terribly accurate and deadly. The Chinese ship *Chen-Yuen* was hit nearly one hundred times. Nothing was left above water of her; of her crew, 450 strong, over 350 were killed or died of wounds. All this was from the fire of six-inch and eight-inch rifles, at a distance from 1,000 to 1,600 yards.

A British officer who visited the *Chen-Yuen* immediately after the battle reported, "The slaughter has been awful, blood and human remains being scattered over the decks and guns." European naval experts tended to discount the battle as a test of modern ships and navies, because it had been fought by what they considered backward countries. A battle between squadrons of the United States and Spain was regarded as offering more significant and conclusive results.

The Spanish and American navies at the outbreak of war appeared to be almost evenly matched—on paper. The United States possessed five battleships to Spain's one, but the Spanish had a big edge in armored cruisers—seven to two. One of the newest Spanish cruisers, *Cristobal Colon,* was unmatched in the American navy. It was much faster than any American battleship, and it possessed armaments superior to any cruiser. Spanish torpedo boats, torpedo gunboats, and destroyers outnumbered the ships of the United States of those classes by a wide margin. The American navy possessed no destroyers at all, although it held a big advantage in protected cruisers. Bob Evans and many others thought that the Spanish torpedo boats already in Cuba, if handled with daring and skill and operating out of the many coves on Cuba's northern coast, could inflict serious damage on an American force blockading Havana. A single daring attack by a swarm of torpedo boats, if pressed home with determination, might easily sink an American battleship.

The reality behind the figures on paper, however, was very different. Many Spanish capital ships dated from the early 1880s or even the 1870s and were no match for the newer American ships. The single Spanish battleship, *Pelayo,* was superior to *Texas* but decidedly inferior to *Indiana* and its sister ships and no match at all for *Iowa.* It took no part in the war. The formidable *Cristobal Colon* lacked the guns of its main battery. Supplied by an Italian firm, they had been tested, found unsatisfactory, and returned to the manufacturer just prior to the outbreak of war. Several Spanish cruisers had not been dry-docked in more than a year, and seaweed growth on their hulls slowed them significantly.

Most importantly, the personnel of the Spanish navy, both officers and men, were woefully unprepared for war, both technically and psychologically. The Spanish admirals considered their ships to be no match for their American opponents, and they fully expected to be bested in battle. In contrast to the regular training exercises conducted in the American navy, Spanish warships seldom, if ever, engaged in target practice. The general in command of the Cuban revolutionaries told his American allies, "The Spanish *never* attack. They *never* attack." Enveloped in a fog of gloom and pessimism, expecting defeat, the Spanish navy steamed out to war.

During the weeks of crisis in late March and early April, *Oregon* had been pounding south through the Pacific, bound for Callao. As the ship approached and crossed the equator, temperatures below decks rose to above one hundred degrees, and the crew slept on deck. Temperatures in the firerooms reached 160 degrees. The chief engineer warned Captain Clark that the supply of fresh water was running dangerously low, and he wanted to avoid fouling the boilers with salt water, which could severely reduce their speed. Clark gathered the crew and explained the problem. He asked for agreement that drinking water be rationed to keep the boilers supplied with fresh water, warning the crew would have only warm water condensed from the boilers. The crew, eager for their ship to be in top condition for combat, enthusiastically agreed. The small amount of ice that the ship could produce was reserved for coal passers and firemen working below. One of the engineers proposed that some of the hard, high-quality Cardiff coal they had loaded in San Francisco be placed on reserve in a special bunker, to be saved for use in combat, to enable the ship to reach its highest possible speed. They were unlikely to obtain coal of equal quality for the rest of the voyage. The crew again agreed with enthusiasm, and gangs worked below in the sweltering bunkers to shift the coal.

Oregon loosed its anchor in the harbor at Callao on April 4. It had steamed four thousand miles in sixteen days. Its longest previous nonstop run had been 1,800 miles. No modern battleship had ever made a nonstop voyage of that length or duration. Waiting at Callao were telegraphed orders from Washington to steam south to the Straits of Magellan, then north to join the Atlantic fleet at Key West. Clark was warned that as the ship approached the Straits, he should keep a sharp lookout for Spanish torpedo boats, especially a large boat named *Temerario* reported to be at Buenos Aires, which might be lying in wait somewhere along the coast of South America to ambush the American battleship on the last leg of its highly publicized voyage. The ship spent only three days in port, taking on stores and fuel. On the evening of April 7, in a dense fog, with sacks of coal stacked on its decks, *Oregon* slipped out of the harbor at Callao and continued south.

For months, Theodore Roosevelt had let everyone know that in the event of war with Spain he would resign his position in the Navy Department to seek an army commission that would allow him to see combat. He ruled out a navy commission because, he said, "I would be use-less aboard a ship." He haunted the office of the secretary of war, begging for a commission in the army and permission to raise a special regiment of "harum-scarum roughriders" from among the cowboys, buffalo hunters, and other men of action he had come to know in the west. Everyone tried to dissuade him, pointing out that he would be much more useful in his current position with the navy than as an army officer in the field, but he was adamant. In a letter to a friend, he ex-plained his thinking in rather uncharacteristically dispassionate prose:

> I say quite sincerely that I shall not go for my own pleasure. On the contrary, if I should consult purely my own feelings, I should earnestly hope that we should have peace. I like life very much. I have always led a joyous life. I like thought, and I like action, and it will be very bitter to me to leave my wife and children, and while I think I could face death with dignity, I have no desire before my time has come to go out into the everlasting darkness. . . . So I shall not go into a war with any undue exhilaration of spirits or in a frame in any way approaching recklessness or levity; but my best work here is done. . . . One of the commonest taunts directed at men like myself is that we are armchair and parlor jingoes who wish to see others do what we only advocate doing. I care very little for such a taunt, except as it affects my usefulness, but I cannot afford to disregard the fact that my power for good, whatever it may be, would be gone if I didn't try to live up to the doctrines I have tried to preach.

He got his commission, and he got his regiment. He could have been appointed the regimental commanding officer, but he admitted to the secretary of war that he lacked experience in military organization, al-though he felt sure he could "learn to command the regiment in a month." He stepped aside to accept a lieutenant-colonelcy, and he asked that command of the regiment be given to a close friend and vet-eran of the Indian wars, a rather remarkable army doctor named Leo-nard Wood. On April 16, he wrote in his diary, "Long is at last awake, and anyway, I have the Navy in good shape. But the Army is awful. The War Department is in utter confusion." Succeeding months would prove the truth of his statement.

His last weeks in office were hectic and crammed, as usual, with ac-tivity. Long later described them:

> His room at the Navy Department after his decision to enter the army, which preceded for some time his resignation as assistant secretary, was

an interesting scene. It bubbled over with enthusiasm, and was filled with bright young fellows from all over the country, college graduates and old associates from the western ranches, all eager to serve with Roosevelt. The Rough Rider uniform was in evidence; it climbed the steps of the Navy Department; it filled its corridors; guns, uniforms, all sorts of military traps, and piles of paper littered the Assistant Secretary's room, but it was all the very inspiration of young manhood.

That was Long's recollection years later. At the time, he wrote in his journal:

My Assistant Secretary, Roosevelt, has determined upon resigning in order to go into the army and take part in the war. He has been of great use; a man of unbounded energy and force, and thoroughly honest, which is the main thing. He has lost his head in this unutterable folly of deserting the post where he is of most service and running off to ride a horse and, probably, brush mosquitoes from his neck on the Florida sands. His heart is right, and he means well, but it is one of those cases of aberration—desertion—vain-glory; of which he is utterly unaware. He thinks he is following his highest ideal, whereas, in fact, as without exception, he is acting like a fool. And yet, how absurd all this will sound if, by some turn of fortune, he should accomplish some great thing and strike a very high mark.

Years later, Long added a hand-written postscript to the typed journal entry: "Later P.S. Roosevelt was right & we his friends were all wrong. His going into the army led straight to the Presidency."

6

"A Fourth of July Present"

A full gale blew driving gusts of rain against the wheelhouse windows as *Oregon* steamed between the headlands flanking the entrance to the Strait of Magellan on April 16. Bilge keels to reduce roll had been added during the dry-docking at Bremerton, and the low-lying battleship rode surprisingly well in the heavy seas, although the foredeck was often awash as far aft as the forward turret, and seawater sometimes even sloshed around on top of the turret. Gun crews stood ready at their stations as Captain Clark drove the ship at top speed through alternating rain and fog, and lookouts scanned the coves on both sides of the channel, where Spanish torpedo boats might be lurking. The cliffs on either side of the channel were barely visible through the rain and mist. Darkness had already fallen and blowing gusts of sleet were coating the decks with ice when the anchors were loosed at Port Tamar to ride out the storm and await daylight.

For nine days, the whereabouts of the elusive battleship had been a matter of speculation in American newspapers. It had not appeared at Valparaiso, as many had predicted it would, and it was rumored to be somewhere out in the Pacific, enroute to reinforce Dewey. Other speculation was that it had been ordered back to California. There was fear in some quarters that the ship might have fallen victim to those impossibly dangerous Spanish torpedo boats that so obsessed American thinking as war with Spain approached.

The next morning, with the storm still blowing hurricane-force gusts, the ship resumed its transit through the Strait and arrived at Punta Arenas, Chile, after nightfall. A few hours after arrival, it was joined by an American gunboat, *Marietta*, that had sailed from Valparaiso to join *Oregon* in the Strait and escort it north through the Atlantic. Both ships urgently took on coal, the crews working through the night and the following day. They departed at daylight on April 21.

There was no telegraph line linking Punta Arenas with the outside world, so the location of the two ships was still unknown to the rest of the world as they headed north for their next coaling stop, Rio de Janeiro. With lookouts constantly alert for Spanish torpedo boats, the two ships steamed at night without lights, especially when they passed the mouth of the River Plate, the entry to Buenos Aires, where *Temerario* was reportedly lurking. *Marietta* was much slower than *Oregon,* and at times they could make only seven knots in heavy seas. However, no Spanish vessel appeared, and *Oregon* and its escort made landfall at Rio on April 30. They learned for the first time that the United States and Spain were formally at war, and the rest of the world learned their whereabouts. On May 1, the headline in Portland's *Oregonian* rejoiced, "The *Oregon* is safe!"

Through March and April in Hong Kong, Dewey fully justified Roosevelt's confidence in his self-reliance and initiative. He put his ships into dry dock to be scraped and painted so as to be at their fastest in combat. He purchased a shipload of high-quality Welsh coal from Cardiff, and when the collier *Nanshan* arrived, he bought the ship itself to add to his squadron as an auxiliary. He bought another ship, *Zafiro,* to serve as a supply ship. He recruited the British crews of both ships into the American merchant marine, and placed a small detachment of American naval personnel aboard each. He ordered all unessential personal belongings and ship's woodwork that would be a fire hazard in battle to be off-loaded from all the ships, as he anxiously awaited the arrival of *Baltimore* from Honolulu with its load of ammunition.

The British in Hong Kong thought Dewey's little force could defeat the Spanish fleet in the Philippines—if the two forces met at sea. The Spanish flagship, *Reina Cristina,* had a displacement only half that of *Olympia,* and the fleet's largest guns were only 6.2-inch, compared with the eight-inch guns aboard *Olympia, Baltimore,* and *Boston.* One of the Spanish ships was wooden-hulled. The Spanish force was obviously no match for the Americans. But Dewey would have to confront the Spanish ships in Manila Bay, under the large-bore guns of shore-based artillery mounted on Corregidor, the fort at Manila, and the Spanish naval base at Cavite. The Spanish were reported to have recently added modern Krupp breech-loaded rifles to the ancient muzzle-loaders that had guarded Manila for centuries, and the entrance to the bay was reportedly mined. Against those defenses, Dewey's ships were deemed to have no chance. Some of the Americans were guests of British officers at a party held at the Hong Kong Club. As they departed, they heard their hosts murmur, "a fine set of fellows, but unhappily, we shall never see them again."

The revenue cutter *McCulloch* arrived from Singapore on April 17, and on the 19th, Dewey had all the ships painted battle gray. On April 22, the long-awaited *Baltimore* arrived with its load of ammunition, and it was immediately placed in dry dock to be scraped and painted. On April 23, a letter from the governor of Hong Kong arrived to inform Dewey that the United States and Spain were at war. His squadron must depart the neutral port of Hong Kong within forty-eight hours, the governor wrote. On the 25th, a telegram from Long arrived with news of the declaration of war and orders for the commodore to "proceed at once to Philippine Islands. Commence operations particularly against the Spanish fleet. . . . You must capture vessels or destroy."

The American ships departed Hong Kong in two groups and moved north to Mirs Bay in Chinese territory. It was neutral territory, like Hong Kong, and therefore technically out of bounds to the American warships, but Dewey was confident the Chinese were too busy with other matters to worry about the presence of his little fleet in one of their remote bays for a few days. He was anxiously awaiting the arrival of a visitor, the American consul at Manila. He had remained at his post until the declaration of war, at a good deal of personal risk, to gather last-minute information about the Spanish fleet and shore defenses. He arrived at Mirs Bay on April 27, and Dewey immediately convened a meeting of his ships' captains to hear the consul's report.

The diplomat confirmed that the Spanish had mounted large-bore Krupp artillery on Corregidor, at Manila, and at Sangley Point near Cavite. They had reportedly mined the bay entrance. He also reported that the Spanish squadron had departed Manila Bay to go north thirty miles to take refuge in Subic Bay. It is a deep, well-protected body of water where the American navy later built its biggest naval base outside the United States itself. It was reportedly also defended by recently installed modern artillery and mines. The Spanish squadron could mount an effective defense there without endangering Manila or its base at Cavite.

As soon as the consul finished his report, at 2:00 P.M., Dewey ordered his squadron to weigh anchor. The band aboard *Olympia* struck up John Philip Sousa's *El Capitán* as the flagship led the little fleet out of Mirs Bay. The navigator set a course for a point on the coast of Luzon just north of Subic Bay, about six hundred miles to the southeast.

The squadron could make only eight knots, the speed of its slowest component, the collier *Nanshan*. They arrived at the approaches to Subic Bay in the afternoon of April 30. Dewey sent *Raleigh* and *Concord* ahead to scout the bay for any sign of the Spanish squadron. When the ships did not return immediately, and some officers said they thought they heard the sound of gunfire from the bay, *Baltimore* was dispatched to investigate. Soon all three ships returned to report no sign of the Spanish.

The Spanish squadron commander, Admiral Patricio Montojo, had indeed taken his seven ships to Subic Bay, only to learn to his intense disgust that the Krupp artillery pieces sent there months earlier had never been mounted. The bay entrance had been mined, but most of the mines had been fished out of the water by Filipino insurgents to extract their powder. Montojo's squadron would be defenseless and trapped. Only twenty-four hours before the arrival of the American squadron, he had taken his ships back to Manila Bay and the protection of the shore-based artillery there. An ancient, wooden-hulled cruiser, *Castilla*, sprang a leak in its propeller stuffing box which was plugged with cement, rendering the propeller useless. The ship, one of Montojo's largest, would have to serve as a stationary gun platform, at best.

When the three American ships returned from their reconnaissance, Dewey halted the squadron to hold a conference of his captains. There was no real need for a meeting, because he had already decided to go on to Manila Bay. But he was in no hurry to proceed. He wanted to arrive after dark, and they had only thirty miles to go. The little fleet steamed at dead slow speed. When darkness fell, each ship showed only a faint truck light to guide the ship immediately astern. A little before midnight, they approached the entrance to Manila Bay.

The island of Corregidor sits astride the entrance to Manila Bay, dividing it into two channels. The narrower channel to the north of the island separates Corregidor from the southern tip of Bataan peninsula. The wider channel to the south contains two small islands, Caballo and El Fraile. Dewey chose the wider southern channel to enter the bay, although he would pass between artillery mounted on both Corregidor and El Fraile. He discounted the danger of mines. He calculated that the water was too deep for contact mines to be effective, and electrically detonated mines probably had been in the water so long as to be rendered harmless by accumulations of barnacles and seaweed. However, the artillery on the two flanking islands could easily sink his ships.

As the column of ships steamed into the bay, both Corregidor and El Fraile were completely dark, suggesting that the Spanish knew of their approach and were waiting. But no shots were fired until the tail end of the column was passing between them. Soot in the funnel of *McCulloch* caught fire, and flames flared briefly into the night sky. Guns flashed on El Fraile, and a shell screamed overhead between *Raleigh* and *Petrel*. One of *Boston*'s eight-inch guns replied. Two more shells from El Fraile fell wide, then silence again descended upon the bay entrance. The guns on Corregidor failed to fire a single shot. The squadron passed unscathed into the bay and steered a course for the city of Manila, a few miles across the bay. Speed was reduced to four knots in order to arrive off the city at daybreak.

Dawn was just beginning to break on a hot tropical morning when the squadron arrived off the Manila breakwater. It was the height of the hot dry season in the Philippines. Below decks on the ships, with all the portholes and hatches secured, temperatures climbed precipitously as the sun rose. A stoker aboard *Olympia* later recalled: "It was so hot our hair was singed. There were several leaks in the steam pipes, and the hissing hot steam made things worse. The clatter of the engines and the roaring of the furnaces made such a din it seemed one's head would burst." On the ships' bridges, binoculars scanned the city waterfront. It was crowded with merchant shipping, but there was no sign of any warships. The Spanish squadron must have taken refuge at Cavite. The American column executed a fishhook turn in front of the breakwater to head southwest toward the Spanish naval base. Flashes erupted from the ramparts of Manila, and shells whirred overhead. They fell far wide of the ships, and Dewey ignored them as he headed for his prey, the Spanish squadron waiting under the protective artillery at Sangley Point. The ships steamed at a stately eight knots in a single column at four-hundred-yard intervals. *Olympia* led, followed by *Baltimore, Raleigh, Petrel, Concord,* and *Boston*. The two unarmed auxiliaries were sent off to a remote corner of the bay to await the outcome of the battle.

Cavite and Sangley Point are like two pincers of a peninsular claw curving northeast into the bay toward Manila. Sangley Point lies to the north, Cavite to the south. Admiral Montojo had drawn up his squadron in an arc curving out from the little bay between the two pincers. The immobile *Castilla* was surrounded by protecting barges filled with sand and rocks. The other ships were moored at both stem and stern to present their broadsides toward the approaching enemy. Behind them, *Reina Cristina,* another cruiser, two gunboats, and several smaller vessels waited, obviously with steam up. When the range between the two fleets closed to three miles, puffs of smoke blossomed from the Spanish flagship and one of the gunboats. A shell ricocheted off the water and tumbled over *Olympia.* Dewey ordered the navigator to follow the five-fathom curve to ensure that the column would pass as close to the Spanish ships as the draft of his ships would allow.

At 5:40 A.M., at 5,500 yards range, Dewey turned to *Olympia*'s commanding officer, Captain Charles Gridley, and coolly issued the order that enshrined the captain's name forever in the lore of the American navy: "You may fire when you are ready, Gridley." The starboard eight-inch gun in *Olympia*'s forward turret roared, a signal to the other ships that they need not hold their fire any longer. A hail of projectiles screamed toward the Spanish ships. The column bore to the right to head due westward and steam parallel with the line of Spanish ships, its port guns firing as fast as the crews could serve their weapons. The Spanish ships replied. Neither squadron used smokeless powder, and soon both were enveloped in thick clouds of smoke that hung over the glassy water of the bay.

When the column cleared Sangley Point after a run of about two and one-half miles, Dewey ordered a reversal of course to make another pass, heading eastward and even closer to shore, to give his starboard batteries a chance. They poured a hail of fire—the eight-inch shells weighed 250 pounds each—into the out-gunned Spanish ships, which gamely, but ineffectually, returned the fire. Lieutenant Ellicott, the intelligence officer aboard *Baltimore,* later described the scene aboard his ship:

> The pall of smoke which hung between the contending vessels prevented the effect of many shots from being seen, but close scrutiny with the glasses gave the comforting assurance after the first twenty minutes that the enemy was being hit hard and repeatedly, and as the range grew less, so that guns' crews could watch the fall of their shots with the naked eye,

many an exultant cheer went up from every ship. Naked to the waist and grimy with the soot of powder, their heads bound up in water-soaked towels, sweat running in rivulets over their glistening bodies, these men who had fasted for sixteen hours now slung shell after shell and charge after charge, each weighing a hundred to two hundred and fifty pounds, into their huge guns . . . under a tropical sun which melted the pitch in the decks.

Below decks, the stokers and firemen and the ammunition passers worked in the stifling heat, unsure of what was happening over their heads. The stoker on *Olympia* recalled:

> We could tell when our guns opened fire by the way the ship shook; we could scarcely stand on our feet, the vibration was so great. . . . The ship shook so fearfully that the soot and cinders poured down on us in clouds. Now and then a big drop of scalding water would fall on our bare heads, and the pain was intense. One by one, three of our men were overcome by the terrible heat and hoisted to the upper deck.

For nearly two hours the Americans weaved back and forth, making three runs to westward and two to eastward. On each run the ships passed closer to shore than on the one before, until they steamed only a little more than a mile from the Spanish ships. They held to their deliberate eight-knot speed and maintained the four-hundred-yard intervals between the ships as if passing in review, as their port and starboard batteries alternately loosed salvos at the enemy. During the fourth pass, the Spanish flagship made a brief, futile effort to charge the American column, drawing upon itself a withering fusillade. Lieutenant Ellicott described the scene:

> It was seen that she was on fire forward. Then a six-inch shell tore a jagged hole under her stern from which the smoke of another fire began to seep out. Right into this gaping wound another huge shell plunged, driving a fierce gust of flame and smoke out through ports and skylights. Then came a jet of white steam from around her after smokestack high into the air, and she swayed outward upon an irregular course toward Cavite until aground under its walls.

Admiral Montojo shifted his flag to the gunboat *Isle de Cuba*, attracting a storm of fire upon that ship.

At 7:30 A.M., after two hours of relentless shelling, the Spanish flagship was on fire and out of action, the immobile *Castilla*'s guns were silenced, and what was left of the Spanish squadron was retreating behind the mole of Cavite. Even so, no one in the American squadron could feel confident that the battle was won, especially with their vision obscured by the pall of smoke that hung over the entire scene. A lieutenant aboard *Petrel* had watched the battle from an excellent vantage point high on the mast. He later remembered:

> I could see that the Spanish ships were hit a number of times, especially the *Cristina* and *Castilla;* but then it seemed to me that our ships were hit many times also, and from the way they cut away boats from the *Raleigh* and from other signs I concluded that the *Raleigh* was suffering severely. I could see projectiles falling in the water on all sides of our ships.

At 7:35 A.M., signal flags fluttered on *Olympia:* "Withdraw from action," and then, "Let the people go to breakfast." News reports of the battle later cited Dewey's breakfast order as evidence of his extreme coolness in battle. The commodore could attend to his men's welfare even in the heat of an action, withdrawing for a brief respite, serenely confident that he could finish the destruction of his enemy at his leisure. The reality was different. Captain Gridley had passed an urgent message to Dewey that only fifteen rounds per gun of five-inch ammunition remained in the flagship's magazines. Dewey knew his closest source of supply was seven thousand miles away in California. He also knew that fifteen rounds of five-inch ammunition could easily be expended by a gun in about as many minutes. The battle was not yet over, and he had to know if his squadron was running short of ammunition. He decided to withdraw to find out about the ammunition supply on the other ships, but he did not want his men to know about an ammunition shortage. A pause for breakfast was as good a reason as any for a temporary withdrawal.

When the squadron had steamed beyond the range of the Spanish guns, the crews were piped to breakfast, and Dewey summoned his captains for a conference aboard *Olympia*. Each captain arrived with the same two thoughts in mind. His ship and crew had miraculously escaped any serious damage, but he expected to hear dire reports of severe damage and casualties from his fellow commanding officers. They all soon learned that the entire squadron had sustained no serious damage and amazingly light casualties. Even *Raleigh* had sustained only superficial damage. Investigation soon established that the message about *Olympia*'s supply of five-inch ammunition had been garbled. Only fifteen rounds per gun had been expended, and an ample supply remained to continue the battle.

Everyone knew the Spanish had suffered severe damage, but they had not surrendered. Dewey had to assume they were still capable of fighting and planned to continue. The shore batteries at Sangley Point remained undamaged and still constituted a threat, although their fire had not been effective. After the battle, the Americans discovered that the guns behind their parapets could not be depressed sufficiently to hit targets as close as the American ships had approached. Apparently, the Spanish had assumed that no ship would dare come so near. However, Dewey did not know this at mid-morning on May 1. A little before 11:00 A.M., the squadron headed back toward Cavite, this time with *Baltimore* in the van. Well in advance of the rest of the squadron, the cruiser closed to within 2,500 yards of shore, and steaming slowly, opened fire on the Sangley Point batteries. Lieutenant Ellicott wrote this account:

> Then followed for ten minutes a duel with the batteries which is attested by the onlooking squadron (not then within fighting distance) as one of the most magnificent spectacles of the day. The big cruiser, slowing and creeping along at a snail's pace, seemed to be in a vortex of incessant explosions both from her own guns and the enemy's shells. At times, she was completely enshrouded in smoke and seemed to be on fire, while every shell she fired was placed on the earthworks as accurately as if she were at target practice. Canacao battery was the first to fall under deadly fire. Its embankments of sand, backed by boiler iron, were torn up and flung into the faces of the gunners until panic took hold of them. Hauling down their flag, they tumbled into an ambulance and drove madly to the protection of Fort Sangley. The whole fire of the squadron was then concentrated on this fort. . . . At last, the Spanish flag came down and a white flag was raised in its place.

The squadron's guns were turned on the single remaining cruiser, *Don Antonio de Ulloa*, moored inside Sangley Point. Its guns were destroyed or disabled, and listing badly, it was abandoned by its crew. It turned turtle and sank.

By 12:20 P.M. the battle was over. Dewey and his little squadron had achieved one of the most devastating, one-sided naval victories ever recorded. Ten Spanish warships were destroyed and almost four hundred Spaniards killed or wounded. The Spanish naval forces in Asia had been totally demolished. No American had been killed, and only a few slightly wounded. No American ship had sustained any serious damage. Dewey's squadron was ready for further combat, if any were needed.

Little *Petrel*, with the shallowest draft of any of the American ships, darted in to the Cavite arsenal to take its formal surrender and burn several small vessels that had been abandoned by their crews. Dewey led the rest of the squadron back to Manila and anchored just off the city. At 2:00 P.M. he sent a message to the Spanish governor-general to the effect that if the Manila batteries fired on his ships, he would shell the city. A reply promptly gave assurance that the batteries would not fire. At sunset, *Olympia*'s band gave its customary concert. Shocked Spaniards lined the waterfront to listen, stare at the foreign warships, and wonder what the next day would bring.

The Spanish in Manila were threatened not only by the guns of the American squadron. The city was surrounded and cut off by Filipino insurgents who might be emboldened by the American naval victory to attack. Dewey had no troops to land and occupy the city or control the insurgents. During the helter-skelter war preparations of March and April, attention had focussed on defeating the Spanish squadron, and no one had given thought to what should be done once that was accomplished. Dewey and his men had to remain aboard their ships, anchored in the bay just off the city, and await orders from Washington. However, he was, as he wrote in his autobiography, "in control of the situation."

The first fragmentary report of the battle arrived in Washington on Sunday evening, to everyone's astonishment. A smashing victory had been achieved scarcely ten days after war was declared. No one had expected the first news of success to come from the remote, little-known Philippines. One of Roosevelt's last actions in the Navy Department before departing for an army training camp in Texas was to send messenger boys off with the news to all the newspapers. However, everyone had to wait a week for a full account of what had happened. Dewey could not cable a report to Washington, because the Spanish governor-general balked at giving the Americans access to the undersea telegraph cable that linked Manila with Hong Kong and the rest of the world. In retaliation, Dewey ordered the cable cut. The little dispatch boat, *McCulloch*, was sent off to Hong Kong carrying Dewey's report to be cabled to Washington. It also carried three newspapermen who had sailed with the fleet and were avid to file their stories of the battle. The

New York *World* correspondent scooped his colleagues by sending his bulletin by "urgent" cable at an unheard-of cost of nine dollars per word.

Within weeks, three transports of troops were ordered urgently to cross the Pacific to reinforce Dewey and occupy Manila. However, two months passed before they arrived. A heavily gunned monitor was also sent to beef up his squadron's firepower when a Spanish fleet that included the battleship *Pelayo* departed from Spain, with the obvious purpose of passing through the Suez Canal and going on to the Philippines. But the fleet got no farther than the south end of the Suez Canal when the wavering Spanish government summoned it back. As Dewey and his men awaited reinforcement, they sweltered through the torrid weeks of a tropical summer aboard their ships in Manila Bay, holding the population of Manila hostage under their guns.

While Dewey and his squadron waited, McKinley and his government struggled with the growing awareness that they must decide whether America was to join the headlong rush of imperialism by taking control of a group of islands, half-way around the world, about which they knew practically nothing. Thanks to the new American navy, the Philippines belonged to the United States, if the Americans wanted them. But if they did, they might still have to fight the Filipino insurgents who had been struggling for years to gain their independence from Spain.

In the White House, the president puzzled over a little map in a schoolbook, trying to identify geographic locations mentioned in Dewey's reports, until an officer from the Coast and Geodetic Survey arrived with a batch of large-scale maps. McKinley sighed, "It is evident that I must learn a great deal of geography in this war." After the war with Spain ended, when the American army was mired in a nasty, seemingly endless anti-guerrilla war in the Philippines, McKinley told a friend, "If only old Dewey had just sailed away when he smashed that Spanish fleet, what a lot of trouble he would have saved us."

Captain Clark and his crew aboard *Oregon* learned of Dewey's victory as the battleship took on coal in Rio de Janeiro. The American minister to Brazil and members of the American community came aboard to celebrate. *Oregon* was safe, as *The Oregonian* had proclaimed, but the most dangerous portion of its epic voyage still lay ahead. As he joined the victory celebration, Captain Clark received an urgent cable from Washington:

> Four Spanish armored cruisers, heavy and fast, three torpedoboat destroyers sailed April 29 from Cape de Verde to the west, destination unknown. Beware of and study carefully situation. Must be left to your discretion entirely to avoid this fleet and to reach the United States by West Indies. You can go when and where you desire. *Nictheroy* and *Marietta* subject to the orders of yourself.

Nictheroy was a small auxiliary cruiser, built as a merchant vessel in the United States, that had been purchased from Brazil as part of the frantic effort to beef up the navy as war approached. Like *Marietta*, it was slower than *Oregon*, and when the battleship departed Rio on May 4, Clark left both of the smaller ships behind so that he could proceed north at top speed. *Oregon* arrived in Bahia on May 8 to take on coal and departed on May 9. On May 15, it made the best day's run of the entire voyage—375 miles in twenty-four hours for an average speed of better than fifteen knots. A twenty-four-hour stop was made in British Barbados on May 18.

American newspapers were full of stories about *Oregon*, its epic voyage, the possibility that it might be intercepted by the mysterious Spanish cruiser squadron, and what would happen if it were. Captain Clark was not worried about a possible encounter with the Spanish cruisers. He knew they were faster than *Oregon* (if they were still capable of attaining their top designated speeds), but the battleship outgunned them. Clark told his officers that if they met the Spanish squadron, he planned to let them see his ship, and then he would steam away at top speed. He calculated that the cruisers would become strung out chasing him. When they were widely separated, he would turn and finish them off, one by one. His plan was never tested, because the Spanish were never sighted.

On May 15, *Oregon* made its American landfall at Jupiter Inlet, Florida, just north of Palm Beach. Clark cabled news of the arrival to Washington and received a prompt reply: "If ship in good condition and ready for service, go to Key West, otherwise to Hampton Roads. The Department congratulates you upon your safe arrival which has been announced to the President."

On May 26, *Oregon* dropped anchor at Sand Key, off Key West, to coal before joining Sampson's North Atlantic Squadron blockading

Cuba. It had steamed 13,879 miles from San Francisco in sixty-eight days, breaking the long-standing coast-to-coast record of eighty-nine days set by the American clipper ship *Flying Cloud* nearly a half-century earlier. It arrived in excellent condition in all respects, ready to take its place immediately in the American battle line. Its remarkable voyage justified the faith of Theodore Roosevelt, Mahan, Luce, and others in the first-rate battleship as the backbone of the fleet, capable not only of defending the nation's coasts but also of taking offensive action in far-off waters.

For Sampson, there was no prospect of an immediate, decisive victory like Dewey's. When war was declared, he, Bob Evans, and other officers wanted to take their ships immediately to Cuba and capture Havana. With the Cuban capital under American control, they reasoned, the Spanish forces on the island would soon capitulate. But their superiors in Washington disagreed. Long and others preferred to follow standard Mahanian doctrine: the navy's objective must be the enemy navy, and the main Spanish naval forces were not at Havana. Four ancient cruisers, one totally immobile and the others barely able to get underway, lay in Havana harbor, along with five torpedo boats. It was not a force to worry about. Washington's attention was focussed on those modern armored cruisers that menaced *Oregon* during the last leg of its voyage. After their departure from the Cape Verde islands, they were loose somewhere in the Atlantic. Cities up and down the east coast still clamored for protection from raids, although the Spanish squadron was presumably headed for Cuba. Sampson and Schley were ordered to intercept and engage them, although no one could be sure exactly where they were or where they were headed. Sampson was ordered to blockade Cuba to intercept the Spanish squadron if it appeared in those waters as expected. Schley's Flying Squadron was held, for the time being, at Hampton Roads in case the Spanish appeared elsewhere.

The Spanish squadron had arrived at St. Vincent in the Spanish Cape Verde Islands, three hundred miles off the African coast, on April 14. It was composed of four armored cruisers, three destroyers, and three torpedo boats. It included the fast and formidable *Cristobal Colon*. One of the destroyers, *Pluton*, with a top speed of thirty knots, was the fastest warship on either side of the Atlantic. In command was Admiral Pascual Cervera y Topete, a fifty-nine-year-old veteran sailor with forty-seven years of service. He was Spain's senior, premier naval officer—decorated, respected, and known as an able leader. He had even served briefly as Minister of Marine before resigning the post in protest, accusing his superiors of preferring political expediency over the national interest.

Like Montojo in Manila, Cervera fully expected defeat as he led his squadron to war. One of his cruisers, *Vizcaya,* was so slow from barnacle and seaweed growth on its hull that he considered it "nothing more than a buoy." *Cristobal Colon* lacked its main battery's guns, so the effectiveness of his best ship was gone. It and his flagship, *Infanta Maria Teresa,* consumed coal at an alarming rate. Much of his ammunition was defective, his ships were undermanned, and their crews had had virtually no target practice.

When war was declared, Cervera was ordered to sail for the West Indies to confront the Americans, but he was given no clear strategic plan of what he should accomplish once he arrived there. The Spanish forces in Cuba desperately wanted his ships to come to their aid, but with that island blockaded by a force superior to his, he was ordered to make for San Juan, Puerto Rico. In response, Cervera warned that "nothing can be expected of this expedition except the total destruction of the fleet." A common topic of conversation in Madrid was the expectation that the Spanish navy faced another Trafalgar.

The squadron departed the Cape Verde Islands on April 29, the cruisers towing the destroyers so that the smaller ships would not have to refuel in mid-ocean. The little torpedo boats were left behind. The fears in Washington that Cervera planned to ambush *Oregon* were totally unfounded. The Spanish admiral was not even aware that the American battleship had departed the west coast to join Sampson. If he had encountered *Oregon,* he would have done everything he could to avoid a fight.

For nearly a month, the American navy and Admiral Cervera played cat and mouse. Cervera could play the game because of the limitations of naval communications in 1898. There was no shipboard radio. Ships at sea were incommunicado, except with other ships that were in sight. On shore, cities were linked by telegraph, and there were even undersea telegraph cables linking many cities. Washington could send a cable to Sampson, for example, which he would receive immediately if he were in Key West. But if he were at sea on blockade, the message would have to be relayed by a fast dispatch boat from the nearest shore-based tele-graph station. For the American ships blockading Cuba, messages usu-ally arrived via stations at Key West or in Haiti. The delays in getting messages to commanders at sea caused a good deal of trouble for the American navy in its efforts to find Admiral Cervera.

Sampson reasoned that Cervera would go to San Juan, and he de-cided to intercept the Spanish squadron there. Leaving some smaller vessels to guard the approaches to Havana in case Cervera slipped by him, Sampson took his biggest ships—*New York, Iowa,* and *Indiana*—along with a few cruisers and gunboats on an expedition that was a minor disaster. For additional firepower against the forts guarding San Juan, he took along two monitors. They had almost no coal bunker ca-pacity, so they had to be towed by *New York* and *Iowa,* reducing the fleet's speed to eight knots. The tow lines repeatedly parted. *Indiana* suffered problems with its boilers, further reducing their speed of advance.

The voyage to Puerto Rico consumed eight days. In the early morn-ing hours of May 12, they arrived off San Juan. *Iowa* opened up on the forts with its twelve-inch guns. Although Sampson had been cautioned by Washington not to risk his ships in duels with shore batteries, the fleet bombarded the San Juan defenses for two hours but with little re-sult. After their first pass across the mouth of the harbor, they knew that Cervera's squadron was not there, and Sampson had to worry that it might slip into Cuba during his absence from the blockade. With the awkward monitors again in tow, the slow return trip westward began.

On the day that Sampson's ships shelled San Juan, Cervera and his squadron appeared at the French-controlled island of Martinique, far to the south. Fearing that the Americans might try to intercept him at San Juan, he had decided to avoid it. The Spanish consul at Martinique hurried out to the flagship when it arrived to tell the admiral of the American attack on San Juan. Although his ships badly needed coal, Cervera immediately headed westward to Curaçao in Dutch Guiana, on the coast of South America. He hoped to find chartered colliers awaiting him there. Sampson learned of Cervera's appearance in the Caribbean two days later, on May 14, while enroute back to Key West. Leaving the battleships to tow the monitors, he ordered *New York* to return to Key West at full speed. The news of the Spanish squadron's appearance so far south prompted Washington to release Schley and his Flying Squadron from Hampton Roads, and they proceeded south to Key West, arriving on May 18. In the absence of Sampson, Schley, to his delight, was ordered to blockade Havana.

The Flying Squadron hurriedly took on coal, but as it was departing Key West in the evening, Sampson arrived aboard *New York*. Schley went aboard the flagship to confer with his superior officer. With his squadron returning to resume the Havana blockade, Sampson decided that Cervera would probably try for the port of Cienfuegos, on Cuba's southern coast, rather than attempt to run the blockade to reach Havana. A railroad and telegraph line linked Cienfuegos with Havana, so it was a logical destination for the Spanish force. Enough time had passed since Cervera's sighting at Martinique to allow him to reach the Cuban coast. Accordingly, Sampson ordered Schley and his squadron to steam immediately for Cienfuegos and set up a blockade. To beef up the Flying Squadron's firepower, he ordered *Iowa* to join Schley as soon as it finished coaling.

When Schley arrived off Cienfuegos on May 20, he had no means of ascertaining whether Cervera was there. Like several other Cuban harbors, the bay at Cienfuegos was land-locked with a narrow, winding entrance, and it snaked back into the hills for several miles. It was impossible for a ship to see into the bay from outside the entrance. However, as soon as he arrived, Schley became convinced, from several bits of circumstantial evidence, that Cervera's squadron was there, and he triumphantly established a blockade.

No sooner had Schley departed Key West than Sampson received a cable from Washington informing him that there was reason to believe Cervera was at Santiago, three hundred miles east of Cienfuegos. The cable, however, did not explain why he was thought to be there. *Iowa* was departing Key West to join Schley, so Sampson put a letter aboard informing Schley of the news from Washington but directing him to maintain the blockade at Cienfuegos. Sampson reasoned that, in the unlikely event that Cervera was at Santiago, he could accomplish nothing there and would sooner or later move to either Havana or Cienfuegos.

Immediately after *Iowa* had departed with Sampson's letter, Sampson learned why Cervera was thought to be at Santiago. A Cuban telegraph operator at Havana, who was serving as a secret agent for the Americans, had sent a report saying that the Havana telegraph office had received a message announcing Cervera's arrival at Santiago. Almost immediately, a report from Madrid confirmed the agent's report. The day after *Iowa*'s departure, Sampson sent off a second letter to Schley via the cruiser *Marblehead*. He instructed Schley to move his squadron to Santiago, but he added a surprising, ambiguous proviso: "if you are satisfied [the Spanish] are not at Cienfuegos." He cabled Washington, "Schley has been ordered to Santiago." Convinced that Cervera was at Cienfuegos, Schley sent a reply saying he proposed to remain where he was. Only after receiving belated information from Cuban insurgents ashore that no Spanish warships could be seen at Cienfuegos did Schley, on the evening of May 24, depart in very heavy weather to search for the elusive Cervera at Santiago.

In fact, Cervera and his squadron entered the harbor at Santiago at dawn on May 19, at almost exactly the same time Schley departed Key West. The single American auxiliary cruiser assigned to watch the harbor entrance happened to be away coaling at precisely that moment, so the Spanish ships were able to slip in undetected. They had stopped briefly at Curaçao, only to learn that the chartered collier carrying their urgently needed coal had gone to Martinique. The squadron had barely enough fuel to reach Cuba, and it was running very low on provisions. Afraid that he might encounter Sampson at San Juan and suspecting that Cienfuegos might be blockaded as well, Cervera made for the only other Spanish-controlled port that he had any hope of reaching.

Cervera's arrival at Santiago did nothing to improve Spain's fortunes in Cuba. Santiago had no rail links with Havana or Cienfuegos. Food was disappearing fast in the city, and there was no hope of resupply, because the city was surrounded and cut off by Cuban revolutionary forces. The city treasury was nearly empty, and inflation had become rampant. The Spanish squadron represented nothing more to the defenders of Santiago than two thousand additional mouths to feed and a tremendous drain on the city's other dwindling resources. Cervera knew he had no chance of winning a battle with the American naval forces in Cuban waters. He wanted only to fuel and secure provisions for his ships as quickly as possible and depart before his presence was detected. But obtaining enough coal and provisions for his six large warships in the besieged city of Santiago proved to be a slow and difficult task. Moreover, where he might go if he was able to depart Santiago was a good question.

In the early morning hours of May 26, Schley's squadron approached Santiago and encountered three American ships that had been watching the harbor entrance. Captain Charles Sigsbee, who had been the captain of *Maine* when it blew up, commanded one of them. He came aboard the flagship. "Have we got them?" Schley asked. "No, they are not here," Sigsbee replied. He and the captains of the other ships, which had been watching the harbor entrance since just after Cervera's arrival, had seen nothing of the Spanish ships. The harbor at Santiago, like the one at Cienfuegos, was landlocked, with a narrow entrance that wound snakelike around a high hill. The long, winding bay was completely screened from the sea, and the city lay four miles inland at the head of the bay. From the open sea, it was impossible to see the city or its harbor.

Schley had no reason to believe that Cervera was at Santiago other than Sampson's ambiguously worded letter. He turned his attention to another matter. He was constantly haunted by fears of running out of fuel. Although his ships had enough coal in their bunkers for several days' steaming, he worried that his squadron would soon exhaust its fuel supply while maintaining a blockade. He had with him a collier, *Merrimac*, containing four thousand tons of coal. The heavy weather had somewhat abated, but coaling in the open sea would nevertheless be a tricky and possibly dangerous business. The big sponsons extending outward from the sides of *Texas* that supported the battleship's *en echelon* turrets made it especially dangerous for the little collier to come alongside if a heavy swell was running. If Cervera was not at Santiago, the commodore decided, his squadron had time to fill its bunkers at some protected port before setting up a blockade.

At sunset, *Brooklyn* winked a signal to the other ships: "Destination Key West via south side Cuba and Yucatan Channel, as soon as collier is ready; speed nine knots." Evans on *Iowa* was bewildered by the order which he delicately described in his memoirs as "an unexpected retreat." Asked by Captain Philips of *Texas* what it meant, Evans replied, "damned if I know, but I know one thing—I'm the most disgusted man afloat." The Spanish in Santiago, watching the fitful maneuverings of the American ships, decided they were "incomprehensible." The squadron slowly disappeared over the horizon, heading west.

Forty miles west of Santiago, Schley received a message from Long in Washington delivered by a dispatch boat from a telegraph station in Haiti. "All Department's information indicates Spanish division still at

Santiago," Long wired. "The Department looks to you to ascertain facts, and that the enemy if therein does not leave without a decisive action." Schley replied, "Much to be regretted, cannot obey orders of the Department. Have striven earnestly; forced to proceed for coal to Key West, by way of Yucatan passage; cannot ascertain anything positive respecting enemy."

Long had been irked by Schley's dilatoriness in proceeding to Santiago, and this message absolutely flabbergasted him. The trap was ready to be sprung on the cagey Cervera, penning him up indefinitely at Santiago, and Schley was inexplicably leaving the scene and giving the Spanish squadron a chance to escape. Long seriously considered relieving Schley immediately of his command and even of ordering a court-martial. Of course, he did not know what Captain Sigsbee had told the unfortunate commodore. He later remembered the day he received Schley's cable as "the most anxious day in the naval history of the war and . . . the only instance in which the Department had to whistle to keep its courage up." He shot off a cable to an incredulous Sampson informing him of Schley's amazing message and ordering Sampson to proceed immediately to blockade Santiago.

The next morning, the heavy weather on Cuba's south coast abated enough to allow one of Schley's ships to take on some coal. The squadron drifted for several hours while the commodore apparently reconsidered his options. Around 1:00 P.M., he suddenly signalled to reverse course again and return to Santiago. By early morning of May 29, the American ships were back off the entrance to Santiago harbor and treated to an electrifying sight. Just inside the harbor entrance, in a position to command the channel, the unmistakable silhouette of *Cristobal Colon* could plainly be seen. Actually, the ship had been there when they made their first visit three days earlier, but in the heavy weather then blowing no one had noticed it. Schley ordered the squadron to form a semicircle around the harbor entrance. "We've got them now," he exulted. "They'll never go home."

Sampson arrived on June 1 with *New York, Massachusetts,* and the recently arrived *Oregon.* The harbor entrance was enclosed by a semicircle of steel. The two fast armored cruisers *New York* and *Brooklyn* anchored the two ends of the arc, with *New York* to the east of the harbor entrance and *Brooklyn* to the west. They were positioned to be the first to engage the Spanish ships if they made a dash to escape. If Cervera tried to leave, he would have to fight his way out. At night, the battleships moved close in and covered the entrance with powerful searchlights to prevent a nighttime escape. The Americans were surprised that the Spanish batteries guarding the entrance did not even try to fire at the searchlights.

Sampson decided to ensure the Spanish fleet's imprisonment by a device he had seen used successfully in the Civil War. He proposed that the collier *Merrimac* be taken into the harbor entrance and sunk. The channel was so narrow that the collier, if sunk sideways across it, would block it completely. On a dark, moonless night, a daredevil volunteer crew took in the old ship, primed with explosive charges to sink it. However, before it could be jockeyed into position across the channel, it was discovered by the Spanish. The shore batteries on both sides of the channel entrance poured down a murderous fire. Maneuvering to avoid the Spanish shells, the little ship struck a mine and sank parallel with the channel, rather than across it, with its bow pointing in toward the harbor. The channel was not totally blocked. The crew was rescued by Spanish sailors in small boats, including Cervera himself, who helped fish some of the Americans out of the water. The courtly Spanish admiral sent a message to Sampson under a flag of truce to inform him that the Americans had been rescued.

With the entrance channel still permitting a possible escape by Cervera's ships, the blockade continued through the month of June. The American ships tried lofting shells over the hills into the harbor to hit the moored Spanish warships, but they fell harmlessly into the water. They shelled the shore batteries in the ancient forts guarding the harbor entrance, but with little effect. The Americans who had been rescued from the *Merrimac* were being held prisoner at one of the forts. They later reported that the shelling did nothing to disable the Spanish guns. The American bombardment threw up tons of dirt and sand, some of it spraying the guns and their crews. But a fort cannot be sunk like a ship. A shell had to make an absolutely direct hit on a gun to disable it, and none did.

On June 14, an American army expeditionary force of nearly sixteen thousand men, which included Roosevelt and his Rough Riders, departed Florida bound for Cuba. It was the largest American military force ever to leave the United States until that time. Santiago rather than Havana had become the focus of American military operations, so the ragtag armada transporting the little army, escorted by *Indiana*, headed for the south coast to land the troops near Sampson's blockading fleet. Thus far in the war, the new American navy had performed superbly, despite a few minor bungles like Sampson's expedition to Puerto Rico and Schley's zigs and zags at Cienfuegos and Santiago. Dewey's spectacular victory and the successful blockade of Cervera more than compensated for these lapses. By contrast, the army's performance so far had been one big bungle. It had shown itself totally unprepared for rapid wartime expansion. Roosevelt's low opinion of the War Department's competence as compared with that of the Navy Department had been fully justified. On June 22, the expeditionary force landed at Daiquiri, east of Santiago, amid confusion and wild scrambling.

The general in command was William Rufus Shafter, a sixty-three-year-old veteran of the Civil War and the Indian wars on the plains. A Medal of Honor winner, he was a thorough professional with a distinguished army record. But in 1898, he was in no condition to command an army on the attack in the tropics. He weighed more than three hundred pounds and suffered terribly from gout. Sporting a huge paunch, he could barely sit astride a horse. Soon after landing in Cuba, he came down with fever.

As the army was landing, Sampson went ashore to confer with Shafter. He came to the meeting ready with a plan for a coordinated attack. Sampson proposed that the army first attack the forts guarding the harbor entrance. So long as it was protected by Spanish guns, his ships could not risk forcing the mined entrance. With fire support from his fleet's heavy guns, he had no doubt the army could easily capture the forts. His fleet could then steam in, clear the mines, and deal with Cervera's squadron. With the forts occupied and the squadron captured or destroyed, the city of Santiago was bound to fall. Shafter at first agreed, but then had second thoughts about his troops attacking masonry forts perched on high cliffs, even with naval fire support. He decided, to Sampson's bafflement, that the army's proper objective should be capture of the city. If the navy wanted to go after Cervera, it could fight its own way into the harbor.

The army moved inland toward Santiago, and on June 24 fought its first action at Las Guasimas. The Rough Riders were in the thick of it, and it was Theodore Roosevelt's baptism of fire. Sixteen Americans were killed and twenty-five were wounded as the army took possession of high ground on the road to Santiago. It was a promising beginning to the campaign. On July 1, the battles of El Caney and San Juan Hill took place—the two most famous land battles of the war, which established Roosevelt's military reputation. At the end of the day, the Americans were victorious, occupying high ground overlooking Santiago, but at a cost of more than one thousand casualties. In less than two weeks, they had learned, somewhat to their surprise, that the Spanish could fight. Their Mauser rifles had proven to be deadly and superior to the Americans' Krag-Jorgensens. The rains of the hurricane season had begun, and the American ranks were being further thinned by spreading yellow fever, malaria, and other diseases.

Two days after the twin American victories, on the morning of July 3, a Spanish relief force of 3,600 men was able to enter Santiago to reinforce its defenders. The Spanish were not strong enough to counterattack and drive the Americans from their positions overlooking the city, but they could make an assault very costly for the attacking force. On the same morning, Shafter sent an urgent cable to Washington: "We have the town well invested on the north and east, but with a very thin line. Upon approaching it, we find it of such a character and defenses so strong it will be impossible to carry it by storm with my present force, and I am seriously considering withdrawing about 5 miles." At almost the same moment, Roosevelt was writing a letter to Lodge: "Tell the President for Heaven's sake to send us every regiment and above all every battery possible. We have won so far at a heavy cost, but the Spaniards fight very hard and charging these entrenchments against modern rifles is terrible. . . . We *must* have help—thousands of men, batteries, and *food* and ammunition."

As Shafter and Roosevelt were writing their alarming messages, *New York* just off-shore was pulling out of the blockade line. Sampson was going to a meeting with Shafter at Siboney, east of Santiago, to decide what to do next. Aboard *Brooklyn*, Schley watched *New York* depart, and he reflected that Sampson could have travelled the few miles to Siboney aboard one of the small auxiliaries, leaving *New York* on the blockade line. *Massachusetts* was also absent, away coaling.

At 9:35 A.M., when *New York* was about five miles east of its usual station, signal flags suddenly flapped on several of the blockading ships. "Enemy fleet coming out!" they announced. Aboard *Iowa*, Bob Evans had just finished breakfast in his cabin when the General Quarters alarm sent him running to the bridge. As he hurried along the spar deck, one of the battleship's guns boomed, the first shot in the last, decisive battle of the war. When he reached the bridge, he saw the Spanish flagship *Infanta Maria Teresa* in plain sight, rounding one of the headlands with battle flags flying.

Everyone later remembered the weather that morning as especially brilliant and beautiful. An early morning haze had burned off, but the heat of a tropical summer day had not yet become intense. The air was crystal clear, and the sun sparkled on the water. The Spanish squadron was a magnificent sight as the ships emerged, one by one. The captain of *Texas* later remembered that "the Spanish ships came out as gaily as brides to the altar. Handsome vessels they certainly were, and with flags enough flying for a celebration parade." The Spanish ships had to steam carefully through the narrow channel to avoid the sunken *Merrimac,* and each emerged in turn to drop its pilot, then pick up speed as it cleared the harbor entrance.

With *New York* five miles to the east and *Massachusetts* away coaling, the arc of American ships was anchored by *Indiana* to the east of the harbor entrance. Then came *Oregon;* then *Iowa,* almost directly south of the entrance; then *Texas;* then, finally, Schley's flagship, *Brooklyn,* to the west. Several smaller auxiliary cruisers and gunboats were interspersed between the capital ships. *Brooklyn* for some reason was out of position. It lay out to sea, almost out of sight of the harbor entrance, leaving a gap to the west. Sampson's orders to his fleet if the Spanish tried to escape were simple. They should charge the enemy ships, engage them, and sink them. Accordingly, full speed ahead was rung up in all the engine rooms, and idled engines were engaged, boiler room fires were stoked, and the American ships picked up speed as they headed for the emerging Spanish ships.

Cervera was aware of the gap in the American line to the west, and as soon as *Infanta Maria Teresa* cleared shoal water, the ship turned west. Even before dropping the pilot, it came under fire from *Iowa.* One of the first shells ruptured a steam line, reducing the ship's maximum speed. As the pilot was leaving the ship, it was turning west, presenting its broadside to the American ships heading toward it, and it commenced a return fire.

Aboard *Brooklyn,* a brief but important conversation took place. Commodore Schley hailed the lookouts. "Can you see the flagship?" he

U.S.S. *Brooklyn*, flagship of Commodore Winfield Scott Schley, at the Battle of Santiago.

Library of Congress photograph

shouted. "No, sir!" came the reply. "The *New York* is out of sight." "Then it's our fight," announced Schley. Aboard *New York*, several miles to the east and much closer to the harbor entrance than to *Brooklyn*, Sampson gave orders to reverse course and head back toward the blockade as soon as the firing began. From the flagship's bridge, the emerging Spanish cruisers could be seen plainly. For years, a controversy would rage about who was in command of the American fleet at the battle of Santiago.

At a meeting with his captains the night before, Cervera had outlined a plan for his squadron's escape. His flagship, the first ship to exit the harbor, would ram *Brooklyn*, the fastest American ship. This might provide a chance for the other ships to escape. As *Teresa* picked up speed west of the harbor entrance, *Brooklyn*, the nearest American ship, came charging in. On the American ship's bridge, an officer called out, "Commodore, they are coming right at us!" "Well," Schley replied, "go right for them."

Ten minutes after *Teresa* emerged, *Vizcaya* steamed into view, and *Iowa* loosed a broadside at it. Then, the magnificent *Cristobal Colon* emerged, flags flying. Although it lacked the ten-inch guns of its main battery, it could still use its six-inch secondary battery. It fired twice at *Iowa*—"two as beautiful shots as I ever saw," Evans later wrote. Both scored hits but caused little damage to the massively armored battleship.

Teresa and *Brooklyn* were closing on each other at a combined speed well in excess of twenty knots. When they were separated by little more than one thousand yards—the range of Spanish torpedoes—Schley ordered, "Put your helm hard aport." The captain had anticipated the order. "It is hard aport, sir," he replied. The ship passed *Vizcaya*, which was steaming in the opposite direction in *Teresa*'s wake, so close that Schley later testified that he could see the individual Spanish sailors on its decks so clearly that "I observed the daylight between their legs."

By its sudden maneuver, *Brooklyn* was steaming straight into one of the fiercest controversies of a controversy-filled war. Schley's flagship was turning *away* from the westward-heading enemy. Moreover, it was turning directly into the path of the onward-charging *Texas*. All the ships were enveloped in clouds of smoke from their funnels and from their guns, and visibility was severely reduced. A sudden puff of wind cleared some of the smoke obscuring visibility from the bridge of *Texas* to reveal a frightening scene. Captain Phillips later described it. "There, bearing toward us and across our bows, turning on her port helm, with big waves curling over her bows and great clouds of black smoke pouring from her funnels, was the *Brooklyn* . . . so near it took our breath away." Phillips shouted into the voice tube, "Back both engines hard!" and the ship shuddered to sudden stop as the reversed screws bit into the water. The massive cruiser with its much higher freeboard than *Texas* towered over the battleship as it glided across the bow. The two ships escaped by a whisker a collision at flank speed that might well have destroyed both of them. But the tangle of American ships as they rushed pell-mell after the fleeing Spanish cruisers was still not sorted out.

Oregon's position on the blockade line put it to the east of the harbor entrance, farther from the Spanish ships than *Brooklyn, Texas,* or *Iowa*. *Oregon*'s engineering officer had insisted on keeping fires lit under all the boilers throughout the blockade. This meant that the ship burned coal at a faster rate and had to coal ship more often than the other American ships. But it also meant that it could work up to top speed much more quickly than the others, which kept only half their fires lit as they idled on blockade.

Oregon was soon forging westward at fourteen knots into the roiling billows of smoke obscuring the converging American and Spanish ships. At about 10:10 A.M., there was a break in the clouds of smoke to starboard of the onrushing battleship, and there loomed *Iowa*, hardly a ship's length away. Captain Clark ordered, "Hard astarboard!" and the ship heeled to port. It seemed to be clearing *Iowa*'s bow. Clark later remembered, "Just then, someone near me shouted, 'look out for *Texas!*' and I turned to see her looming through the smoke clouds on our port bow. For one tense moment, it seemed as if three of our ships might be put out of action there and then." Clark later explained that he ordered *Oregon* back to starboard,

> with the hope that we might clear the *Texas* and that the *Iowa*, seeing that we must either cross her bows or run her down, would sheer sharply to starboard. Captains Phillip and Evans . . . must have instantly grasped the situation and acted on it, for we did pass between them, but by so narrow a margin that I felt that coming to close quarters with the Spaniards would be infinitely preferable to repeating that experience.

The three battleships continued the chase.

The last Spanish cruiser, *Almirante Oquendo*, had emerged from the harbor to join the others fleeing westward, followed by the two destroyers, *Furor* and *Pluton*. The chase by the Americans ships had been slowed by the near-collision caused by *Brooklyn*'s sudden turn, but the two smaller Spanish ships were quickly put out of action. They came under a tremendous fire from the secondary batteries of the American battleships. The Spanish ships fought back, but they were made a shambles by repeated hits by large-caliber shells. *Pluton*, damaged and on fire, was soon down badly by the bow. Aboard *Furor*, steam pipes and boilers burst, a magazine exploded, and the steering mechanism was shot away. The little ship commenced circling helplessly under the rain of American shells. A small auxiliary gunboat, *Gloucester* (which only a few months earlier had been J. P. Morgan's yacht, *Corsair*), closed in on the stricken destroyers, its small-caliber guns firing furiously. The captain, Lieutenant-Commander Richard Wainwright, described their end:

> I could see that the *Pluton* was slowing down, as the distance lessened between her and *Furor*, and it soon became apparent that she was disabled. . . . I now ordered the battery to be concentrated on the *Furor*. We were within six hundred yards of her, and every shot appeared to strike. And now came the most exciting moment of the day: the *Pluton* was run on the rocks and blew up; and at the same time the *Furor* turned toward us. It appeared to be a critical situation. She might succeed in torpedoing us, or she might escape up the harbor. But as she continued to circle, it became evident that she was disabled, and her helm was jammed over. Our fire had been too much for her.

At 10:40 A.M., *Furor* sank.

As *Brooklyn* completed its circling turn to resume chasing the Spanish cruisers, Schley was worried: "So far as we could perceive, there was not the slightest evidence that they had been even injured. The thought passed through my mind that after all our precaution and waiting, those fellows would get away." Bob Evans later recalled that the four fleeing Spanish cruisers "presented the finest spectacle that has probably ever been seen on water." Despite the Americans' confused maneuvers, they had kept up a steady fire on the Spanish ships, which responded much less accurately. Evans remembered that "their broadsides came with mechanical rapidity, and in striking contrast to the deliberate fire of the American ships. A torrent of projectiles was sailing over us, harmlessly exploding in the water beyond."

But the Spanish scored hits, too. A Spanish shell decapitated a sailor aboard *Brooklyn*, spattering Schley with blood. The unfortunate sailor was the only American killed in the entire engagement. *Indiana* had joined the chase, on the flank of the Spanish column. Captain Henry Taylor described its role in events:

> One of our heavy shells struck the *Teresa* early in the action and exploded, doing great damage. Another hit *Vizcaya* abaft the funnels, and its explosion was followed by a burst of flame which for a moment obscured the after-part of that vessel. The *Colon* and the *Oquendo*, as soon as they were clear of Morro Point, fired their first broadsides, apparently at the *Indiana* and *Iowa*, both of which vessels replied vigorously and with excellent effect.

A few minutes after *Brooklyn* resumed the chase, a cheer went up from its crew as a break in the pall of smoke off the starboard quarter revealed the redoubtable *Oregon*, coming on fast "with a bone in her teeth," as white water curled away from the bow. Schley had assumed that the slow battleships could not catch the Spanish cruisers, and it must fall to the speedy *Brooklyn* to catch them, if they were to be caught. But he had not reckoned with *Oregon*'s remarkable engineers, the special coal supply they had hoarded under lock and key, and their refusal to foul their ship's boilers with salt water. *Oregon* was gaining even on *Brooklyn*, firing as it came. Schley recalled that "the *Brooklyn* and the *Oregon* were a sheet of flame. I never saw such a fire and never realized what rapid gun firing really meant before."

Badly hit and slowing, *Teresa* was being passed by the other Spanish cruisers. An officer aboard *Oregon* described her end:

> Smoke and flames were pouring from her upper works, and the sight of her hopeless condition served to double the energy of our ships, for their fire became more rapid and deadly than ever. The *Oregon, Texas,* and *Iowa* hurled their terrific broadsides into her as she turned inshore and steamed slowly for the beach at Juan Gonzales, six miles from Santiago. Only forty minutes had elapsed since the stately *Teresa* had led the column out of the harbor. She boldly went to her death, fighting her guns until overwhelmed by fire and shell.

Oregon charged on, turning its fury on *Oquendo* as the gap between the two ships rapidly closed. Twelve minutes after *Teresa* beached, *Oquendo,* burning fiercely, also turned ashore to go aground in shoal water. *Oregon* raked the doomed ship unmercifully with broadsides as it raced past, intent now on catching *Vizcaya* two miles ahead off the starboard bow.

Brooklyn was almost abeam of *Vizcaya* but two miles or more out to sea. The Spanish cruiser turned to port to head offshore across *Oregon's* bow, its forward guns firing at *Brooklyn,* and its port batteries at *Oregon.* One of the battleship's half-ton thirteen-inch shells exploded on its port bow, and the ship veered back to its former course. A second thirteen-inch shell scored a hit directly amidships, causing the ship to lurch sharply to port and send up clouds of steam and smoke. On fire, *Vizcaya* turned to starboard to go aground like the others. At 11:00 A.M., it struck its colors. *Brooklyn* hoisted a signal: "well-done *Oregon!*" Within ninety minutes of the first sighting of *Teresa,* three of the four cruisers had become grounded, flaming wrecks.

Now began what one of *Oregon's* officers called "the grandest chase in naval history," pitting *Brooklyn* and *Oregon* against the speedy *Cristobal Colon.* It had far outdistanced the other Spanish cruisers. The other American ships, their bottoms foul from months of steaming in tropical waters, could not hope to catch the Spanish cruiser, now barely in sight. *Texas* followed the chase, but *Iowa, Indiana,* and the smaller ships stopped to rescue the survivors from the grounded Spanish ships. One of them was Admiral Cervera himself, who swam ashore from the burning *Teresa* and was taken aboard *Gloucester.*

Colon was six miles ahead of its two nearest pursuers. With a designated speed of twenty knots, it was theoretically faster than either American ship. *Brooklyn* might be expected to have a chance of catching it, but with only eight-inch guns in its main battery, the American cruiser would have to cut several miles from the Spanish ship's lead to get within range. *Colon* was designed to outrun any battleship. However, *Oregon*'s chief engineer, like Captain Clark, had served on his ship's trial board, and he knew what a marvelous piece of machinery it was. He pushed steam pressure far above the standard 160 pounds, and he set double watches at every station in the engineering spaces. *Oregon*'s designated speed was fifteen knots, but it exceeded eighteen knots during the chase of the *Colon*. Below decks, the double-manned teams of stokers shoveled the good Cardiff coal into the fireboxes, and on deck, to everyone's amazement, the faint outline of the *Colon* gradually grew larger and clearer. The gap was being closed. One seaman wrote in his diary:

> The poor men in the fire-room was working like horses, and to cheer them up we passed the word down the ventilators how things was going on, and they passed the word back that if we would cut them down, they would get us to where we could do it. So we settled down for a good chase of the *Colon*. I thought she was going to run a way [sic] from us. But she had to make a curv [sic] and we headed for a point that she had to come to.

An officer aboard *Oregon* described the last act of the Santiago drama:

> Several times the *Colon* turned in as if looking for a good place to run ashore, but each time changed her mind and continued to run for her life. It was ten minutes to one when Captain Clark gave me orders to "try a thirteen-inch shell on her"; and soon an 1100-pound projectile was flying after her. The chief engineer was just coming on deck to ask the captain to fire a gun in order to encourage his exhausted men, and when they heard the old thirteen-inch roar, they knew that we were in range, and made the effort of their lives.
>
> The scene on *Oregon*'s decks at this time was most inspiring. Officers and men were crowded on top of the forward turrets, and some were aloft, all eager to see the final work of that great day. The *Brooklyn* fired a few eight-inch shells, and we fired two eight-inch, but all fell short, and the eight-inch guns ceased firing. The *Colon* also fired a few shots, but they fell short of their mark. Our forward thirteen-inch guns continued to fire slowly and deliberately, with increasing range, and the sixth shot, at a range of ninety-five hundred yards (nearly five miles) dropped just ahead of the *Colon*, whereupon she headed for the shore. Our men were cheering wildly, and a few minutes later, at twelve minutes after one o'clock, a thirteen-inch shell struck under the *Colon*'s stern. Immediately,

Crew members of *Oregon* watching the flight of a 13-inch shell toward the Spanish cruiser *Cristobal Colon*.

Library of Congress photograph

her colors dropped in a heap at the foot of the flagstaff. The bugle sounded, "Cease Firing!" The *Colon* had surrendered, and the last shot of July 3 had been fired.

New York had been following the chase and arrived on the scene immediately after the surrender. Schley ordered a signal raised: "A glorious victory has been achieved. Details later." To the surprise of everyone aboard *Brooklyn*, there was no answering congratulatory signal as *New York* rapidly approached. Schley ordered a second signal: "This is a great day for our country." To his disappointment, the answer from Sampson's flagship said tersely, "Report your casualties." *Brooklyn* replied, with equal terseness, "One dead and two wounded." That evening, Sampson sent off a cable to Washington from the telegraph office at Siboney: "The fleet under my command offers the nation, as a Fourth of July present, the whole of Cervera's fleet."

The cold, businesslike reply hoisted by the squadron flagship in reply to Schley's signal at such a jubilant moment, especially when compared with Sampson's message to Washington, appeared jealous and mean-spirited. It served to intensify the controversy that immediately arose about which flag officer should join Dewey as one of the victors of the war. Sampson was undoubtedly the senior officer in command of the blockade squadron, and his flagship had never been out of sight of the battle. But it was never in a position to take part, affect the outcome, or permit the admiral to direct operations. Schley, in contrast, had been in the thick of the fight. But the sudden turn by his flagship had nearly caused a disaster. It further tarnished his wartime reputation that was already blemished by his fitful maneuverings at Cienfuegos and Santiago.

The dispute was fought in the press and among the navy's officer corps for several years, and both officers had their supporters. Schley, stung by the public criticism directed at him, requested a board of inquiry to review his actions. It convened in 1901, chaired by George Dewey, and sat for three months. Its findings were more critical of Schley than Sampson, although Dewey submitted a dissent that defended Schley.

It is now known, thanks to Edward Beach in his *The United States Navy*, that during the summer of 1898, Sampson was in the initial stages of an illness, probably Alzheimer's Disease, that would kill him within a few years. By the time the board of inquiry convened, he was too ill to testify, and he died soon after, in 1902. Accounts by officers in close contact with him during the blockade and the battle describe him as sometimes acting oddly, quite at variance with his usual self and consistent with early symptoms of Alzheimer's. Photographs taken over a span of a few months in 1897 and 1898 show marked signs of aging. If he was beginning to suffer the effects of that terrible disease, this might explain his uncharacteristic failure to acknowledge his subordinates' spectacular accomplishment at the moment of victory. The signal hoisted by *New York* may have been prepared by one of the admiral's subordinates, since it is normal to assess casualties after a battle. It probably was not made in reply to Schley's signal. Unfortunately, the reputations of both officers suffered in the wake of a battle that should have covered one or even both of them with glory.

Although neither was heralded as a Dewey at Santiago, a second

Roosevelt, the governor of New York, being welcomed aboard *Olympia* in New York harbor by Admiral Dewey in September 1899.

U.S. Naval Historical Center photograph

crushing naval victory had been won, to compare with Dewey's. One American had been killed and one seriously wounded. None of the American ships had been seriously damaged. Six Spanish ships had been totally destroyed, including some of Spain's finest warships. Three hundred twenty-three Spaniards had been killed and 151 wounded, out of a total complement of 2,227 men. The battle effectively ended the war. The siege of Santiago continued for a few weeks, and there was an anticlimactic invasion of Puerto Rico, but the destruction of Cervera's squadron meant that the war was over, and it ended in an American victory.

On August 15, Roosevelt and his regiment stepped ashore at Montauk, Long Island, to a hero's welcome. So popular was the leader of

"McKinley's Bulldog," *Oregon*, in 1898.

U.S. Naval Historical Center photograph

the Rough Riders that he was elected governor of New York less than three months later. But the record of the rest of the army in the war had been far from glorious. As Roosevelt had anticipated, it entered the war woefully ill-prepared, and it had lurched from one embarrassing mistake to another. Fortunately, the little fighting that took place on land had not been decisive.

As many experts had expected, the brief conflict had been a naval war. Naval experts everywhere studied it for the lessons it might hold about warfare between modern capital ships. They noted that the battles had been decided by gunfire. Mines had played a minor role at Santiago, but torpedoes played no role at all in either battle, and there had been no ramming. Modern naval ordnance had proven to be enormously destructive, as it had at the Battle of the Yalu two years earlier. The monitor, an unseaworthy relic of the Civil War, was finally and permanently written off as useless. *Oregon*'s extraordinary voyage and its decisive performance at Santiago confirmed the value of the battleship as the backbone of the fleet.

In the eyes of proud Americans, their new navy had performed superbly, despite the arguments about who should receive credit for Santiago. When a cease-fire took effect in August, both Sampson and Schley were under something of a cloud, but old Dewey, even more than Roosevelt and his Rough Riders, was the man of the hour. He arrived back in the United States in September, 1899, sailing up New York harbor aboard *Olympia* after a leisurely cruise home through the Suez Canal and the Mediterranean. The city gave him a tumultuous welcome, led by the new governor of the state, Roosevelt. Dewey and his crew led a parade of 35,000 men down Fifth Avenue to a great victory arch dedicated to "The Admiral." In Washington, there was a second tremendous turnout, led by the president. Congress created a special rank for him, Admiral of the Navy, and decreed that he could not be placed on the retirement list except at his own initiative. His portrait appeared everywhere. The Admiral's face peered out from the bottoms of ashtrays, from the sides of teapots, and from all kinds of other knicknacks. He was seriously discussed as a presidential candidate.

Oregon also became a popular focus of attention throughout the country. It was dubbed "McKinley's Bulldog" for its squat, low-slung lines, its ferocious guns, and its tenacious pursuit of Cervera's cruisers. Reproductions of dramatic paintings showing the Spanish ships being pursued by *Oregon* and *Brooklyn* sold out as fast as portraits of Dewey. The president of San Francisco's Union Iron Works, where *Oregon* and *Olympia* were built, told the New York Chamber of Commerce, "American fighting ships are the best in the world!"

Perhaps Spain was not a first-class naval power, and perhaps it was true that these two victories did not deserve to be compared with Nelson's triumphs at Trafalgar or the Battle of the Nile. Maybe Dewey was not another Nelson or John Paul Jones. But in the eyes of most Americans in the summer of 1898, the millions of dollars that had been lavished on the navy and its battleships for the past decade and longer had been fully justified.

7

"OUR MARKSMANSHIP IS
CRUSHINGLY INFERIOR"

In August, 1898, Tsar Nicholas II sent a diplomatic message to every government represented at St. Petersburg. *Le Temps,* a Parisian newspaper, called it "a flash of lightning out of the north" that caught all its recipients by surprise. The Tsar proposed that an international conference be convened for the purpose of limiting armaments. He denounced war as a destroyer of civilization and the spiraling cost of armaments as a burden that was becoming intolerable for people in all the advanced, industrial countries. A fledgling international peace movement, recently brought into being by increasing alarm over the world's burgeoning armaments industries, immediately interpreted the Russian initiative as a first step toward achieving that long-sought ideal, permanent and universal peace. The Tsar's proposal was hailed as marking "a new epoch in civilization," and the Tsar himself was dubbed "Nicholas the Pacific." An American newspaper opined that the Russian proposal could be the beginning of "the most momentous and beneficient movement in modern history—indeed, in all history."

Nicholas was thirty years old and had been on the Russian throne less than four years. He was a rather lethargic, dull-witted young man, and his startling proposal was not his idea. It had been formulated jointly by his ministers of war, finance, and foreign affairs, who feared that Russia, industrially backward compared with the countries of western Europe, was falling farther and farther behind in the technologically driven international armaments race. In particular, they feared the growing military muscle of Austria, a traditional opponent of Russia in eastern Europe and the Balkans, and Germany. Their purpose in proposing a conference was not to seek international disarmament as a first step in an idealistic quest for lasting universal peace. Rather, they sought to gain agreement to maintain the status quo in armaments for a few years to give Russia time to catch up with its potential adversaries.

The European Powers, in contrast to the idealists in the international peace movement, received the Tsar's proposal with coolness, if not outright hostility. The reaction of the Prince of Wales in England—soon to become King Edward VII—was typical. "It is the greatest nonsense and rubbish I ever heard of," he wrote in a letter. "The thing is simply impossible. France would never consent to it—nor We." Nevertheless, no government was willing to oppose such a humanitarian effort publicly, and on May 18, 1899, ninety-six delegates representing twenty-six countries, including the United States, gathered in pleasant surroundings in the summer palace of the House of Orange in The Hague, the capital of the Netherlands. The occasion marked the first organized international attempt to limit armaments. The group divided itself into three committees to deal with the three principal subjects on which they had gathered to reach agreement: limitation and reduction of armaments, revision of the laws of war to make them more humane, and the employment of arbitration rather than armed conflict to solve international disputes.

The head of the American delegation was Andrew White, a president of Cornell University turned diplomat who was serving as ambassador to Germany. He was completely overshadowed by a famous member of his delegation, Alfred Thayer Mahan, the naval member. Mahan's international reputation gave him influence within his own delegation and a powerful voice in the proceedings. He could be expected to defend American interests with eloquence and vigor. When Kaiser Wilhelm saw Mahan's name on the list of delegates, he scribbled in the margin, "our greatest and most dangerous foe." Secretary of State John Hay's instructions to the delegation indicated that he did not expect the conference to succeed in reducing armaments. Arms limitations, Hay wrote, "could not profitably be discussed," because it was "doubtful if any international agreement to this end could prove effective." The American navy and army were both smaller than those of the leading European Powers, so the American government decided that any limitation initiatives should be left to them.

The British delegation was headed by Sir Julian Pauncefote, the British ambassador to the United States. The British naval member, Mahan's counterpart, was Admiral Sir John "Jacky" Fisher. Strong-willed and pugnacious, Fisher took a dim view of the entire proceedings and could be expected to line up with Mahan on most questions. His attitude toward revising the laws of war was summed up when he exploded, "The humanizing of war! You might just as well talk of humanizing Hell!" As for a conference placing constraints on his beloved Royal Navy in the interests of promoting peace, Fisher wrote in the autograph book of a journalist covering the conference, "The supremacy of the British Navy is the best security for the peace of the world." When the British prime minister, Lord Salisbury, appointed Fisher to the British delegation, he remarked that Fisher would no doubt fight at the peace conference. Fisher later wrote, "So I did, but not for peace."

The Hague Peace Conference sat for ten weeks. On the day before it convened, Andrew White wrote in his diary, "Probably since the world began, never has so large a body come together in a spirit of more hopeless skepticism as to any good result." Mahan shared the general skepticism and was mostly bored by the discussions. He agreed with Hay that it was impossible to reach any practical agreement on reducing arms, and he opposed nearly every proposal put before the group, usually with irrefutable logic. White disagreed with Mahan on several points, but he had to admire the naval expert's relentless realism. "[Mahan's] views have been an excellent tonic," he wrote in his diary. "They have effectively prevented any lapse into sentimentality. When he speaks, the millenium [sic] fades, and this stern, severe, actual world appears."

As expected, the Conference's achievements were meager. For the laws of war, it chalked up four feeble successes. It voted to outlaw the dum-dum expanding bullet, over British and American objections; to outlaw the use of poisonous gas, although Mahan pointed out that no militarily useful means of using poisonous gas as a weapon had yet been invented; to outlaw firing projectiles from balloons; and to extend the Geneva Rules of Warfare of 1864 to include naval warfare. Its most notable success was passage of an Arbitration Convention to create an International Arbitration Commission, located in The Hague, to seek solutions to international disputes through arbitration.

As nearly everyone foresaw, no agreement at all was reached on limiting armaments. Several delegations were relieved when the head German delegate stood up and declared that Germany opposed *any* limitations. Contrary to the Tsar's assertion, he said, the production of armaments did not place an undue burden on the German people, who were enjoying unprecedented prosperity. The other delegations were pleased that they need not take the lead to put their opposition on record. The Conference's results meant that the great powers could feel absolutely free to go ahead building bigger and better battleships and fielding ever-larger, more lethal armies. Before adjourning, however, the Conference expressed its collective "wish" that another conference to limit arms might be convened at some appropriate time in the future.

When the United States declared war on Spain in April, 1898, the American navy possessed five battleships, and five more battleships were already well along in the construction process. The two oldest of the unfinished ships, *Kentucky* and *Kearsarge,* had already been launched the month before war was declared. The three other ships—which became *Illinois, Alabama,* and *Wisconsin*—had not yet been launched, but their keels had been laid over a year earlier. The "Fifty Million Bill," passed just before the war declaration, provided funds for three more battleships. On May 3, two days after Dewey's victory, they were authorized, to be finally christened *Maine, Missouri,* and *Ohio. Maine*'s keel was laid on February 15, 1899, one year to the day after its namesake's destruction at Havana. Thus, by the time the peace treaty was signed in December, and four months after the Tsar's call for a conference to limit armaments, no less than eight new battleships were being readied for the navy. However, with the war over, the country's attention turned elsewhere, and the pace of construction slowed. The first of the ships to be completed, *Kearsarge,* was commissioned in February, 1900, four years after its keel was laid. The last, *Ohio,* was under construction for more than five years and did not join the fleet until December, 1904.

The *Kearsarge*-class battleships differed little from *Iowa.* They were almost exactly the same size and displacement and had the same designated speed, sixteen knots. The differences lay mainly in armament. With these ships, the navy returned to the thirteen-inch guns of the *Indiana*-class. The number of eight-inch guns was halved, from eight to four, to make room for fourteen quick-firing five-inch guns, which were more effective against torpedo boats.

The biggest difference was also controversial. The eight-inch guns were mounted in turrets placed atop the bigger turrets housing the thirteen-inch guns, in an arrangement called "superimposed turrets." Its advocates pointed out the weight-saving and efficiency obtained by having the two turrets operated by the same machinery and the two sets of guns served by the same ammunition hoists. In its authorization, Congress had set a limit on the ship's displacement, so reducing weight was an important consideration in its design. Defenders of the arrangement also claimed advantages to having the main and secondary batteries concentrated in "two impregnable gun emplacements." Opponents argued that since the turrets rotated together, the two sets of guns always had to point in the same direction, although thirteen-inch and eight-inch guns might well be needed for use simultaneously against different targets. Moreover, use of common ammunition hoists meant one set of guns had to wait for the other to be fired before being reloaded. Neither side in the argument was convinced by the other, and the arrangement was never tested in combat.

The three *Illinois*-class ships differed only slightly from their immediate predecessors. They were the same size, displacement, and speed. There were no superimposed turrets, because, to the dismay of many officers, the hard-hitting but slow-firing eight-inch guns were abandoned altogether in favor of fourteen quicker-firing six-inch guns in the secondary battery. Turret design was improved. The main battery turrets were elliptical, with overhang in the back and an inclined front. These changes provided better balance, more room inside the turret, and allowed the gun apertures to be smaller than in earlier turrets, affording better protection to the crews and machinery inside.

The *Maine*-class ships of the "Fifty Million Bill" were a bit larger than the earlier battleships, being about twenty feet longer and displacing about eight hundred tons more. Their guns were twelve-inch, like *Iowa*'s, but more powerful, because they were designed to use new smokeless powder that produced higher muzzle velocities than the brown prismatic powder that had replaced black powder. The Krupp company in Germany had developed a new armor, tougher than Harveyized armor, and it was placed on the *Maine*-class ships. It permitted the maximum thickness of armor to be reduced from sixteen inches to twelve inches, so the weight of the armor was reduced by several tons.

Before the war, the United States had built only two armored cruisers, *New York* and *Brooklyn*, but they had proven their worth. *Brooklyn* was almost as famous as *Oregon*. Exciting paintings and drawings showing the big cruiser surging in pursuit of Cervera's ships became popular.

Britain had been building armored cruisers, so in 1899, three armored cruisers were authorized by Congress. Several more followed in the next few years, and the ship type achieved its epitome in 1904 with the *Tennessee*-class which displaced 14,500 tons, could make twenty-two knots, and mounted ten-inch guns.

The problem with the armored cruiser was defining its purpose. A ship did not need so much armor to attack merchant ships as a commerce raider, but the armor was not thick enough or the guns large enough to stand up to a battleship. In Britain, the armored cruiser evolved within a few years into the dashing and admired battle-cruiser, which was huge, fast, and heavily gunned but lightly armored. It proved to be highly vulnerable to the fire of battleships at the Battle of Jutland in World War I, when three British battle cruisers and several armored cruisers were quickly sunk by German gunfire. In the early days of World War II, the German battleship *Bismarck* sank the British battle-cruiser *Hood*, the biggest warship in the world, with one well-aimed shot. *Bismarck*, by contrast, withstood an unmerciful pounding from a fleet of British warships and aircraft-carrier planes. It finally sank, according to *The Oxford Illustrated History of the Royal Navy*, because it was scuttled by its crew.

The new *Maine* represented an improvement over *Indiana* or even *Iowa*, and the new armored cruisers were bigger and faster than *Brooklyn*. But the improvements in the capital ships that joined the fleet in the years immediately following the war, as compared with those that became famous in the war, were incremental rather than revolutionary. The navy was getting plenty of new capital ships, but they were essentially ships designed and built to fight another Spanish war. The ten years that separated the new *Maine* from *Indiana* had not produced changes on the same scale as those that had occurred during the ten years that separated *Indiana* from the ABCD *Chicago*. The headlong pace of the technological changes of the 1860s, 1870s, and 1880s in warship design and construction apparently had slowed significantly.

However, the technological revolution continued apace in other fields. One of the most significant and far-reaching innovations occurred when radio communication was introduced on shipboard. As early as 1899, temporary "Marconi devices" were installed on *Massachusetts* and *New York*, which conducted communication experiments at distances up to thirty-five miles with a similarly equipped lighthouse station in New Jersey. In 1902 further experiments were conducted in Washington and Annapolis to determine which wireless equipment the navy should adopt. The Slaby-Arco apparatus, manufactured in Germany, was selected, and in 1903, it was installed aboard seven ships and at five shore stations. A photograph of the temporarily jury-rigged Slaby-Arco equipment aboard *Baltimore* shows a conglomeration of machines festooned with wires, switches, and dials that resembles something assembled in Hollywood for a Frankenstein movie of the 1930s. However, the communication revolution was moving at lightning pace, and by 1904, the navy had fifty-nine radio installations. One result of enabling ships to maintain continuous communication with the shore was a further erosion of the authority of a ship's captain, which only a few decades earlier had been virtually absolute.

Revolutionary technological improvements also emerged in the navy's smaller vessels. The United States had totally ignored the torpedo-boat destroyer, although Britain had always considered it an important part of the fleet. The American navy decided it needed some of these small ships, and within a few years the outline of the familiar "four-piper" that became famous as the workhorse of both world wars began to emerge. The submarine was an American invention that had also been ignored in the United States, and the navy began experiments to produce a practical underwater craft. But most of the navy's money and attention continued to be drawn to the large capital ships that had defeated the Spanish. Alfred Mahan, whose writings were more popular and influential than ever, continued to emphasize the primacy of the unified battle fleet and its most important component, the first-line battleship.

In the wake of the war with Spain, the navy was the darling of the public and Congress. Respected and growing, it basked in the afterglow of Manila and Santiago. There was no repetition of the neglect and decline after the Civil War. The United States had acquired an empire, of sorts, in Hawaii, the Philippines, and Puerto Rico, that justified maintaining a muscular navy for its protection. Naval appropriations blossomed, and spanking new capital ships joined the fleet every year. Even the War College began to flourish. The navy settled comfortably into a prosperous peacetime existence. To the officers and men who had joined the service since 1880, the new ships were not the intimidating "machine shops" that *New York* and *Iowa* had been to the puzzled Bob

Evans and his contemporaries a decade earlier. The younger and middle-grade officers and petty officers had learned their trade in very similar ships. The technological upheavals and turmoil of the 1860s, 1870s, and 1880s appeared to be past.

The younger officers had come to professional maturity amid technological upheaval and turmoil, and they accepted radical change as part of the naval profession in the modern world. The second wave of the technological revolution that transformed the United States Navy between 1860 and 1914 was already beginning to form in the minds of certain naval architects and naval officers on both sides of the Atlantic. It was not, perhaps, as radical as the revolution of the thirty years between 1860 and 1890, but within a few years it would make the victorious squadrons of Manila and Santiago look as quaint and outmoded as they had made *Monitor* and *Virginia* appear.

In the American navy, a young officer named William Snowden Sims looked around and saw much that he considered faulty, both in the design and construction of the shiny new ships joining the fleet and in the use the navy made of them. He bombarded his superiors in Washington with detailed analyses of what he found wrong. Many of his fellow officers agreed with him, and his reports found a few sympathetic readers among his superiors in Washington. But they probably would have ended up being simply noted, filed, and forgotten, except that Sims was unusually persistent and he was favored by a combination of fortuitous circumstances involving Theodore Roosevelt.

Roosevelt and Sims were almost exactly the same age. Sims was born in Ontario, Canada, on October 15, 1858, twelve days before Roosevelt, into a family in rather more modest economic circumstances than the future president's. His father was an American engineer. When he was ten years old, the family moved to the United States and settled eventually in Pennsylvania. It took young William two tries to gain admittance to Annapolis, where he graduated in 1880, the same year Roosevelt graduated from Harvard. During six years of sea duty that followed graduation, he devoted himself to a rigorous program of wide reading and become one of the best-read officers in the service. He spent a year in Paris studying French, followed by another six years at sea, including two years on the China Station during the Sino-Japanese War.

Sims was a handsome, athletic man, much admired for both his intellect and his looks. Every day, he made a point of "wetting his shirt" through vigorous exercise. He could write well, and this, combined with his inquiring mind, wide reading, and knowledge of French, landed him the coveted position of naval attaché in the American embassy in Paris just as the war with Spain was beginning. It was an important wartime assignment, because Paris became a key source of information about the Spanish navy and its operations after the American embassy in Madrid closed. His reports were read with avid interest by many officials in Washington, including Theodore Roosevelt, until he departed to lead the Rough Riders. Sims received communications from Washington commending his reporting, including at least two that carried personal notes from Roosevelt to assure him that his reports were indeed valuable.

In the autumn of 1900, Sims was detached from the Paris embassy to join *Kentucky*, then crossing the Mediterranean to go via the Suez Canal to the Far East. *Kentucky* was the newest American battleship, and Sims was eager to look it over. He had just spent three years as a naval attaché studying the ships of European navies. How did this newest American battleship compare with them? He made an exhaustive inspection of the ship from the bilges to the crow's nest, and he decided it compared very poorly with the battleships of Britain, France, Germany, and Italy. He spent the remainder of the voyage to the China Station drafting a report setting forth his criticisms.

He focussed his attention mainly on the ship's armament. The machinery to supply ammunition to the five-inch guns was so inefficient, he charged, that a maximum rate of fire could not be maintained. Many of the smaller caliber guns that extended out through gunports in the hull could not be used if a sea were running—even a moderate sea—because of the water that was shipped through the open gunports.

He believed that the superimposed turret arrangement was a mistake. Placing the eight-inch turrets atop the main battery turrets simply created a single large target that would attract more concentrated enemy fire than if the secondary battery turrets were situated separately from the main battery. The gun apertures in the main turrets were so large that the crews inside were needlessly exposed. Four twelve-inch shells, he claimed, could enter the turret through the apertures without touching anything. The loading, training, and elevating gear in the turrets was therefore unprotected, as were the crews. The ammunition hoists were open shafts leading directly from the guns to the handling rooms below. One spark from a gun breech or from an explosion of any kind inside the turret could easily fall into the handling rooms immediately adjacent to the magazines. Years later, after he had retired, he described the dangers of *Kentucky*'s design in testimony before a congressional committee: "You could stand on the quarter deck and look into that turret, and you could spit right down into the powder magazine. Now, that is a fact. You could stand in the bottom of the powder magazine, or rather, in the chamber out of the powder magazine, and looking up see a man smoking a cigarette right up on the bridge."

Sims decided that the reason for the poor design of American warships was that each portion of the ship was designed by technical experts interested only in creating the most efficient and economical turrets, or guns, or ammunition hoists, or engines, or steering mechanism, or any of the other many parts of a warship. Each naval bureau was still an independent fiefdom, operating virtually without any central direction or coordination. Each was responsible for approving the design for only a portion of a ship. What was needed, Sims decided, was an overall authority concerned with creating the fighting ship best able to serve out and absorb punishment as an integrated whole. Individual components should be designed with reference to their fit into the overall design of the fighting unit, rather than their technical merits considered individually.

During the voyage to Asia, Sims aired his findings during conversations in the wardroom, and they were met with hostility by the other officers. *Kentucky* and *Kearsarge* had been lauded in the United States as "the greatest fighting machines afloat." Sims's fellow officers decided he had been too long under the influence of Europeans in Paris. They had prejudiced his attitude toward an American ship. But his wardroom colleagues had to admit that he supported his arguments with facts. "After much discussion," he later wrote, "they were sadly obliged to acknowledge the justice of my criticisms."

By the time *Kentucky* arrived in the Philippines, Sims had finished his report, putting forth in calm, professional prose his critique of the ships, and he sent it off to Washington. In the spring, as *Kentucky* lay at Cavite,

Sims received orders transferring him to *Monterrey,* the monitor that had been hurriedly sent across the Pacific in 1898 to reinforce Dewey. It was now stationed at Canton, in China. Although he had been aboard *Kentucky* for only a few months, his transfer was not unusual and apparently had nothing to do with his criticism of the battleship. Enroute to join his new ship at Canton, he stopped at Hong Kong. There he made the acquaintance of someone who would exert a profound influence on Sims and the course of his professional life as a naval officer, a Royal Navy captain named Percy Scott.

Scott commanded a British armored cruiser, H.M.S. *Terrible,* attached to Britain's Asiatic Fleet. Like Sims, he possessed an inquiring mind and a tendency to question orthodoxy. He was interested in science and machinery, and he had already devised several inventions, including a respirator to use in fighting fires and an improved signal lamp. He also possessed a prickly personality that often needlessly aroused opposition to his unorthodox views.

Sims learned that in recent firing practice sessions, *Terrible* had posted phenomenally higher scores than the other British ships— as much as twenty percent higher in the number of hits scored compared with rounds fired. The spectacular performance apparently was not a matter of luck, because Scott's previous ship, *Scylla,* had also toted up unprecedented scores. No American ship had ever done so well in target practice, although the rules set by the American navy for target practice were more lenient than those used by the Royal Navy and made hits easier to obtain. Obviously, Percy Scott was on to something.

In the euphoria that followed the victory over Spain, few Americans took note of detailed studies that were made of the battles at Manila and Santiago. In both battles, all the sunken Spanish ships had been grounded in shallow water, and all except one could be easily examined after the battles. The exception was *Cristobal Colon,* which was almost undamaged when it was run aground on a reef to escape *Oregon*'s thirteen-inch shells. When the Americans pulled it off the reef after the battle, they learned too late that the crew had opened the seacocks. *Cristobal Colon* sank to the bottom in deep water. But the other defeated Spanish ships at both Manila and Santiago sat in shallow water, and they were minutely examined by teams of experts. Every shell-hit was noted and analyzed. Although it was impossible to account for every last shell of every caliber that had struck every ship, a quite accurate survey of hits could be made.

It produced an unflattering picture of the accuracy of American naval gunfire. In Manila, Dewey's squadron had fired some six thousand rounds of various calibers and scored only 142 hits that could be identified. That computed to an accuracy of 2.3 percent. The results at Santiago were worse. More than 9,400 shots were fired, but only 122 hits had been scored, for an accuracy of 1.3 percent. The number of unidentified hits was estimated to be too small to boost percentages significantly. Dewey's ships fired at stationary targets while steaming back and forth on water as still as a mill-pond. Conditions at Santiago were a bit more challenging but only marginally so. What the results might have been if the Americans had been engaged with ships of the British or French navy on the open sea was anybody's guess.

The problem was that the methods used by all navies in 1898 to aim and fire guns had not kept pace with the technological development of the ordnance itself. Gunners at Manila and Santiago aimed their weapons in much the same way that Lord Nelson's gunners aboard *Victory* had done at Trafalgar, despite the fact that the newer weapons were accurate at much longer ranges. They used fixed open sights and depended upon the ship's rolling or pitching to aim the gun at the target. At the split second when the ship's movement brought the gun into line with the target before it dipped downward, the gunner fired. This was called "firing on the weather roll." If the shot missed, the shell might still hit the target by ricocheting off the water. Each gun was aimed and fired independently. The odds against scoring a hit were increased by something called the firing interval of the gunner, the nanosecond of the man's reaction time between his decision to fire and his finger actually pressing the firing button. Each man's reaction time was slightly different, so each gunner had to learn his own firing interval and take it into account in firing his gun. The entire system made the likelihood of scoring a hit very small except at point-blank range on smooth water.

Percy Scott improved the shooting by the ships under his command by, first, replacing open sights with telescopic sights. The telescope sight had actually been devised a decade earlier in the American navy by another innovative thinker named Bradley Fiske. However, when Fiske tested his invention aboard *Yorktown*, the ship's captain, Bob Evans, decided that "in its present shape, it is of no value on board a ship." Perhaps it had been improved when Scott introduced it on *Scylla*. He had crosshairs mounted in the sights, and he ringed the eyepieces with thick rubber padding so the gunners could keep their eye against the sight even when the gun fired.

Scylla's marksmanship improved noticeably in smooth water, but it was still spotty in a rough sea. During one firing practice, Scott noticed that one gunner consistently scored more hits than his fellows. The captain watched him in action and discovered that the gunner did not wait for the ship's movement to bring the target into his crosshairs. He continuously manipulated the gun's pointing wheel to keep his gun aimed constantly at the target. Scott introduced the idea to his other gunners, and so was born the system of "continuous aiming" that transformed naval gunnery.

Sims grasped the revolutionary nature of Scott's new system. He sat down and wrote another report to Washington, explaining in detail how "continuous aiming" worked and the impressive results it achieved on Percy Scott's ships. Part of the reason for Scott's success, he explained, was the extremely efficient machinery that elevated British guns and permitted the gunners to keep a target in their crosshairs throughout the ship's roll. The machinery on American ships was not as efficient and would make continuous aiming more difficult for American gunners, though not impossible. He had discovered one more shortcoming of American warship design.

Hong Kong was the home port of the British Asiatic Fleet, and Sims had a chance while there to examine several British ships. He discovered that the design of British ships was superior to their American counterparts in several respects. He wrote another report, comparing the British *Canopus*-class battleship with the American *Kearsarge*-class, to the latter's disadvantage. He forwarded both reports through his new commanding officer, the captain of *Monterrey*, who read them with interest and sympathy. He sent them to Washington, but he warned the younger officer that "although we ought to stand in the light and be not afraid of the truth no matter how unsatisfactory . . . , the pathway of the reformer is hard."

Sims made copies of his reports and circulated them among fellow officers. Many agreed with his arguments. He heard from friends in Washington that his reports were being circulated in the navy department, and many officers and civilians there also thought they had merit. Several other officers had already expressed concern about the poor results of firing practice in the fleet. But Sims could see no evidence that his reports were producing any changes in the way the navy operated.

In October, he was given proof that his reports were at least being read by higher authority. He was transferred to *Brooklyn*, the flagship of the Asiatic Fleet. More specifically, he was attached to the staff of Rear-Admiral George Remey, the fleet's commanding officer. Sims's reports had passed through the admiral's hands on their way to Washington, and he was impressed when he read them. He arranged to have Sims attached to his staff and given freedom to continue his investigations.

Sims was encouraged by this turn of good fortune, and within a month of joining *Brooklyn*, he decided to take a bold step. He would write directly to the president in Washington. In 1901, the American government and the navy's officer corps were much smaller than they are today. The president was not nearly so isolated from people as he is today. The grounds of the White House, for example, were open to the public. Nevertheless, in 1901, a naval officer on active duty did not write directly to the president, especially if his subject was criticism of the navy. He jeopardized his career if he did so. Sims decided to take the risk, but it was carefully calculated, because Sims knew his letter would be addressed to Theodore Roosevelt.

Roosevelt's election as governor of New York in November, 1898, thrust him into the spotlight of national politics. At age forty, he began to be regarded as a man of destiny. That impression was strengthened less than two years later, in the summer of 1900. The vice-president had died in November, and Roosevelt was selected at the party's convention to be William McKinley's running mate in his bid for a second term. The Republican ticket won in a landslide, and less than a year later, destiny again appeared to intervene in Roosevelt's incredible life. In September, 1901, McKinley fell to an assassin's bullet during a visit to an international exposition in Buffalo, New York, and Roosevelt was suddenly thrust into the White House.

William Sims had never met Roosevelt, but he calculated, correctly, that the new president would take an interest in what he had to report about the shortcomings of the navy's new ships. He also guessed that Roosevelt would have favorable recollections of him personally, because of the reports he had sent as an attaché from Paris.

On November 16, 1901, Sims sent off a long, politely worded letter to Roosevelt. He apologized for writing a personal letter to the president, but when he came to the gist of his message, he pulled no punches.

> The protection and armament of even our most recent battleships are so glaringly inferior in principle as well as in details, to those of our possible enemies, including the Japanese, and our marksmanship is so crushingly inferior to theirs, that one or more of our ships would, in their present condition, inevitably suffer humiliating defeat at the hands of an equal number of enemy's vessels of the same class and displacement.

When Roosevelt received the letter, he had been president for less than three months and was being bombarded with issues and problems. He nevertheless read the letter with interest, as Sims guessed he would. He did remember Sims and his attaché reports as Sims guessed he would, but his recollection was not as positive as Sims probably hoped. He sent the letter along with a brief note to his naval aide, who was his brother-in-law, William Sheffield Cowles.

> Dear Will:
>   I send you the enclosed letter from Sims and accompanying memorandum. Will you please write me back what you think I ought to do? Sims is a good man, but a preposterous alarmist. Prior to the outbreak of the Spanish war, he actually believed that the Spanish vessels were better than ours. Nevertheless, I am inclined to think we are deficient in target practice.

Cowles had a summary of all Sims's reports prepared, and he sent it to Roosevelt with a scribbled note which said in part: "While Sims is an alarmist, he is also a horse & works hard & should receive the encouragement that hard work deserves."

On December 27, Roosevelt sent Sims a reply. He charged that Sims was by nature "unduly pessimistic" and reminded him of his "very gloomy view of our vessels" on the eve of the war with Spain. Roosevelt, of course, thought that the two spectacular American naval victories were irrefutable proof of the superiority of American ships. "Nevertheless," he concluded, "I would a hundredfold over that you erred upon the side of thinking us not good enough than of thinking us too good; and many of the suggestions you made in the past, both upon the need of improving our gun practice and of doing away with or removing faulty construction in our battleships, have been genuinely fruitful. I thank you for writing me; I shall always be pleased to hear from you."

Further encouraged by Roosevelt's response, Sims wrote a second report about H.M.S. *Terrible,* Percy Scott, and his system of continuous aiming. This communication was much longer than any of his earlier reports, and it was couched in blunter, more forceful language. He threw in comments about faulty ship design. His summation was uncompromising:

> The success or failure of a ship must depend on the qualities of her *design* and of her *marksmanship.* We have sinned against all the military principles of the former and have carelessly neglected the latter to such an extent that we have placed ourselves beyond the possibility of success against an equal force of any of our possible enemies including the Japanese. The American people, however, are none the wiser; on the contrary, the Navy has been inordinately flattered by a boastful press, which with the most patriotic intentions imaginable, is too ignorant of such matters to criticize even our most glaring faults.

He finished it on February 15. Admiral Remey forwarded it with an endorsement which said in part: "I deem this paper worthy of the most serious attention, recommending that it be considered by the General Board, and also in connection with the plans of the ships to be built and building. No well-informed man can deny that our situation is extremely dangerous."

Sims knew that the Navy Department, like any bureaucracy, contained plenty of people wedded to the status quo, who as a matter of reflex would resist change of any kind. One of them was Admiral O'Neil, the officer in charge of the Bureau of Ordnance where Sims's reports about continuous aiming finally landed. The admiral arranged a test, apparently for the purpose of proving that this new idea would not work. A six-inch gun was mounted on the seawall at the Naval Gun Factory in Washington and aimed at a target that was moved up and down to simulate the movement of a target at sea as it appeared relative to the gun. In the test, the gunner could not keep his gun aimed at the moving target. He could not overcome the resistance of gravity and the friction in the gun's elevating machinery to raise and lower the heavy gun even five degrees in ten seconds, the equivalent of a ship's roll in a moderate sea, to keep it pointed at the target. Continuous aiming, the admiral announced, was impossible. In his response to Sims's report, he explained that his test's results demonstrated that it would require no less than five men working together to raise and lower a gun fast enough to keep it aimed at a target.

Sims had to use tact in his reply. He pointed out first that continuous aiming was not theory. The records of H.M.S. *Terrible*'s target practice results proved that the system worked. The method used for the Bureau of Ordnance's test was flawed. The admiral and his testers had ignored the basic laws of physics. The test should have been conducted with a gun mounted aboard a rolling ship, not on a stationary seawall. In raising and lowering a gun fastened to a seawall, to keep it aimed at a moving target, the gunner was working against not only the resistance of friction in the gun mounting, but also against the force of gravity and Newton's first law of motion. But on a rolling ship, the ship's motion, in keeping with Newton's law, caused the weight of the gun to work in the gunner's favor, not in opposition to it. When Sims shared the admiral's response with Percy Scott's gunnery officer on H.M.S. *Terrible,* that officer wrote back: "He seems to forget that you are not moving the gun and bringing it to rest, but that the energy you expend is only necessary to overcome the friction which prevents the gun from remaining horizontal. The energy required is small—it is no harder for a man to do than it was for my old nurse to turn her sewing machine for hours together." The whole episode was but one indication that resistance to change was still alive and well in the American navy, despite the experience of a forty-year revolution in technology.

In February, Sims was given further proof that his message was getting through. He was appointed Inspector of Target Practice for the Asiatic Fleet. Through the spring and summer, as he was able to put his ideas into practice with the ships of the Asiatic Fleet, he had the satisfaction of seeing their marksmanship in target practice improve noticeably. In March, he wrote a second, longer letter to Roosevelt. This time, he did not receive a reply, but he felt sure the letter had been read, and he was right. Roosevelt sent it to Rear-Admiral Henry Taylor, the new head of the Bureau of Navigation, with a note: "I am really very much impressed with Sims's letters. . . . We do not want to deceive ourselves. If there is any basis at all for Lieutenant Sims's complaints, not merely as to the inefficiency of the men but of the instruments with which they work, we must carefully go into the facts and take all possible measures for correction."

Taylor was an excellent choice to fill the powerful position he held. As captain of *Indiana,* he had gained combat command experience at the battle of Santiago. Enlightened, open to suggestions, possessed of vision for the future of the navy, he had been impressed with Sims's reports. He ordered them distilled into a single memorandum which was distributed throughout the navy. In August, Roosevelt gave further evidence that he had begun to share Sims's concerns about the quality of the navy's gunnery when he sent a note to the captain of the presidential yacht, *Mayflower.* "I should like some suggestions from you," he wrote to the captain, "as to how we can use the *Mayflower* as in a certain sense an experimental vessel for marksmanship."

In September, Sims was ordered to report urgently to Washington. Mystified, he hurried back to learn he was appointed Inspector of Target Practice for the Atlantic Fleet, the navy's main battle fleet, despite holding only the rank of lieutenant. He owed his good fortune to Admiral Taylor, who as head of the Bureau of Navigation controlled officers' assignments. Sims had offended a good many people in the Navy Department with his acerbic criticisms, so when Taylor decided to bring Sims back from Asia to put him in charge of target practice, there was strong opposition from many senior officers. Taylor invited a group of both Sims's opponents—who were mostly older, senior officers—and his supporters—who were younger, junior officers—into his office for a conference. "How about it?" he asked. "Is Sims the real thing?" The younger officers won out, and in the teeth of opposition from several senior officers, Taylor made the assignment.

Here was Sims's golden opportunity to prove the validity of his arguments. But the navy was also, in a way, flinging down a challenge to the officer who had been badgering his superiors for several years to change the way it aimed its guns. Many other officers were dissatisfied with the results of fleet target practice. The American navy's marksmanship clearly needed improvement. Go ahead and fix it, Lieutenant Sims, they seemed to be saying. Show us what you can do.

In November, 1902, within a month of Sims's return from Asia, the entire Atlantic Fleet gathered at Culebra, an island off Puerto Rico, for massive maneuvers under the command of Admiral Dewey. The gathering took place at Roosevelt's insistence. Even in the wake of the war with Spain, navy ship commanders were given little chance to operate as part of a fleet. Ships still usually operated alone or occasionally in small squadrons. One of the Roosevelt's goals was to mold the battle fleet into a strong, cohesive force that operated as a team.

Sims was on hand for the innovative training maneuvers, and he travelled through the battle fleet in his new assignment, spreading the gospel of continuous aiming like an apostle preaching a new religion. Over dinners in wardrooms, he would spend the whole meal explaining his ideas. He described his proselytizing to a friend who happened to be the officer he had replaced as Inspector of Target Practice: "I visited every ship in the squadron officially and asked to be given the opportunity to talk with all the line officers including the gunners. . . . Then I went over the whole business, illustrating with sketches. . . . It usually took me from three to four hours, and sometimes I visited three ships in the same day."

Continuous aiming was not the only innovation he sought to introduce. The usual method of scoring the results of target practice was to compute the number of hits against the number of shots taken. Sims insisted that what was important was the number of hits made *per minute*. The rate of a ship's fire, as well as the accuracy, should be taken into account when its effectiveness was assessed. An accurate but slow-firing gun crew might be put out of action before it could score a hit.

Within months, target practice results began to improve noticeably. A report was sent to Roosevelt in March. He responded by telling the assistant secretary of the navy, Charles Darling, that he was "greatly pleased," not only with the target practice results, but also with the "zeal and intelligence with which the high officers having the general supervision of the work in charge are handling the subject." On March 30, Sims reported to Admiral Taylor, "the *Indiana* beat the record of the China Station today with her six-inch guns—with an average of 40.6 percent hits. Many of the men have hardly ever fired her guns before." *Alabama* posted the best record with an overall average of sixty percent hits with all its guns. Thirty-three individual gunners made perfect scores. In June, a Drill Book for gunners, prepared by Sims, was issued to the fleet.

Continuous aiming improved the navy's marksmanship, but it represented only a first step in a long process to enable warships to exploit the full potential of their ordnance. The technology devised by man had outstripped his ability to use it to optimum advantage. Until as late as 1900, the Royal Navy considered effective battle range to be two thousand yards, about a mile, only a little farther than in Lord Nelson's day. Their guns were capable of firing several times that distance with fair accuracy, but the gunners could not aim them at targets so far away with equal accuracy. Until the invention of smokeless powder, battle smoke badly obscured gunners' vision after a few rounds had been fired. But even after the introduction of smokeless powder and telescopic sights, the gunners' range of vision was limited compared to the range of their guns. The guns were still aimed and fired independently by gunners working the guns themselves. By 1903, effective range in the Royal Navy had been extended only to about three thousand yards, well short of the maximum distance a twelve-inch gun could throw a shell.

The first step to extend effective firing range was to station a spotter aloft, as high as possible, who could follow the fall of shots and call for range corrections. Battleships which had hitherto been low-slung vessels, except for tall funnels, sprouted high masts, soon to become tripods of three masts, supporting a small cubicle to house the spotter. The spotters reported that the guns must fire in salvos to allow range corrections to be accurately assessed. It was impossible to know which gun was responsible for which splash or hit when each was fired independently. The first halting steps toward long-range central fire control were being made.

The struggle to extend effective firing ranges to equal the ranges at which naval ordnance was capable to throwing a shell was long and difficult. The problems were maddeningly complex and involved mathematical calculations only a few experts could completely understand. The naval gun was fired from a moving platform that might also be rolling and pitching in a heavy sea. It was expected to hit a target several miles away that was also moving. Moreover, the target, also rolling and pitching, might at any moment change speed and direction, and at extreme ranges it was invisible to the ship's captain on the bridge. All the constantly shifting variables of the firing ship's course and speed and the target's range, course, and speed had to be instantly calculated and the information somehow fed into the complex mechanisms that aimed and fired the guns. The monstrous guns and turrets that weighed tons had to be capable of being moved instantly in response to the commands of central fire control to stay on target. It is a wonder that in an age long before the invention of computers, targets could be hit at all under such conditions.

In 1903, the first manual on fire control was published in Britain. By

William Sims's determined efforts to improve American naval gunnery produced such spectacular results that they attracted notice in the press, like this cartoon published in 1904.

U.S. Naval Historical Center photograph

1904, the British Mediterranean Fleet, under the command of the hard-driving Jacky Fisher who had fought at the Hague Peace Conference, was firing effectively at ranges up to eight thousand yards. In 1906, a British optical company, Barr and Stroud, devised a "coincidence range finder" that could estimate the distance of a ship miles away within an accuracy of a few yards. In the same year, a British inventor named Arthur J.H. Pollen approached the Admiralty to announce he had invented a fire control device that could accurately aim guns at extreme ranges at moving targets. The Admiralty, excited by the prospect of stealing a technological march on other navies, entered into a contract with the inventor. But after several years of encountering mounting costs and repeated difficulties in producing a working model, the British government finally withdrew from the agreement without Pollen's revolutionary device ever having been tested.

This evolution toward effective long-range central fire control would

William Sims, right, with Roosevelt aboard the presidential yacht *Mayflower*, for the departure of the Great White Fleet from Hampton Roads.

Library of Congress photograph

continue right through World War I and beyond. In late 1912, a senior officer of the Royal Navy demonstrated to the first lord of admiralty a fire control device he had invented. A chair, mounted high aloft in the spotter's aerie, was fitted with telescopes, controls for deflection and elevation, and a pistol-grip firing mechanism connected to the main battery guns. A range finder below transmitted data to the firing officer in the chair who could thus aim and fire all the ship's guns simultaneously. The device was the creation of William Sims's old friend, Percy Scott— by then Admiral Sir Percy Scott—and the first lord of admiralty whom he persuaded to adopt his invention was Winston Churchill.

By late 1903, target practice results in the American battle fleet had improved so significantly that William Sims was attracting admiring notice. A senior officer suggested that he should be immediately promoted to rear-admiral. Since he had only just been promoted to lieutenant-commander, that was considered too radical a jump in rank, and the idea was rejected. Admiral Taylor offered him command of a cruiser, but he turned it down, saying his work on improving gunnery was still incomplete.

He still had not met the president. One day, he happened to meet the secretary of the navy, William Moody, who asked if he had ever called on the president. When Sims answered that he had not, Moody suggested that he leave his card at the White House. An invitation to dinner with Roosevelt followed in January, 1904. Sims later recalled: "The President on that occasion showed the keenest interest in the progress of gunnery; he asked repeated questions and instructed me to keep him fully informed regarding developments." A personal relationship was established that continued until Roosevelt's death.

8

"The Only Logical Battery for a Fighting Vessel"

When Theodore Roosevelt was suddenly and unexpectedly catapulted into the presidency on September 14, 1901, his forty-third birthday still lay more than a month in the future. He was, and he remains, the youngest man ever to hold the office. Yet Roosevelt came to the presidency with richer, more varied experience in public office than any of his fellow presidents. He had served with vigor and distinction at all three levels of American government: municipal, state, and federal. He had served in the army in combat. The only gap in his experience, if it can be called that, was that he had never served in Congress. He did have legislative experience, however, in the New York state legislature, and he counted as close personal friends some of the most powerful members of Congress, notably Henry Cabot Lodge.

His knowledge of naval affairs has never been matched by an incoming president. Several American presidents have come from the army's officer corps, but no professional sailor has ever been elected president, although several presidents served briefly as naval officers before taking office. Only Theodore Roosevelt's cousin, Franklin, approached him in knowledge and understanding of the navy, having also served as assistant secretary of the navy before becoming president.

As soon as he took office, Roosevelt continued the call he had been sounding for years to build up the navy. Sometimes it was a plea, sometimes a demand, depending upon his audience. William Chandler, the former navy secretary, was one of the members of Congress concerned about the headlong growth of naval appropriations, and he urged Congress to adopt a more conservative attitude toward them. In early November, less than two months after taking office, Roosevelt wrote to him: "If by conservatism in naval expenditures, you mean that we should stop building up the Navy, I radically and totally differ with you.

I think that no greater calamity could happen to this country at present than to stop building up the Navy."

In his first annual message to Congress, submitted on December 3, he devoted as much or more space to the navy than to any other subject, including his cherished dream of building a Central American canal. His theme was the same that he had used in his thundering speech at the Naval War College in 1897. "Far from being in any way a provocation to war," he wrote, "an adequate and highly trained navy is the best guaranty against war, the cheapest and most effective peace insurance. The cost of building and maintaining a navy represents the very lightest premium for insuring peace which this nation can possibly pay." He seconded the secretary of the navy's annual report in calling for construction of three new battleships and "heavy armored cruisers . . . [and] auxiliary and lighter craft in proportion." Four thousand additional seamen and one thousand additional marines should be recruited, he proposed, and the size of classes at Annapolis should be expanded.

In Congress, members like William Chandler questioned the wisdom of continuing to increase naval appropriations. Soon after Roosevelt took office, an influential senator, Eugene Hale of Maine, wrote to the secretary of the navy, who was still John Davis Long, to say that he opposed *any* increase in the navy. Hale's views were not to be ignored. He was serving as majority leader in the Senate and was considered an expert on naval affairs. Soon after entering the Senate in the 1870s, he was offered the position of secretary of the navy by President Rutherford B. Hayes, but he turned it down. In the Senate, however, he was involved in naval affairs. For years, he supported the build-up of the navy, but he finally came to believe that no matter how much naval appropriations were increased, the navy would always want more. In 1901, Hale and others saw no discernible threat to the country that required an expanded navy. As chairman of the Senate Naval Affairs Committee, Hale would continue his opposition throughout Roosevelt's presidency.

Henry Cabot Lodge told Roosevelt that Hale's opposition was "not wholly surprising." He advised, "When you see him, I would be the soul of good nature and let him know firmly you are bent on your policy. If he stands out, we must beat him." Lodge thought that the Naval Committee in the House "will be with you all right," but he added, "I want

you to see [William] Moody in this connection. He is naturally with us
. . . and if he backs the Naval Committee they will win easily."

The following spring, John Davis Long resigned after having served
five years as secretary, and Roosevelt appointed Moody to replace him.
Roosevelt had five different secretaries of the navy during his presidency,
but he actually acted as his own secretary and personally dealt with both
Congress and the navy itself on most important issues. His vigorous es-
pousal of naval expansion early in his presidency bore fruit, despite the
opposition of Chandler, Hale, and their allies. In July, 1902, when he
had been in office less than a year, Congress authorized construction
of two battleships, to be the largest and most powerful yet built in the
United States.

After William Sims's transfer to Washington to assume charge of the
battle fleet's target practice, he had little time to devote much attention
to warship design, the other obsession that had occupied him on the
China Station. His criticisms of *Kentucky* had revealed faults that were
corrected in ships built subsequently. For example, the turrets of the *Illinois*-class battleships incorporated some of the improvements Sims advocated from his study of *Kentucky*. Ammunition hoists, however, continued to be open shafts connecting the turrets directly with the magazines,
until accidental explosions a few years later killed several sailors aboard
a couple of ships and finally prompted designers to adopt the inter-
rupted-shaft hoists that Sims had advocated. As Sims was aware, such
incremental improvements were not the only possible changes looming
in warship design.

The battleship was firmly established as the ruler of the sea. The
aircraft carrier and the submarine would end the battleship's reign, but
its overthrow by them lay decades in the future. Hardly anyone in the
first decade of the twentieth century could foresee it. Navies needed
other kinds of ships, but few naval experts disputed the proposition that
control of the sea demanded fleets of battleships. Nothing was capable
of contesting control by a fleet of battleships except another fleet of
battleships.

There was growing fear of the torpedo, because the force of the underwater explosion of a torpedo's warhead against a ship's hull was intensified by water pressure and was therefore greater than the explosion

of the largest shell fired from any gun. It could be devastating against the most heavily armored ship. A single torpedo could conceivably sink a battleship, and a few far-seeing people could envisage the potential for destruction that was to be had by marrying the torpedo with the submarine. As early as 1904, the remarkably prescient Admiral Jacky Fisher in Britain wrote, "I don't think it is even *faintly* realized—the immense impending revolution which the submarine will effect as offensive weapons of war."

However, Fisher was writing about potential for the future, not the present. By 1904, no torpedo boat or submarine had ever sunk a battleship, nor had they even come close to sinking one. The range of a torpedo was much less than the range of even secondary battery guns. Bob Evans was reflecting the view of most naval experts when he observed, "A ship will occasionally be destroyed by torpedo boats or submarines— as a man will occasionally slip on a banana peel and break his neck." The dominant sea power, Britain, had more battleships than any other country, and it continued to build them at a furious pace, because Germany was obviously attempting to catch up by starting a massive building program of its own.

Roosevelt specifically stated that he did not want the United States to emulate Germany in its attempt to challenge British dominance. But he was committed to establishing his country's position as a leading sea power nation, and he was determined to build battleships to equal any in the world. For years, American battleships had not only proliferated but had grown steadily in size. *Maine* and *Texas*, designed in the 1880s, displaced a little more than 6,500 tons. The first true battleships of the *Indiana*-class grew to a little more than ten thousand tons, and the new *Maine*-class, built after the war with Spain, displaced nearly thirteen thousand tons. In 1899 and 1900, Congress authorized no less than five new battleships, which became *Virginia, Nebraska, Georgia, New Jersey,* and *Rhode Island*. These *Virginia*-class ships displaced nearly fifteen thousand tons. No new battleships were authorized in 1901, principally because the shipyards and steel mills were glutted with orders for all the ships under construction. The two battleships authorized by Congress in July, 1902, the first authorized during Roosevelt's presidency, became the first two ships of the *Connecticut*-class. *Connecticut* and *Louisiana,* as well as four later sister ships, displaced sixteen thousand tons and mounted four twelve-inch, eight eight-inch, twelve seven-inch, and twenty three-inch guns, as well as several smaller quick-firing three-pounders and one-pounders.

Connecticut and its five sister ships were the final product of a long process of evolution. The *Connecticut*-class ships were later called "the final flowering" of the American pre-dreadnought battleship. *Connecticut* was designed to be the equal of any existing battleship in the world. But it was, in essence, a larger, slightly faster, moderately more lethal *Iowa*. Its basic design differed little from the much older vessel's. Its bunker capacity was greater and its engines generated more horsepower than *Iowa*'s, because it was a bigger ship. But the engines were still reciprocating engines and therefore liable to breakdowns at top speed. Its designated speed, eighteen knots, was only two knots faster than that of *Indiana* and no faster than that achieved by *Oregon* in its chase of Cervera. Like *Iowa*, it mounted four twelve-inch guns as a main battery. However, they were designed to use smokeless powder, and they had a longer range and greater muzzle velocity than *Iowa*'s guns. The effective range of main battery guns had grown to exceed eight thousand yards.

During the first years of the twentieth century, there were stirring among naval architects and naval officers in several countries some revolutionary ideas about how battleships should be designed and armed. For two years or more before *Connecticut*'s keel was laid in March, 1903, naval experts discussed whether the technological improvements in naval ordnance and the extensions of the effective range of main battery guns called for a radical change in battleship design. Why, they asked, should a battleship carry so many different sizes of guns? *Connecticut* mounted a total of forty eight-inch, seven-inch, and three-inch guns but only four twelve-inch pieces. The steadily increasing range and accuracy of main battery naval guns made it unlikely that the smaller caliber guns would ever be needed in a future battle. Somewhat ironically, recent target practice results, as well as the surveys of the battle damage at Manila and Santiago, revealed that large-caliber main battery guns were more accurate than the smaller secondary battery ordnance. Very small caliber, quick-firing guns were still needed for protection against torpedo boats. But the outcome of any future engagement between fleets of battleships and cruisers would probably be decided by the large guns on both sides firing at extreme ranges before the intermediate caliber guns could be brought into play.

Gun spotters aboard a ship like *Connecticut* found it virtually impossible to identify which calibers of guns caused which hits or splashes. Some naval experts argued that the magazine space used to carry all the different sizes of ammunition for the smaller guns could be better used to store more ammunition for the main battery. For purposes of efficiency and better fire control, a battleship's main battery should be expanded and confined to guns of a single caliber. The number of main battery guns could easily be increased if bigger ships were constructed. A sixteen-thousand-ton battleship was not the biggest that could be built. Ships of twenty thousand tons or larger were possible.

The prodigious leaps in the effective range of main battery ordnance carried implications for tactics as well as design. Until the turn of the century, standard tactics called for a fleet to close with the enemy and pound him with everything it had at close range. This, in effect, had been Sampson's orders at Santiago. It was a concept not much different from the accepted wisdom of Lord Nelson's day. This did not mean that new tactics required in the age of steam would necessarily be more difficult or complicated than those used by ship or fleet commanders in the age of sail. Always, those commanders had to take into account the direction and force of the wind. Just before or during a battle it might change direction, or die out, or suddenly freshen and thereby totally change the tactical situation. Commanders in the age of steam could not ignore the wind completely, but it was not the overriding factor for them that it had been for Nelson and his contemporaries. In a sense, there was a kind of art in tactical maneuvering during the age of sail that disappeared with the coming of steam.

With steam-powered warships after the turn of the century able to fire accurately from ever-lengthening distances, new tactical principles were obviously needed to replace those accepted twenty or even ten years earlier. A fast battle fleet armed with accurate long-range ordnance could choose the range at which to carry on a battle with a slower enemy armed with older guns. It might maneuver to remain miles from the enemy and demolish him with impunity. Speed and maneuverability took on increasing importance. The trade-offs among the size, weight of armor, speed, and range of a warship, and the number and size of its guns, became more complicated. They inevitably influenced, and were influenced by, new tactical ideas. Some experts doggedly maintained that thickness of armor and the total weight of metal thrown by a broadside must remain the primary considerations for designing a battleship. They believed that since intermediate battery guns could be fired more rapidly than the large main battery pieces, they should be retained. Other experts, their numbers increasing every year, argued that speed and the number of guns in a ship's main battery had become more important. Large-caliber guns had to be fired more slowly than smaller guns, but since their shells were so much bigger, the total weight of explosives fired from an expanded main battery increased exponentially.

These ideas had been mulled over by naval reformers in several countries for years. In 1901, while William Sims was still in Asia, one of his fellow officers named Homer Poundstone, who had been an Annapolis classmate, designed a battleship armed with only two sizes of gun, a main battery of twelve large-caliber guns and several small, quick-firing, anti-torpedo-boat guns. Poundstone called his creation U.S.S. *Possible,* but Sims christened it *Skeerd o'Nuthin.* His choice of a name was interesting as well as amusing, because it denoted the same idea as the name the British chose for the revolutionary battleship they built a few years later, *Dreadnought.* Poundstone's design became an object of fascination in the Navy Department, but it was never built.

In 1903, *Jane's Fighting Ships* published a radical design by the Chief Designer for the Italian navy, Vittorio Cuniberti. The Italian navy had decided Cuniberti's ship would be too costly and difficult to build, so he called his creation "an ideal battleship for the British Navy." It displaced seventeen thousand tons and boasted a designated speed of twenty-four knots, significantly faster than any existing battleship and probably impossible for any heavily armored battleship to achieve at that time. It mounted twelve twelve-inch guns and eighteen three-inch quick-firers. Cuniberti's ship was never built, but the publication of his design in the bible of the world's navies spread the idea of the fast, all-big-gun battleship.

Not surprisingly, Roosevelt knew about the ideas being proposed for an all-big-gun battleship. If he, and not Congress, had possessed the authority to appropriate the money to construct ships, and if he had possessed the power to appoint a chief of naval operations, the United States might have become the first nation to build one. But then, as now, Congress controlled the purse strings. In its appropriation bills for warship construction, it customarily specified maximum displacement and a cost ceiling. Any quantum leap in battleship size or radical change in armament would have required Congressional concurrence in the appropriation bill.

Within the navy itself, senior authority under the secretary of the navy was fragmented. There was no chief of naval operations, no single senior officer with broad authority. A General Board existed, an outgrowth of a temporary body created during the war with Spain. It was chaired by the venerated and venerable Admiral Dewey, but it possessed no legal authority. It could be influential, but its functions, legally, were strictly advisory. The chief of the Bureau of Navigation was considered the senior officer on duty, but he had no authority over other bureau chiefs. Each bureau was still a virtually independent fiefdom, and each bureau chief reported directly to the secretary. Since a politically appointed secretary seldom possessed the experience or technical knowledge of a senior career naval officer, he was seldom in a position to make informed judgements about the many, often conflicting, proposals and advice he received from the bureau chiefs. Mahan, Luce, Evans, Sims, and others had for years advocated creation of a naval general staff, headed by a senior officer who would be the secretary's principal advisor with authority over the bureaus, but without success. There were sharp differences of opinion among the bureaus about the all-big-gun battleship idea, and the Bureau of Construction, which was responsible for designing new ships, was against it.

In 1902, Roosevelt somehow learned about Homer Poundstone's creation, *Skeerd o' Nuthin*. On December 17, he wrote to Poundstone, "It is excellent; though I am not sure that I can get Congress to take the view I should like it to take on the subject." He was enjoying notable success in getting expanded naval appropriations, but Congress soon confirmed that he could not get everything he wanted. In March, 1903, less than a year after authorizing *Connecticut* and *Louisiana*, it took a collective deep breath and approved construction of five battleships. Three of them were specified to be of the sixteen-thousand-ton *Connecticut* class. They became *Vermont, Minnesota*, and *Kansas*, the last ships of the Great White Fleet to be built.

However, Congress can function only by adjusting differences of opinion among its members, and the other two battleships became products of Congressional compromise between Roosevelt's supporters and their opponents, the budget cutters. The authorization bill specified a displacement of no more than thirteen thousand tons for the two ships and a cost ceiling $700,000 less than for any of the other three ships. They would be three thousand tons lighter and seventy-five feet shorter than the size that had become standard for battleships. The two ships, *Mississippi* and *Idaho,* represented a step backward in warship design. They carried the same armament as *Connecticut* but at a sacrifice of power, range, and speed. Both proved to be unsuitable as battleships, and they were unpopular in the fleet right from their commissionings. Within a few years, they were sold to Greece. Both were sunk in 1941 by the German Luftwaffe while lying at anchor in the harbor at Salamis.

By 1904, a full-blown debate was raging in the navy over the wisdom of the all-big-gun battleship. One of its early supporters was Bob Evans. He had taken command of the Asiatic Fleet while William Sims was still attached to it, and he had supported the switch to continuous aiming. Evans had Roosevelt's ear, and when he returned to Washington, he argued in favor of the new battleship design. On October 5, Roosevelt wrote to Sims, who had been preoccupied with his target practice duties, "Evans insists that we ought to have on our battleships merely big twelve-inch guns and fourteen pounders, with nothing between. What do you think of this?" Roosevelt had long since become a fan of William Sims. In April, he had written to Secretary of the Navy William Moody, "what a useful man [Sims] is!" Sims replied the following day, saying that Evans was correct. "The great majority of our naval officers who interest themselves in such matters," he wrote, "have long since been convinced that this is the only logical battery for a fighting vessel."

Roosevelt was prompted to query Sims because Congress had authorized another battleship the previous April. This became *New Hampshire* and was intended to be the sixth ship of the *Connecticut* class. It was being designed to carry the same mixture of main and intermediate battery ordnance as the other ships of that class. Two days after receiving Sims's letter, Roosevelt sent a message to the navy's Board of Construction to suggest that *New Hampshire* be designed as an all-big-gun ship. It should carry a main battery of eleven-inch or twelve-inch guns and three-inch guns for defense against torpedo boats, Roosevelt proposed. There should be no intermediate batteries.

The Board of Construction and its parent body, the Bureau of Construction, were not yet ready to make such a leap into the unknown, even though the proposal came from the president himself. The Congressional authorization specified a sixteen-thousand-ton ship, and the

Bureau seized upon that limitation as an argument to reject Roosevelt's proposal. The ship would be too small to carry a great number of large-caliber guns. On October 17, the Board of Construction sent a reply to Roosevelt. Nearly three years earlier, it explained, a design for a ship such as Roosevelt proposed had been rejected (Poundstone's *Skeerd o'Nuthin*). Recently, Rear Admiral O'Neil, the Chief of the Bureau of Ordnance (who had sought to prove to Sims that continuous aiming did not work), had returned from a trip abroad to report that the *Connecticut*-class battleships were the equal of anything being built in Europe. "After prolonged and mature consideration," the Board of Construction's letter concluded, it remained convinced that "nothing has transpired during the past year which would justify extensive changes in the main battery of vessels building or recently designed." *New Hampshire* would be built as another *Connecticut*.

The Board of Construction had a powerful ally, who also commanded Roosevelt's attention and confidence, in the person of Alfred Thayer Mahan. Mahan was ranged against Evans, Sims, and the other supporters of the new battleship design. His opposition did not derive simply from obstinate, unthinking resistance to change. For several years, Mahan had been watching with concern the increasing size and cost of battleships. As they continued to grow larger and more expensive, Mahan feared that the country could afford to build fewer and fewer in future years. The individual battleship might continue to grow bigger and more powerful, but if its numbers in the fleet grew progressively smaller, and it became progressively more expensive to build, the navy would be increasingly reluctant to risk it in battle.

The subsequent history of the battleship confirmed Mahan's argument. During World War I, both Britain and Germany exhibited reluctance to risk their expensive battleships in a decisive battle. The battle of Jutland was a strategic victory for Britain but a tactical draw, because of the un-Nelsonian caution and hesitation exhibited by both sides. In 1938, a Royal Navy officer, Commander Russell Grenfell, wrote that there had developed "an increasing tendency to think more of preserving the great ship from damage than of using her to damage the enemy . . . , to think of the battleship in terms of 'can we keep her safe' than of 'can she sink the enemy?'"

Moreover, Mahan argued, faster and faster ships might be built, but they would have to operate in a fleet of older, slower ships. Their speed would be controlled by the speed of the slowest ship in the group. The advantage of greater speed would be cancelled out. Newer, faster ships would always be hobbled by older, slower ships. In sum, the naval philosopher argued, the navy would be better off with a greater number of smaller battleships resembling those already in the fleet, rather than an ever-dwindling number of bigger, faster, more powerful, and more expensive ships that would always become outmoded with the advent of the even bigger, faster, more powerful ships that would always succeed them. Mahan was worried about twin problems for the navy that had begun to manifest themselves decades earlier: technological obsolescence and mushrooming unit costs caused by technological innovation. In naval and military affairs, these are literally matters of life and death, and they demand serious attention. They have continued to be military and naval problems throughout the twentieth century.

As early as 1902, in a letter to Roosevelt, Mahan had argued on tactical grounds against the growth of battleship size and cost.

> The primary consideration is that the battleship is meant always to act with others, not alone. Strategically, and yet more tactically, this demands homogeneousness. In the battle ship, one is designing a class, not a unit. . . . War depends largely upon combination, and facility of combination increases with numbers. Numbers, therefore, mean increase of offensive power, other things remaining equal.

The naval historian harkened back to the sailing era's seventy-four-gun ship. He explained that in its day it was held to be the optimum size for a warship by "professional consensus" among naval officers, although larger ships were built. In a similar manner, the size of modern battleships should be limited by consensus among the world's naval officers, Mahan believed, and he thought that most naval officers would agree that a displacement of twelve thousand to fifteen thousand tons was the optimum size for a modern battleship. If naval officers and not civilian administrators were responsible for designing warships, Mahan argued, an international consensus against the continued growth of battleships would emerge.

One problem with Mahan's argument was that a growing number of American naval officers favored bigger, faster, and more heavily armed battleships, if they could be built. Few sailors would deliberately choose to go into battle in a ship smaller and slower than the enemy's. Naval commanders in the age of sail liked the seventy-four-gun ship because it was more nimble than the slow, unwieldy 100-gun three-decker. In the age of steam, a larger battleship need not necessarily be slower or less maneuverable than smaller existing ones.

Another problem was the difficulty of reaching an enforceable international agreement to limit the size of battleships. Even if naval officers agreed among themselves to limit battleship size, their governments would have to agree, too. So long as just one country built bigger, faster battleships, every other country would feel compelled to follow suit. Roosevelt saw the problem, but he nevertheless adopted the idea and promoted it, half-heartedly and ultimately without success, for discussion as a measure to limit armaments at the Second Hague Peace Conference held in 1907. The other powers refused even to discuss it and would not agree to place it on the conference agenda.

In Britain, the all-big-gun battleship idea fared rather differently. On October 21, 1904, four days after the Board of Construction rejected Roosevelt's proposal for *New Hampshire,* Jacky Fisher sat down at his desk in the Admiralty in London as the new first sea lord of the Royal Navy. It was the ninety-ninth anniversary of Nelson's victory at Trafalgar, "a good fighting day to begin work," Fisher wrote to a friend. First sea lord was the senior position for an officer of the Royal Navy, roughly comparable to the chief of naval operations in the United States Navy today, but possessing even more authority and prestige.

The tough, hard-driving, flamboyant Fisher brought with him to his new assignment a 120-page paper he had written that constituted a blueprint for a total overhaul of the Royal Navy. Among its sweeping reforms were two that provoked controversy and debate. Fisher proposed sending 154 obsolete warships, including several battleships, to the scrap yard, and he proposed initiating a massive building program that included immediate construction of an all-big-gun battleship.

Fisher was prompted to devise his revolutionary plan by the accelerating naval arms race being thrust upon Britain by Germany. With the support of Kaiser Wilhelm, Fisher's counterpart in Germany, Grand Admiral Alfred von Tirpitz, was determined to build a German navy to equal or even surpass Britain's. Fleet laws passed by Germany in 1898 and 1900 specifically flung down a challenge to Britain's supremacy at sea. In the latter year, the law stated that the German battle fleet must be "so strong that even for an adversary with the greatest seapower, a war against it would involve such dangers as to imperil his position in the world." The law laid out a long-term building program that would provide Germany with a fleet of thirty-eight battleships and proportionate numbers of other ships by 1920.

British politicans and the British public might be divided on many issues, but on one issue there was absolute unanimity throughout the country: the Royal Navy must be supreme in the world. There was opposition to some aspects of Fisher's sweeping plan, notably to his proposed scrapping of so many apparently perfectly good battleships. But with a massive German building program in progress just across the North Sea, he could count on solid support in the government. He was determined to force the Royal Navy to make such a leap into the future and build such a powerful fleet of such advanced, powerful ships that British naval supremacy would continue, no matter what von Tirpitz might be able to accomplish.

On the day he took office, Fisher presented his blueprint paper to the first lord of the admiralty, the British equivalent to the secretary of the navy. "I sat him in an armchair in my office," Fisher later recounted with obvious glee, "and shook my fist in his face for two and a quarter hours without a check; then he read 120 pages of foolscap, and afterwards collapsed." Fisher immediately set about with his usual remorseless determination to put his plan into effect. He worked sixteen-hour days, seven days a week, until his wife expressed concern about his health to King Edward VII. The king wrote out an order forbidding the first sea lord to work on Sundays, but Fisher ignored it.

The 154 obsolete ships were struck from the navy's rolls "with one courageous stroke of the pen," wrote Prime Minister Arthur Balfour with admiration. On December 22, a committee to design the new, revolutionary battleship was formed. It included Rear-Admiral Prince Louis of Battenberg, a future first sea lord and father of Lord Louis Mountbatten, another future first sea lord and last British viceroy of India. Another member was Captain John Jellicoe, who was to command the British Grand Fleet at the battle of Jutland. Fisher himself was not a committee member, but he closely oversaw its work.

On February 22, 1905, the design committee submitted its proposal for construction of the ship that became the famous *Dreadnought*. In March, the first lord of admiralty informed Parliament of the plan and gained approval of the cost estimates. Through the spring and summer, machinery, construction materials, and armor were ordered and stock-piled. On Monday, October 1, 1905, *Dreadnought*'s keel was laid at Portsmouth Naval Yard.

While Fisher with ruthless singleness of purpose was ramming through his plan to overhaul the Royal Navy, the United States was continuing the greatest naval buildup in its history, but not according to any master plan. By early 1905, there were thirteen battleships in the fleet and twelve under construction, one more was authorized, and Roosevelt and the navy were preparing funding requests for still more. Roosevelt's drive to expand the navy was given a strong assist by the German naval buildup. The German Fleet Laws of 1898 and 1900 attracted notice in Congress. They did not provoke the level of concern in the United States that they aroused in Britain, but Germany appeared increasingly bellicose, and the new German policy prompted many members of Congress to support Roosevelt's program. Roosevelt apparently was able to gain Congressional approval for five battleships in a single year, 1903, because of the publicity about Germany's plan for naval expansion.

In 1902, in a lecture at the Naval War College, the naval constructor, J. J. Woodward, pleaded for a plan to guide the construction program for which he was responsible. "The most important question of general interest to the naval service of the United States at the present moment is that concerning the necessity of the adoption by this country of a definite naval program," he stated, "and a part of such policy concerned with the determination of a program of naval construction of new vessels to be built for the navy during the next few years." In 1903, Secretary of the Navy Moody, apparently prompted by developments in Germany, asked Dewey's General Board to draw up such a program for future construction. The plan submitted by Dewey's group was breathtaking in scope and kept secret for ten years. It proposed a year-by-year building program to create by 1920 a navy of forty-eight first-line battleships with numbers of smaller warships and auxiliary vessels in proportion. The calculations of Dewey's board were obviously influenced by the German plan in the Fleet Law of 1900. If the fleet it proposed were built, by 1920 the United States Navy would rank second in the world after Britain—assuming Britain continued to build ships at its current rate—and ahead of Germany.

However, then, as now, military expenditures in the United States were not determined by a single master plan. They were decided by a multitude of forces and influences both in and out of government. Members of Congress adopted the positions they took on the issue as much because of pressure from their constituents as because of their assessment of what kind of navy the country needed. In Britain, maintaining a navy superior to Germany's was regarded as nothing less than a matter of national survival, while in the United States the German naval challenge was watched with less alarm. Various members of Congress supported the administration's naval construction program for various reasons. Some were moved to do so by concern about naval strategy or international politics; others, for domestic political or economic reasons.

Congress and the navy were acutely aware that private business was very much involved in questions about the size of the navy. Secretary Moody, in his annual report for 1902, included a list of more than thirty large companies involved in the construction of warships. Notable among them were the steel giants, Bethlehem and Carnegie, that produced armor and gun steel. By 1902, the two companies were being "commanded," according to the president of Bethlehem Steel, to double their armor-making capacity in order to supply what was needed for all the new battleships and cruisers. Charles H. Cramp, owner of the enormous shipyard in Philadelphia that bore his name, stated in 1901: "The profit on armor-making is something enormous. The people who make money on their ships are not the persons who design and construct them, nor the persons who take two or three generations to get information enough to design a battleship. . . . Why, I would be willing to take a battleship and build the ship at cost if we got the profit on the armor." Cramp's shipyard had already built several battleships, and since he continued to submit bids to build more, he also was presumably making a profit. His company was included on Moody's list, as were such other industrial leaders as Union Iron Works in San Francisco and the Colt Firearms Company.

Members of Congress, especially those representing districts or states where these companies were located, knew that the armor makers and shipbuilders wanted to be kept busy with government orders. With Roosevelt's approval, emphasis was given to the big, expensive glamor vessel, the battleship, that required the most armor and the biggest, most expensive guns. Roosevelt wrote to the chairman of the House Naval

Committee that "heavy cruisers were very well in their way, but heavy battleships are what we need. We do not need light cruisers at all." He was supported by Admiral Dewey, who wrote to the president, "it would be on very rare occasions that a commander-in-chief would not prefer to add another battleship to his fleet in preference to an armored cruiser." Although other kinds of ships were built, the navy was becoming top-heavy with battleships.

Congress could find the money to pay for this massive naval construction program, because American wealth and prosperity exploded during the last three decades of the nineteenth century. Between 1865 and 1914, a nation with a mostly agricultural economy was transformed into one of the world's industrial giants, and a mostly rural society became increasingly urbanized. The country's population was trebled by a flood of immigrants, but per capita income grew even more. Financial panics in 1873 and 1893 triggered severe economic depressions, but between 1877 and 1893 the economy mushroomed.

The headlong pace of railroad construction contributed significantly to this expansion. In 1860, perhaps thirty thousand miles of railroad existed, most of it poorly designed and incapable of supporting heavy traffic. By 1914, more than 250,000 miles of heavy-duty track carried most of the country's freight and passenger traffic. In 1880, total American steel production was 1,300,000 tons, less than in Britain or France. By 1910, more than fifteen million tons were being manufactured, and the United States had become, by a wide margin, the world's leading steel producer. In 1897, the nation embarked on a period of economic expansion that would continue, with only a few brief downturns like the 1907 panic, until 1930. Roosevelt enjoyed the good fortune of serving as president during the early years of this unprecedented period of growing prosperity, and the navy benefited from his determination to channel a part of it into making it second only to Britain's.

On March 3, 1905, Congress authorized construction of two more battleships. Their design provoked a tug-of-war within the navy that reflected the disagreement over the all-big-gun ship. Admiral Dewey's General Board recommended building eighteen-thousand-ton ships carrying ten twelve-inch guns—all-big-gun ships—but the Bureau of Construction disagreed. The Bureau insisted on holding displacement to sixteen thousand tons, which precluded arming the ship with a main battery of ten large-caliber guns. But the Bureau agreed to compromise by omitting an intermediate battery and expanding the main battery to eight twelve-inch guns. So, as the Portsmouth Navy Yard was marshalling all its resources to build *Dreadnought,* Congress authorized construction of the two battleships which became *Michigan* and *South Carolina.* They were built according to the Bureau of Construction's compromise proposal.

In 1905, the Senate Committee on Naval Affairs—which was chaired by that arch-critic of naval expansion, Eugene Hale—issued a document entitled *A Compilation of the Annual Naval Appropriations from 1883 to 1905.* As the committee chairman no doubt intended, it revealed the astonishing amounts of money that had been spent on America's "new navy." Naval expenditures during that period had totalled more than a billion dollars, which was about three times total government expenditures in 1883 and nearly twice what they were in 1905. Appropriations for construction alone had totalled more than $250 million. Since 1901, annual appropriations had grown from $85 million to $118 million. Clearly, the concerns of Mahan, Senator Hale, and others about the headlong growth of naval spending were not unfounded.

On the day after passage of the authorization of *Michigan* and *South Carolina,* Roosevelt was inaugurated for his first, and only, full term as president. He had already served nearly a full term, but as an unelected president. Five days later, he wrote a letter to his close friend and fellow Rough Rider, General Leonard Wood, who was serving as military commander in the Philippines. He ruminated about his first term and looked forward to his second. "Congress," he wrote, "does from a third to a half of what I think is the minimum it ought to do, [but] I am profoundly grateful that I get as much." He explained in some detail his plans for the navy.

> When I became President three years ago, I made up my mind that I should try for a fleet with a minimum strength of forty armor-clads; and though the difficulty of getting what I wished has increased from year to year I have now reached my mark and we have built or provided for twenty-eight battle-ships and twelve armored cruisers. This navy puts us a good second to France and about on a par with Germany; and ahead of any other power in point of material, except, of course, England. For some years now, we can afford to rest and merely replace the ships that are worn out or become obsolete.

The early battleship *Texas* had clearly become obsolete and needed to be replaced. The same would soon be true for *Iowa* and the redoubtable *Oregon* and its sister ships of the mid-1890s.

PEACEFUL SAM

Roosevelt's buildup of the army and navy prompted opposition in Congress and in the press, as demonstrated in this cartoon published in 1904.

Library of Congress photograph

In his annual message to Congress in December, Roosevelt made official a slowdown in the furious pace of naval construction that he had been advocating so strenuously for four years. It did not appear necessary, he wrote, to increase the fleet "beyond the present number of units." It was necessary only to replace "worn-out or inefficient units." One new battleship a year would be enough to accomplish that. Henry

Cabot Lodge thought he was making a mistake by making such a public announcement. If he wanted for any reason to speed up construction again in the future, Lodge reasoned, this announcement in an annual Congressional message would put him at a disadvantage with his opponents in Congress. Admiral Dewey and his General Board continued to cling tenaciously to their long-range plan to build a fleet of forty-eight battleships. Nevertheless, for the present, the administration would seek authorization for no more than one capital ship a year.

The Russo-Japanese War, which broke out in February, 1904, finally produced the battles between fleets of battleships that naval analysts had been awaiting. The Russian Pacific Fleet was crippled by a daring surprise attack that touched off the war on February 8. It was launched at night by Japanese torpedo boats as the Russian ships lay at anchor at Port Arthur. Four Russian capital ships were badly damaged. In a subsequent battle at sea, more Russian ships were sunk or damaged. On August 10, the bulk of what was left of the Russian Pacific Fleet, including six battleships, tried to escape from Port Arthur to Vladivostok. A Japanese fleet which included four battleships and four armored cruisers intercepted it. The Russian force was badly defeated and scattered. A British naval attaché, Captain Pakenham, was aboard the Japanese flagship. He reported that Japanese gunfire at long range decided the battle.

> Compared with peace practice, ranges of 10,000 and 12,000 metres sound preposterous, but they are not really so. Firing begins to look possible at 20,000 metres, reasonable at 14,000 metres; close range may be counted as setting in at about 10,000 metres. . . . When 12-inch guns are firing, shots from 10-inch pass unnoticed, while, for all the respect they instill, 8-inch or 6-inch guns might then just as well be pea-shooters.

With his Pacific Fleet destroyed or rendered useless, Tsar Nicholas II sent his Baltic Fleet on a futile mission to the Far East to deal with the Japanese. It made an incredible voyage around Africa, across the Indian Ocean, through the Straits of Malacca, and north through the China Sea. It had almost reached its destination at Vladivostok when it was intercepted on May 27, 1905, by the Japanese in the Straits of Tsushima that separate Japan from Korea. What ensued was the greatest action between fleets of battleships until the battle of Jutland.

The Russians were numerically superior in capital ships, with eight battleships, three armored cruisers and three monitors, to the Japanese fleet's four battleships and eight armored cruisers. Nevertheless, most naval experts expected a Japanese victory, and they were not disappointed. The battle was a resounding victory for Japan. Twenty Russian ships, including four of the newest battleships, were sunk, seven surrendered, and two sank after the battle. Six were able to escape to neutral ports where they were interned for the remainder of the war. More than four thousand Russians were killed and six thousand taken prisoner. Of the thirty-eight ships that had departed the Baltic, only two reached Vladivostok. The Japanese lost three torpedo boats. Japanese casualties totalled 116 killed and 538 wounded.

The battle was eagerly studied to extract its lessons, especially the reasons for such a crushing victory by the Japanese navy. They were not difficult to discover in superior Japanese leadership, personnel, and materiel. The Japanese commander, Admiral Heihachiro Togo, was infinitely more capable than the Russian admiral, Zinovy Rozhestvensky. He was able to use the Japanese ships' superior speed to execute the classic maneuver "crossing the T," which all naval commanders since the days of sail sought an opportunity to make. It permitted the weight of a fleet's entire broadside to be brought to bear against an enemy able to respond with only a few guns firing dead ahead. The Japanese officers and crews were better trained and motivated than the Russians. Several senior Japanese officers were graduates of Annapolis. Many members of the Russian crews had been raw landsmen when they began their long, grueling voyage. They were exhausted as they neared its end, while the Japanese sailors, in their own home waters, were rested and eager for battle.

The differences in the ships were equally decisive. The Russian battleships were smaller than their Japanese counterparts, and several were old and obsolete. After their long voyage, the Russian ships were in no condition to fight a battle. They were heavily overloaded with stores and coal taken on in Vietnam for the last leg of their voyage to Vladivostok. The ships were filthy, with their decks and cabins piled high with crates of food supplies and sacks of coal. They were so overloaded that their armor belts were mostly underwater. After their long voyage, their bottoms were foul with underwater growth, which, together with the overloading, significantly reduced their speed. As a result, they were as much as seven knots slower than the newer Japanese ships, a difference that by itself could almost guarantee a Japanese victory.

Like Yalu, Manila, Santiago, and the earlier actions in this war, the battle was decided by gunfire. Torpedoes were used, but only late in the action after the Russians had, in effect, been defeated, and mines were not a factor at all. What was perhaps most important as a lesson for the future was that the issue was decided during the first hour of battle—although it lasted into the next day—by large-caliber guns firing at long range. The first shots were fired at 1:55 P.M. At 3:20 P.M., the captain of the Russian flagship recorded in his notebook that the battle had been lost. The captain later testified that he "had never seen or imagined such accuracy of fire, the shells coming one after another without interruption, and hitting so frequently that he could not count the number of hits."

The British naval attaché, Captain Pakenham, was again on hand aboard Admiral Togo's flagship, and he again reported the devastating effect of the largest Japanese guns fired at long range. The Japanese twelve-inch shells were four feet long and gave forth an eerie wailing sound as they tumbled through the air. They exploded even if they hit only the water, and they threw up geysers sixty feet high. They were filled with a new explosive mixture devised by the Japanese, called *shimose*, that burned fiercely when it exploded, instantly setting ablaze even the paint on a steel bulkhead. The captain of the Russian flagship described what happened when a Japanese twelve-inch shell struck: "They burst as soon as they touched anything. Handrails were quite sufficient to cause a thoroughly efficient burst. Iron ladders were crumpled up into rings, and guns were literally hurled from their mountings." The Russian ships were crammed with wooden decks and panelling, coal, and other combustibles. Fires broke out everywhere as exploding twelve-inch shells spattered shimose over everything. The Russian flagship alone was hit by more than one hundred twelve-inch shells. The doomed ships were enshrouded in flames, flying shrapnel, and bloody human remains.

The Russian fleet was pounded by a hail of shells from both the large-caliber main batteries of the Japanese battleships and by eight-inch and six-inch fire. Analysts later decided that much of the smaller caliber fire probably came from cruisers closing in on the stricken Russian ships after they had been severely damaged by Japanese main-battery fire. The most formidable Russian ships were put out of action or badly damaged early in the engagement at long range before intermediate caliber guns or torpedoes could be used. The arguments in favor of the big, fast, all-big-gun battleship had been proven in the crucible of combat.

On February 9, 1906, at Portsmouth Navy Yard, a crowd of a thousand or more dignitaries and guests watched King Edward VII, on his second try, smash a bottle of Australian wine on the bow of the completed hull of *Dreadnought*. Then, wielding a chisel and a wooden mallet made from the timbers of Nelson's *Victory*, the king cut the last symbolic rope holding the great ship on the ways, and it slid into the water. Scarcely four months had elapsed since its keel was laid.

Dreadnought's launching attracted prominent coverage in the American press, in part because Fisher insisted on maintaining complete secrecy about its design. For the first time, a warship was being built in secret. Only people authorized by the Admiralty were permitted near the ship. American newspapers reported that Britain was constructing, at an unbelievably rapid pace, a mysterious "monster battleship" that would render all existing warships obsolete. Information about its principal features became known, but the secrecy Fisher insisted on maintaining obviously intrigued both editors and newspaper readers.

Under the furious prodding of Jacky Fisher, construction continued at a breakneck pace. Even if the ship itself could be completed according to Fisher's telescoped schedule, manufacturing its twelve-inch guns would require many additional months. So Fisher confiscated the guns already manufactured for two other battleships under construction, setting back their completion but speeding up *Dreadnought's*. On September 1, construction was sufficiently advanced so that the ship was placed in reserve commission, and the first crew members reported aboard.

On October 2, 1906, a year and a day after its keel-laying, *Dreadnought* headed out into the English Channel on its sea trials. Its completion represented an astonishing record. Battleships customarily required three or four years to build, and this biggest battleship yet built had been completed in one-third the usual time. The ship performed beautifully in all respects. On October 17, it fired its guns for the first time. No one could be certain what would happen when a salvo from eight twelve-inch guns was fired. The broadside of any existing battleship anywhere totalled only half as many guns. The ship's designer, Sir Philip Watts, was aboard to witness the event. Another observer later described the scene. "He looked very grave and serious," he wrote, "I am quite sure he fully expected the decks to come down wholesale. Presently, there was a muffled roar and a bit of a kick on the ship. The eight guns had been fired and scores of men between the decks had no idea what happened." On December 3, *Dreadnought* was accepted into the Royal Navy.

The ship was as revolutionary in design as Fisher intended. It mounted ten twelve-inch guns in five turrets arranged so that six guns could fire dead ahead, six guns astern, and eight guns on either broadside. Surprisingly, it displaced only 17,900 tons. Its armament was not its only new feature. Fisher eliminated the forward-slanting ram bow that had continued on battleships as a relic of the battle of Lissa. *Dreadnought*'s knife-like bow was perpendicular (ironically, the only ship that *Dreadnought* ever sank in battle was a German submarine that it rammed during World War I). For the first time on a British battleship, the quarters of the captain and the other officers were moved forward from the stern to amidships, nearer the bridge. Fisher insisted the ship be made as nearly unsinkable as possible. Not only was the hull divided into compartments, as warships hulls had been divided for decades, but there were no doors connecting one compartment with another. Each compartment was totally sealed off from the others. Anyone below decks in one space who wished to move to the adjacent compartment had to ascend to the deck above and then descend.

Most revolutionary of all was *Dreadnought*'s propulsion plant. It was powered by turbine engines. Fisher took a tremendous gamble when he insisted on turbines, because no ship approaching the size of *Dreadnought* had ever been driven by them. They represented the cutting edge of marine propulsion technology. The familiar reciprocating engine that had powered ships for decades operated on the principle of steam pressure expanding to drive pistons which, in turn, transmitted power to the shaft that turned the propeller. The power generated by early steam engines was limited, because the level of steam pressure had to be kept low for safety. As engine design and material improved, higher steam pressure became possible. That permitted engine power to be increased by using the same steam again in a second set of pistons operating at a somewhat lower pressure (the double expansion engine), and even a third set at even lower pressure (the triple expansion engine). As early as the 1890s, battleships were powered by triple-expansion engines.

Among the reciprocating engine's advantages were long-life, simplicity of operation and maintenance, and dependability at normal operating speeds. Disadvantages for a warship included limits to the speed the ship could attain and susceptibility to breakdown when operated at top speed for extended periods, because of vibration that could damage both the machinery and the hull. Engine rooms were hot, noisy, and dirty. A British admiral vividly described working conditions in an engine room:

> When steaming at full speed in a man-of-war fitted with reciprocating engines, the engine room was always a glorified snipe-marsh; water lay on the floor plates and was splashed about everywhere; the officers often were clad in oilskins to avoid being wetted to the skin. The water was necessary to keep the bearings cool. Further, the noise was deafening; so much so that telephones were useless and even voice-pipes of doubtful value.

By the turn of the century, engines capable of generating twenty thousand horsepower were being built, but the power of the reciprocating engine was nearing its maximum practical potential because of the size to which it had grown. The lowest pressure third expansion cylinders of a battleship's engines had become nearly ten feet in diameter. With the bracing and foundation structure needed to control the tons of metal in such enormous pistons being reversed on every stroke, the reciprocating engines required to propel a battleship of sixteen thousand tons displacement at eighteen knots had grown to monstrous proportions.

The turbine engine operates on the principle of a current of pressurized steam, water, or gas exerting force against a series of curved blades mounted on a central spindle to keep the spindle endlessly spinning. Turbine engines had been installed in a few small craft in the 1890s, mostly as experiments to produce speed, and the results had been spectacular. A British destroyer with turbine engines reached a speed of thirty-six knots. But turbine engines of the size needed to propel a ship like *Dreadnought* had never yet been built. The tolerances for the thousands of blades turning the central spindle were minute, and doomsayers predicted that a microscopic maladjustment sooner or later would cause instant and wholesale destruction of the blades and consequent crippling of the engines.

They were wrong. Fisher's gamble paid off handsomely. The big battleship easily reached a speed of twenty-one knots during its sea trials, and there was virtually no vibration felt in the ship. The engines were designed to operate on either fuel oil or coal. Fisher preferred oil, but in 1906, few places in the world could supply it, so the ship was designed to use either fuel. The engine rooms were a wonder to behold. Engineers accustomed to the ear-splitting racket, the clouds of steam, the puddles of water on the deck plates in engine rooms of existing battleships marvelled at the new ship's clean, amazingly quiet engineering spaces.

Dreadnought did not instantly render every existing battleship useless, as a few excitable journalists claimed. But it did signal the beginning of a new battleship era. No other country possessed such a ship, and no other country even had plans to build one. But every country with any pretensions to being a naval power soon began to draw up plans. The two American battleships authorized in early 1905, *Michigan* and *South Carolina*, were designed to carry eight twelve-inch guns. All four turrets were mounted on the centerline, so the ships could fire a broadside of eight guns, the same as *Dreadnought*. Some naval historians have therefore called them the first American dreadnoughts, but they did not meet that standard in all respects. They were powered by reciprocating engines. With a designed speed of 18.5 knots, they could not approach the British ship's top speed. They displaced only sixteen thousand tons, the same as the mixed battery *Connecticut*-class. Perhaps most significantly, there was no Jacky Fisher in the American navy to push the pace of their construction to the limit. Their keels were not laid until December, 1906, two months after *Dreadnought*'s sea trials. They joined the fleet only in 1910, more than three years after *Dreadnought* was commissioned.

In the United States, debate over the wisdom of the all-big-gun ship dragged on. On August 29, 1905—more than two months after the battle of Tsushima, when preparations for construction of *Dreadnought* were moving swiftly along—Roosevelt wrote to the American minister in China: "The only point about which there seems to be any doubt in naval circles is as to whether the battleship of the future shall have nothing but twelve-inch and three-inch guns, or whether there shall be an intermediate battery of eight- or seven-inch guns." Two influential people, Senator Hale and Alfred Thayer Mahan, led the opposition. Both men worried about the explosive growth in naval expenditures during recent years and the prospect of a continuing rise in coming years. Mahan also continued his arguments, based upon tactical and strategic principles, in favor of smaller, homogeneous battleships.

In an article published in the June, 1906, issue of the Naval Institute's *Proceedings,* Mahan presented his analysis of the battle of Tsushima. The lessons he extracted from it were precisely the opposite of those derived by Captain Pakenham and others. The superior speed of the Japanese fleet, he argued, was not a decisive factor in its victory. "Togo, by good scouting and choice of position," he wrote, "secured beyond reasonable hazard his strategic object of bringing the Russian Fleet to battle. . . . What is contended here is that speed at its best is a less valuable factor in a battleship than fighting power." Japanese intermediate-caliber guns, he maintained, had been as responsible as the main batteries for damage to Russian ships. He based his reasoning on certain assumptions and probabilities. "The lighter pieces [in the Japanese squadron] were to the heavy in the proportion of $2^{1}/_{2}$ to 1, and we may be justified in assuming that calibre for calibre there were at least four discharges of the secondary to one of the heavier, with the consequent probability of a proportionate number of hits." As a clincher, the naval philosopher offered a "moral" argument against the fast, all-big-gun ship.

> The fleet which has . . . placed its dependence on long-range fire has with it assumed the moral tone and temperament associated with the indisposition to close. . . . The navy which, for any reason, habitually seeks to keep its enemy at a distance, in order to secure a preliminary advantage, usually fails to achieve more than a defensive success for the occasion, and in the long run finds itself brought to battle at an unexpected moment, under conditions unfavorable to it, both materially and morally.

A naval commander should close with his enemy and slug it out, like a man. It was an argument that harkened back to the tactics of Mahan's beloved age of Nelson and John Paul Jones.

Any piece of writing by Mahan was bound to attract attention, and this one was no different. There was favorable comment in the press, and the mixed battery advocates in the navy and Congress felt vindicated. Roosevelt read it, and it may have checked at least temporarily his inclination toward the all-big-gun ship, because he invited Mahan to Sagamore Hill, where they discussed it on July 31. On August 30, his secretary, William Loeb, wrote a note to William Sims, asking on behalf of the president for Sims's reaction to Mahan's article.

Sims must have sat down with zestful anticipation to respond to Roosevelt's request. He did not relish rebutting Mahan, because they were personal friends and allies in the fight to create a naval general staff to replace the independent bureau system. But he welcomed the opportunity to respond, especially in a letter to the president, to arguments that opposed what he considered crucial steps that the navy must take to remain an effective fighting force. On September 24, he sent a long letter to Roosevelt.

Sims summarized three lessons about battleship design that Mahan had derived from his study of the battle of Tsushima: (1) speed should not be increased at the expense of equivalent weight of gun power; (2) main battery guns should not be substituted for equivalent weight of intermediate ordnance; (3) because of budgetary limitations, ship size should not be materially increased, in order that plenty of ships could continue to be built. Politely, but with devastating logic supported by massive evidence, Sims methodically refuted each argument. He dismissed Mahan's "moral" argument as based upon a faulty understanding of modern naval gunnery. He politely and gently closed by speculating that Mahan was not in possession of all relevant information about Tsushima when he wrote, so he drew erroneous conclusions "founded largely upon mistaken facts." In a slightly different form, the letter appeared in the December issue of the Naval Institute's *Proceedings* under the imposing title, "The Inherent Tactical Qualities of All-Big-Gun, One-Caliber Battleships of High Speed, Large Displacement and Gun Power." It was also published in Brassey's *Naval Annual* in Britain.

Roosevelt sent Sims's letter to Mahan before it appeared in print and invited a response. Mahan replied with a brief, rather lamely phrased letter on September 30 in which he admitted he was "not fully equipped in tactical resource," was not conversant with modern gunnery, and was too busy with other matters "for an exhaustive study of tactics." Nevertheless, on October 22, he sent Roosevelt a second, lengthy response to Sims's arguments. He repeated the conclusions in his original article and argued that Sims, not he, based his reasoning on faulty or incomplete information about Tsushima. He included a long explanation, complete with diagrams, of a theoretical battle between two fleets, one of all-big-gun ships and one of mixed battery ships, to show that the latter would defeat the former. The outcome was based upon numerous assumptions and suppositions that worked only if a slow-thinking, lethargic commander was in charge of the fast, all-big-gun fleet. Not surprisingly, the whole war-gaming exercise recalled the tactics of a battle from the age of sail.

Mahan's letters of rebuttal were not persuasive. The naval historian had been blown out of the water by Sims, and for good reason. In analyzing an action between modern battleships, Mahan was out of his depth. Most of his naval career had been spent aboard sailing ships, and most of his attention since his retirement had focussed on historical studies of the age of sail or geopolitical analysis. He had always been bored by technology and machinery. His last naval command had been the ABCD *Chicago,* which was already a somewhat quaint relic of a past era when Mahan took command of it in the mid-1890s. Mounting a main battery of Captain Pakenham's "pea-shooter" eight-inch guns, the whole of *Chicago* could have been placed on the foredeck of *Dreadnought.* Yet Mahan had found it intimidatingly large and somewhat bewildering when he took command. Mahan had little knowledge of, and absolutely no experience with, modern warships or gunnery, as his analysis of Tsushima made painfully clear. In his debate with Sims, he had been routed, as Roosevelt recognized.

Sims had bested Mahan, but he probably would have willingly conceded that his intellect did not match the naval philosopher's. Sims was no philosopher. He readily accepted the naval milieu in which he lived and worked. The changes he advocated in ship design and departmental organization were not fundamental or philosophical. Mahan's mind ranged much further and deeper to grapple with such questions as the basic purpose and mission of the navy, how it related to the nation's foreign policy, and how it could be best employed as a policy instrument by the nation's leaders. Sims's writings were important in the context of the times when he wrote them, but today they are of interest only to the naval historian. The best of Mahan's writings have survived the contemporary context in which he wrote them to remain relevant today and probably for the foreseeable future.

The Sims-Mahan debate on paper had little effect on events, because when Mahan sent Roosevelt his weak riposte to Sims's letter, the entire issue of proper battleship armament and size had already been rendered moot by Congress. On June 29, 1906, it authorized the single annual new battleship that Roosevelt had asked for in his annual message the previous December. For the first time, Congress did not specify maximum displacement in its authorization. If there was to be only one battleship for the year, and for each succeeding year, the navy submerged its differences and decided it wanted the biggest, fastest, most heavily-gunned ship that could be built. Roosevelt, of course, agreed. The ship became *Delaware*. It was designed to displace twenty thousand tons, reach a speed of twenty-one knots, and mount ten twelve-inch guns. Sims and the other big-ship advocates had won.

9

"They Should Realize I Am Not Afraid of Them"

On February 6, 1904, two days before the outbreak of the Russo-Japanese War, Roosevelt had a conversation with the German ambassador to the United States, Speck von Sternburg, about the looming conflict. He considered von Sternburg a close personal friend, and he customarily spoke to the German diplomat with considerable openness and candor. Roosevelt often operated as his own secretary of state, as he customarily served as his own secretary of the navy. He carried on very personal diplomacy through a wide circle of friends and acquaintances, who included businessmen, journalists, intellectuals, and diplomats, both American and foreign. His own ambassadors were sometimes left in the dark about the president's actions. In particular, Roosevelt maintained close, candid contact with three senior European diplomats: Cecil Spring-Rice of Britain (who had served as best man at Roosevelt's wedding to Edith), Jules Jusserand of France, and von Sternburg. For months, the likelihood of war between Japan and Russia over Manchuria and Korea had appeared to be growing, and by early February, war appeared imminent. Roosevelt told von Sternburg, "The sympathies of the United States are entirely on Japan's side, but we will maintain the strictest neutrality."

The sympathies of the United States were with Japan in large part because Roosevelt's own sympathies lay in that direction. Roosevelt was a man of strong beliefs and prejudices, and they were reflected in the policies he adopted as president. He considered close, cordial, cooperative relations with Britain the cornerstone of American foreign policy. He admired and respected Germany's military and industrial might, but he thought that Germany would be the most likely opponent if the United States were forced to go to war in the foreseeable future. He felt contempt for China as a weak country that had allowed itself to be controlled and manipulated by stronger countries. He had admired Japan since its victory over China in 1895. Roosevelt particularly respected military prowess, and he had noted that the Japanese troops in the international Relief Force that raised the siege of the legations in Peking in 1900 during the Boxer uprising were reported to be the best disciplined and most effective of all the national contingents. He disliked Russia as a semi-barbaric country whose leaders could not be trusted. In any conflict between Japan and Russia, anyone who knew Roosevelt could easily deduce where his sympathies lay.

Throughout 1904, it was easy for Roosevelt and the United States to maintain neutrality while favoring Japan. The Japanese won victory after victory. Bob Evans, who had predicted the outbreak of war as early as the previous October, when he noticed unusual activity in the Japanese fleet during a visit to Nagasaki, commanded the Asiatic Fleet. The main elements of his command were in the Philippines, and he was ordered to keep his ships well clear of the areas of conflict.

On January 1, 1905, the long siege of Port Arthur ended in the most important Japanese victory yet to occur in the war, when the city's Russian defenders surrendered. But the Japanese paid a fearful price in their repeated frontal attacks on the stubbornly defended fortress, having suffered more than 55,000 casualties. A great battle around Mukden in March engaged the largest armies ever assembled for a single battle until that time. The Russian defenders totalled more than 280,000 men, supported by more than 1,200 pieces of artillery. The Japanese attackers were slightly less numerous, but they formed a more cohesive, better trained, and better motivated fighting force. They won, but again they suffered enormous casualties.

Just after the battle of Mukden, Japan secretly approached Roosevelt to request that he mediate an end to the conflict. Since early in the war, Roosevelt had let it be known through many diplomatic channels that he would be available to serve as a mediator in negotiations to end the war. Roosevelt's diplomatic objectives in Asia were to defend the "Open Door" in China—the great diplomatic triumph of his Secretary of State, John Hay—and preserve the balance of power, especially between Russia and Japan in northeastern Asia. After Russia completed the Trans-Siberian Railroad and gained control of the Liaotung Peninsula and the South Manchurian Railroad in Manchuria, Roosevelt saw Japan as a counterweight to the growing Russian presence which threatened the Open Door in China, as well as the balance of power in northern Asia. But the string of Japanese victories in 1904 and early 1905 threatened to tip the balance in the other direction, in Japan's favor. The United States was in no position to take military action on the Asian mainland to achieve Roosevelt's objectives, but the president could take steps to end the war before Japan's presence in Manchuria became too extensive and too well entrenched.

Neither country was eager to end the war before it achieved a conclusive victory. But Japan realized it was being bled white by the grinding struggle. Russia was less affected, but Russia's leaders had been shaken by the revolution that had broken out in January and by summer was being suppressed only with difficulty. The Russian defeat at Mukden followed by the Japanese naval victory at Tsushima convinced Russia that it could not win, while Japan decided its victories had given it the secure foothold it sought on the mainland in Manchuria and Korea. Negotiations arranged by Roosevelt took place in Portsmouth, New Hampshire, in August.

Thanks to Roosevelt's tireless behind-the-scenes diplomacy, a peace settlement was achieved in September. The negotiations threatened to break down completely over Japan's insistence on receiving an indemnity from Russia to pay its crushing war debts. Russia as insistently refused to pay anything, and only Roosevelt's persistent efforts persuaded the Japanese to forgo the indemnity in the interests of gaining an agreement. There was anger in Japan when the treaty provisions were made public. Many Japanese felt that their country had won a war but had been denied the full fruits of victory.

Japan had paid a fearful price in blood and treasure to achieve victory, and it had not gained everything it wanted in the peace settlement. But it emerged from the war with its position as the strongest country in Asia confirmed. It occupied a commanding position on the Asian mainland by virtue of its control of Korea and the southern half of Manchuria. The prowess shown by the Japanese army gained it profound respect among the world's military leaders. The Japanese navy emerged from the war the strongest naval force in Asia. It ranked only fifth among the world's navies, but the other naval powers maintained only small squadrons in Asian waters, consisting mainly of cruisers and gunboats. No other country maintained a squadron in Asia to match Japan's battleships. The clockwork precision of maneuver and pinpoint accuracy in gunnery exhibited by the Japanese navy in its crushing victories over Russia gained it respect and even admiration. The navy's impressive performance also generated supreme self-confidence, marked by more than a touch of arrogance, among senior Japanese naval officers.

Japan's strong position was further enhanced by the alliance it had signed with Britain in 1902 that the British reconfirmed and strengthened in 1905, immediately after Japan's victory over Russia. For Britain, an alliance with the strongest naval power in Asia allowed the British to pull major fleet units back home to confront the growing German naval challenge in European waters. For Japan, with powerful Britain as an ally, the alliance provided assurance that Japan was secure from attack on either the home islands or its new possessions on the mainland. No other power, or combination of powers, could challenge the combined fleets of Britain and Japan in Asian waters.

As early as 1895, in the wake of Japan's victory over China, Alfred Thayer Mahan watched Japan closely and warily, convinced that the Japanese had hopes, if not plans, for expansion in Asia and the Pacific. He had urged that the United States annex Hawaii, because he was convinced Japan had its eye on the islands as an outpost in the eastern Pacific. He persuaded Roosevelt that Hawaii should be annexed, but Roosevelt admired Japan and regarded its position as a counterweight to Russia in Asia as more important than the possible threat it might pose to American interests. The Japanese navy's spectacular victories in the war with Russia, however, prompted him to give greater heed to Mahan's warnings. If Japan had any plans to use its superb navy to expand its power into the Pacific, Roosevelt meant to make clear his determination to oppose it.

The focus of his concern was America's new colonial possessions in the Pacific. They included Samoa, Guam, and Hawaii, but the largest and most important was the Philippines. On July 4, 1902, Roosevelt proclaimed the nasty war against Filipino guerrillas that the American army had been fighting since 1898 to be won. The American government turned its attention to several problems to be resolved in its new colony: what kind of government should rule the islands; how should the United States discharge its responsibilities in such fields as education, public health, and economic development; should the islands eventually be granted independence, and if so, when?

One of the most important of the immediate problems, for which a wholly satisfactory solution was never found, was how to defend the islands from external attack. They lay far off in the western Pacific, much closer to Japan and the Asian mainland than to the United States. They were garrisoned by American troops, but defending the thousands of islands in the archipelago was really a naval responsibility. If the United States did not control the seas surrounding them, an American army in the Philippines could not hope to hold out indefinitely against an enemy army that succeeded in landing and establishing a foothold.

But there were no adequate bases in or even near the Philippines to support an American battle fleet. The old Spanish naval base at Cavite was woefully inadequate to support modern warships. In the whole of the Pacific, the American navy possessed only two bases capable of providing support to a modern battle fleet, at Mare Island, in California, and at Bremerton, Washington. Only one dry dock, at Bremerton, was capable of taking a modern battleship. The Philippines were seven thousand miles away.

Even if an adequate base or bases were built, the navy faced a dilemma if it was to defend the country's new possessions in the Pacific. Should basic Mahanian doctrine be violated, and the battle fleet be divided between the Atlantic and the Pacific? When the Russo-Japanese War broke out, Bob Evans had three battleships in his Asiatic Fleet, supported by a miscellaneous gaggle of lesser craft. It was not an integrated fleet, as Evans was quick to point out. It would be incapable of resisting a determined attack by Japan or any other major naval power on the Philippines.

The vast bulk of the American battle fleet remained in the Atlantic, and most senior officers thought it should remain there. There was growing worry that Germany, with its expanding High Seas Fleet, might be tempted to flout the Monroe Doctrine and try to establish a colony in the western hemisphere. That would pose a much greater threat to the security of the United States than any Japanese move against the Philippines. In the autumn of 1902, when Roosevelt's massive fleet maneuvers took place at Culebra in the Caribbean, a dispute with Germany over Venezuela flared and appeared to confirm worries about the Kaiser's possible designs on South America.

By 1906, the United States had followed Britain's example and pulled all its battleships out of the Pacific, back to the Atlantic Fleet.

Roosevelt aboard the presidential yacht *Mayflower* to watch maneuvers of the Atlantic Fleet in 1906. To the right of Roosevelt is the fleet's commander, Rear Admiral Robley D. "Fighting Bob" Evans; to his left is Cornelius Vanderbilt.

U.S. Naval Historical Center photograph

The biggest ships in the Asiatic Fleet were four armored cruisers, but Admiral Dewey and his board drew up a plan to send the battle fleet to the Pacific within ninety days if it was needed to defend American territory from attack. Everyone therefore agreed that the country needed a major naval base in the western Pacific. It must contain facilities to support a large battle fleet, and it must be a bastion with strong defenses to repel an attack from either land or sea. But there was disagreement about where such a base should be built.

In 1901, after suppression of the Boxer uprising in China, the navy proposed that the United States build a base on the coast of China. It selected a site on the coast of Fukien province, opposite the island of Formosa. The idea was practically stillborn. Japan had occupied Formosa after its victory over China in 1895, and it considered Fukien province within its sphere of influence in China. When the American ambassador in Tokyo broached the idea to the Japanese, they vehemently opposed it as a threat to Japanese interests in China. More importantly for the navy, the cornerstone of American policy in China was John Hay's Open Door, proclaimed in 1899. The United States stood committed to defending China's territorial integrity, and establishing a major naval base in China would violate everything the United States professed to stand for in its China policy. There would be no base in China.

The Philippines was the logical place to locate a base, but there existed sharp, persistent disagreement about precisely where in the islands it should be built. The Naval War College sent an officer to examine possible locations. He traveled all over the archipelago and selected a site near Iloilo, a city in the Visayas, the central islands of the group, about seven hundred miles south of Manila. Topographically, the choice was a good one for a naval base, but it made little sense strategically or politically, and it gained few backers in Washington.

Admiral Dewey had his own plan. He possessed significant influence as chairman of the General Board, and his personal prestige continued to be great. Dewey was regarded as an expert on the Philippines, so his ideas about the location for a base were heeded. Ever since his arrival there for the battle that made him famous, he dreamed of an American naval base at Subic Bay, the sheltered, deep-water anchorage thirty miles north of Manila. It could easily accommodate a large fleet of the largest battleships. It was well placed to guard the approaches to Manila Bay. It could easily be defended from seaborne attack. It was, in short, ideal from the navy's point of view, and it was close to Manila, the political, economic and social center of the islands. Spain had apparently come to the same conclusion. A few months before the outbreak of war with the United States, the Spanish had begun to build a base at Olongapo City, on the shore of Subic Bay. They began to move equipment from Cavite and to ship heavy coastal defense guns to be installed in permanent fortifications. But the war prevented completion of the Spanish plans.

Dewey's dream was opposed by Leonard Wood, Roosevelt's old comrade in arms in the Rough Riders. By 1905, he was a major-general in command of American army troops in the Philippines. He, too, possessed great personal prestige and influence, and he was exchanging regular correspondence with his friend and admirer, the president. Wood argued that a naval base at Subic Bay could be defended against a land attack only by an army of 100,000 men, and the United States had no intention of placing an army of that size in the islands. Perhaps it was an ideal location for a base from the navy's point of view, but the army was responsible for defending it from a landward attack. The army saw a definite resemblance of the navy's proposed base site to Port Arthur, the doomed Russian naval base and fortress in Manchuria that had fallen to the Japanese. Defending it, Leonard Wood declared, would require all American troops in the islands and leave defenseless the country's vital center, Manila. Wood urged that the base be located at Manila Bay under the protection of the coastal defenses planned for Corregidor and Cavite to defend Manila. Cavite, he told Roosevelt, was the best location for the naval base.

The debate dragged on for years. Funds were appropriated to improve the old Spanish base at Cavite, and Roosevelt approved funds to build limited facilities at Subic Bay. But a decision on building the major naval bastion was postponed. It could be put off, because no one expected an attack on the islands from any quarter in the foreseeable future. Japan was the only likely aggressor, but the Japanese were still recovering from their war with Russia. Moreover, their alliance with Britain made them an unlikely enemy of the United States, and Japanese-American relations were cordial.

In the summer of 1905, as Roosevelt was arranging the peace negotiations between Japan and Russia, the secretary of war, William Howard Taft, visited Japan and held talks with the prime minister, Count Katsura. The two men reached an agreement: Japan would make no threatening moves against the Philippines, while the United States would acknowledge Japan's control of Korea. Since Japan had no plans or even desire to attack the Philippines, and the United States was in no position to contest Japanese control of Korea, the agreement was easily reached. Taft had no authority to make such a deal, and when he cabled a report to the president, he added, "If I have spoken too freely or inaccurately or unwisely, I know you can and will correct it." Roosevelt immediately cabled a reply which said, "Your conversation with Count Katsura absolutely correct in every respect. . . . I confirm every word you have said." The unplanned exchange became enshrined in diplomatic history as the Taft-Katsura Agreement. The Philippines might be defenseless, but the international politics of Asia in early 1906 made the likelihood of an attack on them very remote.

On July 19, 1905, a squadron of four American cruisers arrived off Nantucket Shoals after a thirteen-day trans-Atlantic voyage from Cherbourg. In command was Rear-Admiral Charles D. Sigsbee who had commanded *Maine* at Havana in 1898. His flagship was *Brooklyn*, veteran of the Spanish war and the Asiatic Fleet. In a place of honor aboard the cruiser lay the reason for the squadron's voyage. In an eighteenth century lead coffin, encased in polished mahogany, the body of John Paul Jones, the father of the United States Navy, reposed.

Jones died in Paris in 1792 during the aftermath of the French Revolution and was buried in the city's Protestant Cemetery. In the course of succeeding decades, the precise location of his grave was forgotten as the city swallowed up the cemetery, which was built over with houses. In 1899, the American Ambassador to France began a search to locate the grave. Only in April, 1905, was a lead coffin exhumed which contained a remarkably well-preserved body that was recognizable as resembling a marble bust of Jones. Two medical experts within a few hours were able to establish with certainty that it was the remains of John Paul Jones. They were even able to perform an autopsy to determine that he had died from multiple natural causes, including pneumonia.

Roosevelt ordered the cruiser squadron led by *Brooklyn* to return the body to the United States for burial at Annapolis. Several cities, including Washington, D.C., sought the honor of being the location of the famous patriot's tomb, but Roosevelt insisted that the most appropriate site was the chapel of the Naval Academy.

At Nantucket Shoals the cruisers were met by seven battleships under the command of the admiral in charge of the North American Squadron, Bob Evans, for the voyage south to Chesapeake Bay and the Naval Academy, where the coffin was transferred ashore to await its permanent interment in the chapel. On April 24, 1906, commemorative services were held, with Roosevelt as the principal speaker, as the body was placed in a temporary vault under the main staircase of Bancroft Hall on the grounds of the Academy.

Congress was slow to appropriate funds for a permanent vault, and a marble sarcophagus and tomb, modeled on the tomb of Napoleon in the Invalides, was not constructed in the crypt of the Academy chapel until several years later. On January 26, 1913, with suitably solemn ceremony, the father of the American navy was finally laid to permanent rest.

At 3:30 P.M. on November 8, 1906, President and Mrs. Roosevelt stood on the after starboard deck of *Mayflower* as it pulled away from the dock at the Washington Navy Yard for an overnight voyage to Hampton Roads. "Goodbye," shouted the president as he waved to a crowd of reporters and well-wishers on the dock. "I'm going down to see how the ditch is getting along." The "ditch" was the Panama Canal. Like expansion of the navy, inaugurating construction of the canal was an accomplishment in which Roosevelt took particular pride.

Building a canal had been envisioned for decades, and to judge from looking at the narrow neck of Central America on a map, it did not appear especially difficult. In 1879, a French company was created by Ferdinand de Lesseps, the builder of the Suez Canal, to dig a canal across the isthmus of Panama. But de Lesseps found that the difficulties of cutting through the jungles, swamps, and mountainous spine of Panama were much more formidable than digging a canal across the flat desert isthmus of Suez. With his work force decimated by tropical disease, progress was agonizingly slow, and his company was liquidated in 1889.

De Lesseps's failure did not dampen American enthusiasm for building a canal, because it would confer obvious benefits upon the United States, both economic and strategic. The incredible voyage of *Oregon* in 1898 dramatically highlighted the importance of a canal for national defense, and after the United States acquired its possessions in the Pacific, the strategic importance of a canal increased.

Many obstacles—diplomatic, political, technical, even medical— had to be overcome before construction of an American canal could begin. The second Hay-Pauncefote Treaty signed with Britain in 1901 cleared away one diplomatic problem. Should the canal be built across Panama, as the French had tried and failed to do, or by the longer but easier route through Nicaragua, as many engineering experts urged? Should it be a canal with locks or a sea-level canal? A lock canal across Panama was decided upon only after much investigation and debate. A French company that had succeeded de Lesseps's had been digging sporadically since 1895, and its equipment, legal rights, and concessions had to be acquired. The deadly tropical diseases—malaria, cholera, plague, and especially yellow fever—that had decimated the American army in Cuba in 1898 had to be combatted. Panama was the northern province of Colombia, and a long diplomatic imbroglio with Colombia over gaining rights to build a canal ended only in late 1903, when Panama, with American support, successfully revolted and gained its independence. In late 1904, an American work force took over from the French company, and construction began in earnest. Thus, the Americans had been at work for two years when Roosevelt made his visit.

In Hampton Roads, the president and his party transferred from *Mayflower* to the battleship *Louisiana,* escorted by two cruisers, for the voyage south. It would be the first time a president left the jurisdiction of the United States while in office, and there was much doubt about the wisdom of his doing so. The White House took pains to assure the country that the office travelled with the president, who would be kept in touch with Washington by wireless. The idea of Roosevelt going personally to inspect his "ditch," like a general visiting the front lines, caught the country's imagination, and the trip was given extensive, positive coverage in the press.

The flag quarters of *Louisiana,* the country's newest battleship, had been enlarged for the president and his wife by knocking down several bulkheads, and they were made comfortable with special furnishings. The big, new *Connecticut*-class battleship awakened Roosevelt's pride in the navy. He wrote to his seventeen-year-old son, Kermit, "it is a beautiful sight, these three great warships standing southward in close column, and almost as beautiful at night when we see not only the lights but the loom through the darkness of the ships astern." To his oldest son, Ted, he wrote, "it gives me great pride in America to be aboard this great battleship and to see not only the material perfection of the ship herself in engines, guns, and all arrangements, but the fine quality of the officers and crew."

But after only a few days at sea, this most naval-minded of presidents wrote to Kermit, "I, of course, feel bored, as I always do on shipboard." He did his best to fight the boredom by reading the prose works of John Milton and a German novel, by inspecting the ship with the captain, by eating meals with the crew, and by "walking briskly up and down the deck" with Edith. In one of the firerooms, in front of an audience of stokers and ship's officers, he tried his hand at shoveling coal into a firebox. As he heaved a shovelful toward the furnace door, the ship rolled slightly. The coal missed the opening and spattered over the white uniform of an officer standing nearby. "Not a man cracked a smile," one witness reported. A second shovelful found its mark, to everyone's relief, no doubt, and the shovel was sent to the White House as a souvenir.

The president spent three days in Panama. Roosevelt had deliberately chosen the month of November for his visit, because it is the rainy season and he wanted to see conditions for construction at their worst. He was not disappointed. It rained incessantly for the entire visit. He slogged through downpour and mud, looking into everything, grinning and waving at sodden, bedraggled crowds of Panamanians and American workers brought out to witness the historic event. The high point of the visit occurred when Roosevelt climbed aboard a monstrous steam shovel and had the operator show him how to move the levers to operate the huge machine.

On the return voyage, he wrote to Kermit:

Now we have taken hold of the job. . . . [T]here the huge steam shovels are hard at it, scooping huge masses of rock and gravel and dirt previously loosened by drillers and dynamite blasters, loading it on trains which take it away to some dump, either in the jungle or where the dams are to be built. They are eating steadily into the mountain, cutting it down and down. . . . It is an epic feat, and one of immense significance.

On December 17, he sent to Congress a "Special Message Concerning the Panama Canal" to report on his visit. He dwelled especially on the astonishing progress made in health and sanitation to combat yellow fever, cholera, and plague. He was full of praise for everyone involved in the epic project. "It is a stupendous work upon which our fellow countrymen are engaged in down there on the Isthmus," he wrote. "No man can see these young, vigorous men energetically doing their duty without a thrill of pride."

When the canal was finished, it would alleviate a major strategic headache for the navy in discharging its responsibilities to defend American territory in both the Atlantic and the Pacific. But a completed canal obviously lay years in the future.

On October 11, less than a month before Roosevelt departed for Panama, relations with Japan took a sudden and dramatic turn for the worse. The cause was not a new international crisis, but rather an action taken by the school board of the city of San Francisco. The board decreed that children of oriental heritage—Chinese, Japanese and Korean—henceforth must attend a special school set aside for them. On October 25, the Japanese government submitted a formal protest against the "stigma and odium" which such a segregation order visited upon Japanese immigrants in the United States.

Immigration from eastern Asia had been a political and social problem in California for decades. The early immigrants were Chinese driven from China during the middle decades of the nineteenth century by the devastation of the Tai-ping rebellion and attracted to California by the gold rush. As early as the 1850s, grumblings on the west coast about Chinese immigrants became protests, and the California state legislature took steps to curb immigration from China. Growing numbers of Californians considered the Chinese dirty, clannish, untrustworthy, and totally incapable of being assimilated into American life. In 1894, a treaty was signed with China to exclude laborers entirely and severely restrict immigration by other classes. Chinese were denied citizenship.

American public opinion was not unanimous in opposing Asian immigration. The extensive construction of railroads after the Civil War, especially in the west, depended heavily on Chinese laborers. Many American businessmen not only welcomed Chinese immigrants but actively advertised in China to attract them. The pragmatic businessmen knew that Asians worked hard, could be easily trained, and were willing to work for what native-born Americans considered starvation wages.

Until the Russo-Japanese War, Japanese immigrants were few. After the war, their numbers dramatically increased. They began to arouse the same resentment that the Chinese had long attracted. The whole issue of oriental immigration became increasingly nasty and contentious, both in American domestic politics and the country's foreign relations in Asia. The Chinese government for years had lodged repeated protests in Washington about treatment of its nationals, especially in California. But China under the dying Manchu dynasty was a weak, moribund country that could do little but protest. Roosevelt had always evinced contempt for China, and while he took vigorous steps to see that Chinese visitors to the United States were treated courteously, he did not worry about China taking drastic action against the United States in retaliation. Japan was a different proposition.

The segregation order in San Francisco was prominently reported in Japan, and it offended Japanese pride, not least because Japanese were being lumped together with Chinese and other Asians for whom the Japanese themselves felt a considerable measure of contempt. There was a sensationalist press in Japan, like the newspapers of Hearst and Pulitzer that had agitated for war with Spain. It seized upon the issue and published inflammatory articles. Even reputable newspapers took up the cause. On October 22, the *Mainichi Shimbun* wrote: "Stand up, Japanese nation! Our countrymen have been HUMILIATED on the other side of the Pacific. Our poor boys and girls have been expelled from the public schools by the rascals of the United States, cruel and merciless like demons. . . . Why do we not insist on sending ships?" The crisis quickly escalated, and on October 27, Roosevelt wrote to his son Kermit: "I am being horribly bothered about the Japanese business. The infernal fools in California . . . insult the Japanese recklessly and in the event of war it will be the nation as a whole which will pay the consequences." Roosevelt did not really think war with Japan was threatening, but he wanted to put an end to an unnecessary irritant in relations with the most powerful country in Asia. Just before departing for Panama, he gave the secretary of state a formal order directing him to use the armed forces if necessary to protect Japanese in the United States, "if they are menaced by mobs or jeopardized in the rights guaranteed them under our solemn treaty obligations." In his annual message to Congress in early December, he called the school board's order a "wicked absurdity," hinted that he would take strong measures if it were not rescinded, and urged Congress to pass a law allowing Japanese immigrants to become citizens. The Californians were not cowed. The *San Francisco Chronicle* retorted, "Our feeling is not against Japan but against an unpatriotic President who unites with aliens to break down the civilization of his own countrymen." Elsewhere in the country, popular sentiment generally supported Roosevelt, and by early in the new year, he decided to take action.

He invited the members of the San Francisco school board to Washington to work out a solution. A party of eight men came in February to meet with the president. The character of their leader may be an indication of the quality of men with whom Roosevelt had to deal. The group was led by San Francisco's mayor, a politician and former bassoon player named Schmitz who was under indictment for graft. Roosevelt used a combination of persuasion and coercion to gain an agreement. The mayor and the school board members agreed to allow

Asian children to enroll in public schools with other children, and Roosevelt pledged to curtail the influx of Japanese immigrants. He was able to arrange a "Gentlemen's Agreement" with Japan through a series of diplomatic notes in which the Japanese government promised to restrict issuance of passports for travel to the United States by laborers in exchange for the school board's rescinding the objectionable school order.

By spring, the Gentlemen's Agreement was in place, the segregation order was repealed, and the crisis with Japan appeared to have been defused. But resentment in California against orientals still ran high, and in May, riots in San Francisco directed against Japanese prompted Japanese newspapers to resume their attacks. Leaders of the political opposition in Japan called openly for war. This was generally recognized in both countries as a domestic political ploy directed against the party in power, rather than a serious call for action, but it contributed to the tension. In June, more gasoline was poured on the flames when six Japanese employment bureaus were denied licenses to operate in San Francisco. Roosevelt wrote to the secretary of state, Elihu Root, "I see that a new San Francisco fool has cropped up to add to our difficulties with the Japanese." In mid-July he wrote to Root, "I am more concerned over this Japanese situation than almost any other. Thank heaven we have the navy in good shape."

Roosevelt and Root continued to believe that there was no real possibility of war with Japan over what was happening in California, but relations between the two countries were obviously strained. On June 7, after the cabinet held a long meeting to discuss the Japanese situation, the secretary of the interior wrote in his diary, "The general feeling is that war with Japan is inevitable before the Panama Canal is finished—not immediately, for the Japanese are not ready."

On June 15, the Second Hague Peace Conference convened in the capital of the Netherlands. Like the first conference, it was called by Tsar Nicholas II, but Roosevelt was its real initiator. As early as 1904, he had proposed convening a second peace conference, but with the Russo-Japanese War in progress, the time was inappropriate, and the idea was put aside. After the war, he revived the proposal, but the Russians informed him that the Tsar wished to be the sponsor as he had been in 1898. Roosevelt readily agreed to step aside, and he quipped to a friend that American politicans' eagerness to receive credit for certain presidential appointments "is not a bit more amusing than the attitude of the Czar about the Hague Conference."

Roosevelt did not advocate disarmament or even a reduction in armaments. His objective was to freeze the status quo, to seek an international agreement to limit armaments by which he meant stop the growth in expenditures for arms. As he had explained to Leonard Wood in March, 1905, the navy had grown to the size he believed was needed by the United States. He advocated only replacing worn-out or obsolete ships, not further expanding the size of the battle fleet. Hale, Chandler, and their supporters in the Senate had complained for years about the steady increase in naval appropriations. An international arms limitation agreement would gain their support and would not pose danger to the security of the country, so long as the navy could be maintained at its current strength relative to the other naval powers, and kept up to date. In the summer of 1905, Roosevelt wrote to a friend, "I think without exposing ourselves to even the appearance of inconsistency we shall now be in shape to ask for the stoppage of the increase of armament."

He was not the sponsor of the conference, but he took the lead in preparing the ground for discussion. He seized upon Alfred Mahan's idea of limiting the size of battleships as one possible, practical step that might prove acceptable to other countries. In December, 1904, Mahan had written to him, "It has occurred to me, as an agreement tending to lessen the expense of armaments, that nations might agree on a limitation of the tonnage of single ships." In September, 1906, when agreement had been reached to hold a second peace conference at The Hague, Roosevelt wrote to a friend in Britain, "I recognize the great difficulty of coming to an agreement as to [arms] limitations; but it does seem to me that it would be possible to come to some agreement as to the size of ships."

He faced an uphill fight. France and Russia made clear at the outset their opposition to arms limitations of any kind, despite the Tsar's sponsorship of the peace conference, and Britain was equivocal at best. Calling for restrictions in the size of battleships in the autumn of 1906 flew in the face of current realities. In October, *Dreadnought* steamed out on its sea trials, and Jacky Fisher was busy drawing up plans for more "monster" battleships and cruisers. In the same month, in a letter to the British foreign secretary, Sir Edward Grey, Roosevelt shifted his ground from limitation of size to numbers.

I have hoped that we could limit the size of ships and am not yet convinced that this is impossible; but the big new ships are unquestionably so much more efficient than the comparatively small ships even of the most recent date as to make it evident that your own people, as well as some others, will be extremely reluctant to go into any such movement unless they are sure that it will not result to their own disadvantage; and the practical difficulties in the way may be enormous. If we can get an agreement by the various nations that no more than a certain number of ships, agreed upon among them, will be built by any one, that might accomplish something.

He sent special envoys to the European capitals to plead his cause, and he continued his correspondence with Grey in London. In February, he wrote, "The chief thing would be the relief of the strain upon the budgets of the different nations; and this is a very desirable end, for which I shall do whatever is in my power." But no one was persuaded. Germany was adamantly opposed, and the German chancellor, von Bulow, delivered a speech in the Reichstag in May putting on the public record Germany's opposition to even discussing arms limitations in The Hague. The British and the Germans got into a spat, each accusing the other of preventing consideration of such a boon to humanity. In the face of so much opposition, Roosevelt instructed the chief American delegate to the conference: "If any European power proposes consideration of the subject, you will vote in favor of consideration and do everything you properly can to promote it." But if no one else proposed it, the diplomat was told, the Americans were not to raise it. No one else did, so the subject was not even mentioned.

Roosevelt made a valiant effort to get arms limitation on the conference agenda, but it is hard to avoid the conclusion that his heart was not in it. His communications with Grey and others lack the usual Rooseveltian force and directness. Roosevelt no doubt wanted to see an agreement reached, in part to avoid the need to press Congress for continuing increases in naval appropriations, and in part because his views about war had mellowed. In 1907, he was not the fire-eater he had been a decade earlier when he delivered his call to arms at the Naval War College. He still believed in "just" wars, but he also believed that everything possible should be done to avoid wars among the "civilized" nations of the West. Even so, he apparently could generate little enthusiasm for his own proposal to build small battleships when larger ones were not only possible but already being built.

The Second Hague Peace Conference sat until October, 1907, longer than the first peace conference, but its accomplishments were even fewer than the earlier conference's. Disappointment was widespread. A British historian later wrote, "the second Peace Conference at the Hague . . . was a waste of time, energy, and money, for the limitation of armaments was ruled out." The delegates did agree that another conference should be convened at some appropriate time in the future.

On June 14, Roosevelt asked the War Department what plans had been made by the Joint Board in case of conflict with Japan. The Joint Board was a defense planning body created to coordinate activities of the army and navy. It was chaired, like the navy's General Board, by Admiral Dewey. Tension ran high in the relationship with Japan, with the likelihood of further provocations occurring in California. In such circumstances Roosevelt's request was not unusual, even though he did not expect war with Japan. Dewey replied on June 18 to recommend, among other steps, that "the battle fleet should be assembled and dispatched for the Orient as soon as practicable."

The navy had been considering sending the battle fleet on a "practice cruise" to the Pacific for two years or more, but there were differences of opinion among senior officers about taking such a major action, and nothing was done. The absence of adequate bases, for example, even on the west coast, was noted. In fact, during that period, the few battleships in the Asiatic Fleet had been withdrawn to the Atlantic.

In January, when the school crisis with Japan was rapidly heating up, Alfred Mahan wrote to Roosevelt that he had read a newspaper item speculating that four battleships were to be shifted from the main battle fleet in the Atlantic to the Pacific. Mahan wrote to express his opposition to dividing the battle fleet. Roosevelt immediately replied that he was surprised that Mahan should think he would be guilty of such "utter folly" as dividing the fleet. He had no more intention of sending four battleships to the Pacific, he wrote, than he had of "going thither in a rowboat myself." However, he mentioned nothing about the possibility of sending the entire fleet.

Roosevelt convened a meeting on June 27 at Sagamore Hill to discuss Dewey's recommendations. It included the secretary of the navy and, surprisingly, the postmaster-general, as well as a senior officer from the army and the navy. In the course of a discussion that lasted about 90 minutes, Roosevelt ordered several actions, including moving defense guns from Cavite to Subic Bay, stockpiling coal at Subic Bay, and immediately withdrawing the Asiatic Fleet's four armored cruisers back to the west coast. He also approved Dewey's recommendation to shift the battle fleet from the Atlantic to the Pacific, but only as far as the west coast. It should go in October as a training exercise. When he was asked how many battleships should make the voyage, the minutes of the meeting recorded that Roosevelt replied, "If the Navy has fourteen ready, he wanted fourteen to go; if sixteen, eighteen, or twenty, he wanted them all to go."

Precisely when he decided the fleet should move to the Pacific is uncertain. It may have been before the June meeting or even before Dewey's Joint Board formulated its recommendations, because the idea had been discussed for years. Nor does anyone know the precise time—probably, though not certainly, later—when he decided to send the fleet clear around the world. By July 10, he was referring in private correspondence to a "world cruise." Exactly how much effect the tension with Japan had on his decision is also uncertain.

His recollections in later years were varied and somewhat contradictory. Near the end of his presidency, when relations with Japan had returned to mutual cordiality, he wrote, "My policy of constant friendliness and courtesy toward Japan, coupled with sending the fleet around the world, has borne good results!" In October, 1911, when he had been out of office more than two years, he wrote:

> I had been doing my best to be polite to the Japanese and had finally become uncomfortably conscious of a very, very slight undertone of veiled truculence in their communications in connection with things that happened on the Pacific Slope; and I finally made up my mind that they thought I was afraid of them. . . . [I]t was time for a show down. . . . I had great confidence in the fleet.

In his *Autobiography*, published in 1913, he wrote, "My prime purpose was to impress the American people," and he quoted with apparent approval a report published in Britain at the time of the cruise that he was seeking to mobilize public support for a program to build more battleships.

He probably had several purposes in mind simultaneously when he made the decision. The Hague Peace Conference had refused to discuss arms limitations, and he may have already decided to ask Congress for money to build battleships. He probably had the Panama Canal in mind. A long voyage around South America to the west coast by the whole battle fleet would focus attention on the strategic importance of the canal and perhaps speed up its completion.

Impressing the Japanese was definitely among his motives. In late July, when plans were well underway for the cruise, he wrote to an American diplomat, "I am exceedingly anxious to impress upon the Japanese that I have nothing but the friendliest possible intentions toward them, but I am none the less anxious that they should realize that I am not afraid of them and that the United States will no more submit to bullying than it will bully." In other private correspondence, he referred to the "practice cruise" as a training exercise to test in peacetime whether the fleet could move quickly to the Pacific in time of war. He told the acting secretary of the navy, "The fleet is not now going to the Pacific as a war measure."

No public announcement of the decision was made after the June 27 meeting. A report in the New York *Herald* on July 1 broke the story, apparently based on a leak. The president had "determined upon an important change of naval policy," it said. Sixteen battleships and two armored cruisers under the command of Rear-Admiral Robley Evans would sail via the Straits of Magellan to the west coast. Evans commanded the North Atlantic Squadron, but he had been told nothing. When he read the news stories, he was convinced they were in error.

The news reports sparked cries of alarm from several quarters, notably in Europe. The invasion of the Pacific by a massive fleet of battleships was certain to disturb and perhaps anger the Japanese, the alarmists predicted. The bellicose Roosevelt was deliberately provoking a war with Japan. However, the Japanese ambassador in Washington issued a statement promptly on July 3 saying that the movement of American warships from one American port to another was not considered by Japan to be an unfriendly act, even if they went as far as the Philippines. The reaction of the Japanese press was muted when it did not express approval. The *Japan Weekly Mail* on July 13 expressed the hope that the fleet would continue on to the Orient so that the Japanese could show the sincerity of their friendship and hospitality.

For several weeks after the news stories appeared, the White House for some reason officially denied that such a decision had been made, although the secretary of the navy had been granted permission at the June 27 meeting to make a public announcement. On July 3, the White House issued a denial that was obviously very carefully phrased. "There is no intention of sending the fleet at once to the Pacific," it said. "For the last two years, the Administration has been perfecting its plans to arrange for a long ocean cruise of the battleship fleet." It might go to the Mediterranean or to South America, the statement claimed, and the timing was still undecided. Only hours after this statement was issued, the secretary of the navy announced from his home in Oakland, California, that "eighteen or twenty of the largest battleships would come around Cape Horn on a practice cruise, and would be seen in San Francisco harbor."

Not until August 1 did a statement issued by Roosevelt's personal secretary, William Loeb, confirm the navy secretary's announcement. Evans and other senior naval officers were summoned to a conference at Sagamore Hill in mid-August to formulate plans, and on August 23, a statement issued by the White House finally announced officially that sixteen battleships would make a voyage via the Straits of Magellan to San Francisco. They would return by a route not yet decided, it said.

East coast newspapers protested. The populous eastern seaboard would be stripped of its defenses and left open to attack, they argued. The ruinous potential cost of the voyage was invoked. There were frantic appeals to Congress to stop the fleet from going. That arch-critic of naval appropriations, Senator Hale of Maine, issued a statement as Chairman of the Senate Naval Affairs Committee. The fleet would not make the voyage, he said, because Congress would not appropriate the money. Roosevelt retorted that he had enough money to send the battleships to the Pacific. If Congress wanted to refuse to vote the money to bring them back, they could stay there, he said. In September, he wrote to a member of Congress, "I am Commander-in-Chief, and my decision is absolute in the matter." The opposition and cries of alarm did not worry him. On September 2, he wrote to Henry Cabot Lodge, "the people as a whole have been extremely well pleased at my sending the fleet to the Pacific."

10

"The Most Important Service That
I Rendered to Peace"

On January 12, 1908, the American battle fleet made landfall outside
Rio de Janeiro. The Americans were met by a Brazilian warship that
escorted them into the harbor where they anchored off the city by mid-
afternoon. Along the city waterfront milled a huge crowd of hundreds of
thousands of people who had gathered in the early morning and waited
patiently for hours to extend a tumultuous welcome.

Rio was the fleet's second port of call. After its departure from
Hampton Roads on December 17, it made its first stop to take on coal
at the British-ruled island of Trinidad. The welcome extended there had
been cordial but muted. Vendors were eager to sell the thousands of
sailors souvenirs and knicknacks, but the British colonial government
offered only a polite greeting, and the general population appeared only
mildly interested in an unprecedented visit by sixteen battleships. The
fleet spent Christmas at the island and took on coal from chartered colliers before departing on December 29.

The enthusiastic hospitality at Rio contrasted sharply with the cool
politeness at Trinidad. It was the first of a long string of warm welcomes
that the fleet encountered all over the world, as cities vied with each
other to turn out the biggest, friendliest crowds and to host the most
lavish social events.

Upon arrival, Bob Evans was handed a telegram from Washington
warning him that an attempt might be made by terrorists to damage
one or more of his ships. Even before the fleet departed Hampton
Roads, Washington received reports from embassies in Europe about
unsubstantiated rumors that anarchists might attempt to damage the
ships, in order to take advantage of the intense publicity surrounding
the cruise to call attention to their cause. Vague reports from Canada
warned against Japanese sabotage. At Trinidad, half of a stick of dyna-

mite was found in the coal transferred to one of the battleships from a chartered Norwegian collier. It was obviously an unexploded remnant of explosives used to mine the coal, but coupled with the warnings about terrorists, the discovery was given a sinister interpretation. The secretary of the navy, Victor Metcalfe, tended to lend exaggerated importance to every rumor about terrorists and insisted on passing the reports to Evans. He and the American ambassador to Brazil quickly decided to ignore the vague rumors, especially when the "terrorists" in Rio named in some of the reports turned out to be respectable businessmen.

Evans had been in poor health for several years as his war wounds caused him increasing pain and restricted his mobility. Probably he was given command of the fleet for the cruise to the west coast only because of Roosevelt's insistence. During the festivities on the occasion of crossing the equator before the arrival at Trinidad, he suffered an attack of rheumatism that grew worse as time went on. By the time he arrived in Rio, he was bedridden and under a doctor's care. He had to be assisted by two officers when he went ashore to return calls on local officials, and at subsequent stops, he did not even attempt to go ashore.

Aboard *Mayflower* at Hampton Roads, Roosevelt had confided to Evans that the fleet would indeed proceed around the world as so many people had speculated, but there had been no official announcement. On the voyage south through the Caribbean, Evans used the new shipboard innovation, the wireless, to inform the squadron and ship commanders about the world cruise. A shore station picked up the message, and there was a minor public flap when the news was published in the United States. Evans had to employ ingenuity with newsmen in Trinidad to say that he was expressing only his personal belief that a world cruise was intended, not an official decision. An official announcement was not made until the fleet arrived in California.

A flotilla of six destroyers had departed the United States on December 2 to meet the battleships at Rio and escort them onward to the west coast. The smaller ships had to make several stops to take on coal, so they did not arrive in Rio until January 17. The combined fleet departed on January 21. By the time the battleships weighed anchor and bid farewell to Rio, many of the senior officers were happy to leave behind the tiring round of official social events they were required to attend. The receptions and dinners hosted by the Brazilians were but a taste of things to come during the next fourteen months.

Robley D. "Fighting Bob" Evans with Roosevelt aboard the presidential yacht *Mayflower.*
Library of Congress photograph

The fleet was scheduled to bypass Buenos Aires and go directly to Punta Arenas in the Strait of Magellan for its next coaling stop. The publicity about the Brazilian welcome prompted the Argentine government to request a stop. It could not be made, in part because the approaches to the city were too shallow for battleships, and in part because of the arrangements already made to have colliers waiting at Punta Arenas. The Argentinians' disappointment was compounded by a minor diplomatic imbroglio that occurred when a message of congratulations from the Argentine president to Washington prompted only a response from the American secretary of state, delivered by the American chargé d'affaires in Buenos Aires. In Brazil, the Argentinians knew, a similar message from the Brazilian president had prompted a reply from Roosevelt, together with a message from the secretary of state to the Brazilian foreign minister. To placate the ruffled Argentinians, Evans sent the destroyer flotilla to pay a call at the Argentine capital, to everyone's satisfaction. A squadron of Argentine warships steamed out to rendezvous with the battle fleet and fire salutes.

Punta Arenas, Chile, at the Atlantic entrance to the Straits of Magellan, was the next coaling stop. The southernmost city in the western hemisphere, it had the raw, bleak look of a western frontier settlement in the United States, and for good reason. Gold had recently been discovered along the Straits, and the settlement had become a boom town. Bob Evans wrote of it, "one can find here deserters from every naval service in the world and, in addition, men of every nationality who, for one reason or another, prefer to keep out of range of the Pinkertons and police generally." To everyone's surprise, this uninviting town of small, one-story wooden buildings with corrugated iron roofs became the scene of another round of social events, notably an elaborate dinner hosted by the governor. Liberty parties going ashore were greeted by a large sign erected by the Chamber of Commerce that read, "Special Prices for the Fleet." After visits to a few shops, they decided it meant especially high prices.

The Chilean government had sent a cruiser, *Chacabuco*, to welcome the Americans and escort them through the Strait. Aboard were the American minister to Chile and the admiral in command of the Chilean navy, who hosted a dinner aboard the ship. The admiral brought a request from the president of Chile that the fleet stop in Valparaiso. The next scheduled stop, where chartered colliers were waiting, was Callao, Peru. The fleet could not therefore make a stop, but Evans readily agreed to swing through the harbor at Valparaiso and give the Chileans an opportunity to see the fleet.

On February 7, led by *Chacabuco* the fleet departed Punta Arenas to pass through the Strait. Steaming at four-hundred-yard intervals through patches of fog and mist, they completed the passage without incident, to emerge again twenty-two hours later into the long swell of the open sea. It was the largest fleet of battleships ever to enter the Pacific.

On February 14, with *Chacabuco* still in the van and escorted by a flotilla of Chilean torpedo boats, *Connecticut* led the fleet into the harbor at Valparaiso. Evans had last visited Valparaiso in 1891, when he faced down nine Chilean warships in the midst of an international crisis. The atmosphere this time was totally different. The waterfront and the hills surrounding the city were covered by throngs of people, estimated to total more than a half-million. The president of Chile stood on the deck of a Chilean warship to review the passing battleships as salutes were exchanged, bands played, and onlookers cheered. "The whole scene," Evans decided, "was most beautiful and impressive."

In Callao, the crews again faced the irksome task of coaling, and in Lima, nine miles away, another round of social events awaited. For ten days, the officers and men were "simply swamped with kindness and hospitality," according to Bob Evans. He was unable to leave his flagship to attend any of the functions, but he hosted a formal dinner aboard *Connecticut* for their Peruvian hosts.

One notable event during the festivities in Lima was a bullfight especially arranged for the visitors. More than three thousand men and six hundred officers attended. Few of the Americans knew anything about bullfighting, and most of the sailors expected to see an evenly matched contest between the man and the animal. Some thirty years before Ernest Hemingway's *Death in the Afternoon* enlightened the American public on the subject, they quickly corrected their misconception. The bullfight is not a sport, but rather a ritual with an outcome as foreordained as the end of a Shakespearean tragedy: the death of the bull. The Americans quickly began cheering for the bulls, probably to the distress of their Peruvian hosts, since two toreadors were badly gored and had to be carried from the bull ring. Before the afternoon was half over, most of the Americans had departed with feelings of revulsion and disgust.

At 8:30 A.M. on March 12, the fleet anchored in Magdalena Bay in Baja California, two days ahead of schedule. Evans reported to Washington that the ships actually were in better condition and more battle-ready than when they departed Hampton Roads, because the crews had constantly been kept at various drills during the days of steaming between port calls. The fleet would remain in Magdalena Bay for an extended stay, to take target practice before completing the last leg of the voyage to the American west coast. American ships often repaired to the spacious and isolated Mexican bay for target practice, and the navy had even seriously considered acquiring permission from the Mexican government to build a major American naval base on its shores.

Immediately after the anchors were loosed, the ships' wireless facilities were taxed to the limit. The newspaper reporters aboard all clamored to file stories about the arrival, and there was a glut of official messages to be sent as well. Only one naval radio shore station, at Point Loma in San Diego, was in range, so the ships had to take turns sending their messages. The stamina of the operators at both ends of the circuit was taxed to the limit, clearing all the official messages and news reports.

When target practice ended, Bob Evans transferred to a small auxiliary vessel and was taken north for medical attention at Paso Robles Hot Springs in California near Santa Barbara. For weeks, he had realized that his health would not permit him to remain with the fleet when it departed San Francisco to continue its world cruise. On March 18, he announced his forthcoming retirement from the navy. He was the last naval officer on active duty who had served in the Civil War. But he remained in command of the fleet. He planned to take advantage of rest and treatment ashore in order to be on hand for the arrival in San Francisco, where he would formally relinquish his command.

The fleet departed Magdalena Bay on April 10 to steam north to San Diego, its first port of call back in the United States. The city pulled out all the stops for a gala four-day round of ceremonies and social events. In Los Angeles, a small army of volunteers invited all the crew members of all the ships to dinner. Three thousand five hundred sailors accepted and consumed five thousand pounds of barbecued beef, three hundred pounds of fresh butter, and hot rolls by the thousands, among mountains of other comestibles. Each bluejacket was given two California oranges, a more unusual and appreciated treat for a sailor in 1908 than today.

On May 5, Bob Evans rejoined *Connecticut* for the grand climax of the voyage, the arrival at San Francisco. Two battleships that had been refitted on the west coast, *Nebraska* and *Wisconsin*, joined the fleet, so eighteen battleships, escorted by a flotilla of destroyers and a squadron of lesser craft, steamed through the Golden Gate to a gala welcome. They were met by the eight armored cruisers of the Pacific Fleet that had arrived earlier. The fleet of forty-one warships, the largest fleet of American warships to be assembled since the Civil War, passed in review through the bay. Secretary of the Navy Metcalfe took the salute aboard *Yorktown*, Bob Evans's old gunboat.

There was a grand parade of bluejackets and marines through downtown San Francisco, led by Evans riding in an automobile. Ignoring the intense pain in his legs, the popular admiral smiled and waved to the cheering throngs of hundreds of thousands of people lining the parade route. Less than three years earlier, virtually the entire city had been destroyed by the great earthquake and fire. The fleet's well-publicized arrival called attention to the city's remarkable rebirth.

On May 9, Fighting Bob Evans's two-starred admiral's pennant was lowered for the last time on *Connecticut,* although he was unable to be on board for the ceremony. He relinquished command of the fleet to Rear-Admiral C. M. Thomas, his second-in-command, and departed by train for his home in Washington, D.C. Released from the demands of high command and the confines of a ship, his health improved, and he spent his last years writing his memoirs and lecturing about the navy. He died at his home on January 3, 1912, and was buried in Arlington National Cemetery.

Bob Evans's last public appearance as commander of the battle fleet occurred at a reception for the fleet hosted by the San Francisco Chamber of Commerce, where he delivered a short speech. His remarks were curiously defensive as he asserted the excellence of American battleships and American sailors. He showed flashes of anger, and he explained with characteristic bluntness that the cause of his anger was a certain man Evans noticed sitting in the audience.

He was Henry Reuterdahl, an artist and writer who had sailed with the fleet to make sketches and paintings of events. Reuterdahl was also something of a naval expert, being the American editor for the British publication, *Jane's Fighting Ships.* Immediately after the departure from Hampton Roads, an article carrying Reuterdahl's byline was published in a popular American periodical, *McClure's Magazine.* Entitled "The Needs Of Our Navy," it was a catalogue of naval shortcomings. American battleships were poorly designed, Reuterdahl charged. The bureau system was outmoded and inefficient. The promotion system for officers held back young, talented officers and stifled initiative. Reuterdahl supported all his charges with detailed information that could have come only from within the navy itself.

The article's origins went back several years. Reuterdahl wrote it in 1904, in collaboration with William Sims. But Sims feared that airing such criticisms in public would jeopardize the reforms he was working to bring about from within the navy, and he persuaded Reuterdahl not to publish it. In June, 1907, a magazine called *Our Navy,* which was thought to reflect the views of certain senior naval officers, published an article criticizing battleship design. Its appearance just then may have been prompted by the news reports about the battle fleet's forthcoming cruise to the Pacific. In July, the magazine published a follow-up article. By autumn, when arrangements for the battle fleet's cruise were well underway, the articles had sparked considerable discussion of possible defects in the ships.

On October 4, Henry Reuterdahl had a conversation about the cruise with S. S. McClure, the founder and publisher of *McClure's Magazine*, perhaps because Reuterdahl had been invited to sail with the fleet. McClure considered himself a journalistic crusader, and in the course of their conversation, Reuterdahl showed him the 1904 article. McClure was intrigued, but he told Reuterdahl that no magazine could publish such charges unless they were investigated and fully confirmed. McClure, like Reuterdahl, was acquainted with Sims, and he checked with Sims, and perhaps with other officers. Sims assured him that the article was accurate, which was not surprising, since virtually everything in it had originated with Sims. This time, Sims agreed to publication. Reuterdahl reworked and updated it with the help of one of McClure's top writers. It was published in the January, 1908, issue of the magazine, which actually hit the newstands just after the fleet sailed in December.

There was nothing new in the article. It was a summary of all of Sims's criticisms, going back to his original 1901 report on *Kentucky*. Gun apertures on the older battleships were too large. Armor belts were underwater when ships were fully loaded and therefore useless. Ammunition hoists were open shafts connecting turrets with handling rooms, thereby inviting accidental explosions. Intermediate and anti-torpedo-boat batteries were useless if a moderate sea were running, because the guns were mounted too low in the hull and fired through open apertures. The navy's bureau system encouraged inefficiency and stifled progress. The promotion system held back promising young officers. And so on.

If the article's contents were not new, their publication by a popular magazine in non-technical language any layman could understand was. The battle fleet, with great fanfare, had just departed on its great cruise, and the public now read that the ships, far from being the "greatest fighting machines in the world," as the navy claimed, were so poorly designed as to be possible death traps for their crews.

Coming in the wake of the *Our Navy* attacks, Reuterdahl's article triggered a storm of protest and controversy in the navy and in Congress. There were demands for an inquiry to establish whether the charges it made were true. Anyone in the navy could immediately recognize in it all the complaints made for years by William Sims and other insurgent officers. Secretary Metcalfe sent off toughly worded letters to Sims and a few other officers, demanding to know, absolutely and categorically, whether the officer had anything to do with the article. For months after publication of the *Our Navy* articles, the navy had been issuing statements denying that the battleships were deficient. Any officer proven to have been involved with Reuterdahl was sure to be in trouble.

On November 21, 1907, Sims had been appointed Roosevelt's naval aide in addition to his position as inspector of target practice. He had been with Roosevelt aboard *Mayflower* for the fleet's departure from Hampton Roads. Whether the appointment had anything to do with his agreeing that McClure should publish Reuterdahl's article is uncertain. He must have known that the navy as an institution would be upset by it and that his hand in it would be recognized immediately. Perhaps he thought that working in the White House as an aide to the president who had such confidence in him would shield him from any punishment or reprisal.

Sims took Metcalfe's letter to Roosevelt. Sims later wrote that Roosevelt read it and exclaimed, "What! Haven't you been insubordinate?" Sims replied, "Well, there have been others. What about the 'round robin?'" The president reportedly laughed. Sims was referring to an effort by a group of officers several years earlier to abolish Sims's gunnery innovations. They used the traditional naval device of a "round-robin" letter, in which the signatures were signed in a circle, so that all the signers were equal, and no name stood above the others at the head of the list. When Roosevelt heard about the round-robin letter, he ordered it quashed. Roosevelt had, of course, supported Sims's crusade for gunnery reform, improvement in ship design, and reform of the navy's bureaucracy. The president summoned Metcalfe to his office to order Metcalfe's letters recalled, and the navy's inquisition ended.

Congress, however, still wanted to look into the matter, and on February 25, Senator Hale, as chairman of the Senate Naval Affairs Committee, convened a series of hearings to investigate. A firm opponent of expanded naval appropriations, "monster" battleships, and reorganization of the navy department, Hale was a staunch defender of the status quo and was determined to refute or stifle the criticism in Reuterdahl's article. According to Sims's biographer, Hale saw his hearings as "a weapon with which he could club into silence the reformers who had so long plagued him."

Hale insisted that his investigation be limited to battleship design, not the navy department's organization or other matters, and the hearings focussed particularly on two complaints: that open shaft ammunition hoists were dangerous, and that battleships' armor belts were too narrow and situated too low on the hull to be effective. A parade of senior officers from the bureaus countered all of Reuterdahl's charges with detailed, technical testimony arguing that American battleships were as well, if not better, designed as those of any other country. They pointed out that many of the deficiencies cited by Reuterdahl in such older battleships as *Oregon, Iowa* and *Kentucky* had been corrected in later ships. Even the older ships, the navy argued, "had been built up to the best conception of the naval architects of the day."

Several reformers, including Sims, were also called as witnesses and were given a difficult time by the inquiring senators, notably Hale. But they were able to make persuasive arguments that even the latest battleships suffered from defective ammunition hoists and armor belts. They were able to introduce briefly their most significant and long-pursued idea for reform: abolition of the bureau system and creation of a naval general staff. But Senator Hale quickly cut them off and refused to discuss that subject at all.

The reformers made such a good showing, despite Hale's opposition, that the chairman suddenly and without warning called his committee into executive session in the middle of the testimony of one officer, and soon after, he abruptly adjourned the hearings. No report or recommendations were ever issued. Only the transcript of the hearings themselves was published. The outcome was therefore uncertain, but the Reuterdahl article had not been persuasively refuted.

The entire affair put Roosevelt in something of a quandary. He was loath to believe that the battle fleet and the navy as whole were as deficient as Henry Reuterdahl described, and he was no doubt delighted when the embarrassing hearings were abruptly terminated. But he had confidence in his naval aide's judgment, and he wrote to Secretary Metcalfe, "it seems to me that the armor belts ought to be higher." On March 26, when the acrimonious debate was no longer being carried every day in the newspapers, he wrote to one of his former naval aides who had testified at the hearings as a reformer that he thought that Sims and the other reformers "performed a real service by fearlessly calling attention to defects in our naval architecture."

So when Bob Evans spoke at the San Francisco Chamber of Commerce in May, his beloved navy had been the target of stinging public criticism for months, in particular the battleships of his great battle fleet which had just completed a record-making voyage with notable success. Moreover, the man responsible for starting it all was sitting in his audience. Evans agreed with some of the arguments made by Sims and others, but with his navy under fire from the public, he felt compelled to defend it. "It is not armor belts or waterlines that win battles," he told his audience, "it is the men who shoot the straightest and hardest and can stand punishment the longest. If you have such men—and we have just that kind of stuff in our navy—it makes no difference whether the armor belts are of leather or wood or eggshells." As his parting shot, he growled, "if you want to keep the peace, give us more battleships, and fewer statesmen."

The inconclusive outcome of the Hale hearings had satisfied no one, especially Sims's insurgents, and Sims persuaded Roosevelt to convene a conference to discuss the insurgents' complaints. It met at the Naval War College in late July and sat for two weeks. Roosevelt came up from Oyster Bay to open it and deliver a rousing speech about the importance of the navy.

Long before the conference convened, the lines had been drawn between the insurgents and "the enemy," as Sims called the officers from the bureaus who defended the designs. It was inevitable that the two sides would never reach agreement. They devoted most of their time and energy to arguments about the design of the two dreadnoughts, *Delaware* and *North Dakota,* that had been authorized in 1906 and 1907 and were under construction. Sims and his supporters pointed to several flaws in the design, including the old problem of armor-belt location. The insurgents' criticisms were probably valid, but it is probably also true that they were not about fundamental flaws that would render the ships useless or dangerous. For example, the debate about the armor belts came down to arguments about raising or lowering them by a matter of inches.

Discussion also touched upon the two ships authorized the previous April, *Utah* and *Florida,* that were still in the design stage. Sims argued that the main batteries should be fourteen-inch guns, but he was voted down. The two ships were built mounting twelve-inch pieces, like so many of their predecessors. Although the insurgents failed to gain any changes in the four ships' designs, they were able to gain agreement that a committee including sea-going officers would be involved in the design of future battleships.

On July 7, 1908, the battle fleet passed through the Golden Gate and began to breast the long Pacific swells, bound for Hawaii. It still consisted of sixteen battleships, but the coal-guzzling *Maine* and the leaky *Alabama* had been replaced by the newer *Nebraska* and *Wisconsin*. In command was Rear-Admiral Charles Sperry, who had commanded one of the squadrons on the voyage around South America. Admiral Thomas, who had replaced Evans, was near retirement age and in poor health, so Roosevelt chose Sperry to command for the remainder of the cruise. He proved to be a good choice for the assignment, showing ability as an adept speechmaker and diplomat as well as an able naval commander.

Upon arrival in Hawaii, the fleet anchored at Honolulu, because Pearl Harbor was not yet the site of a naval base. It was still an empty, somewhat isolated bay. However, several officers made a special trip from Honolulu to have a look at it, because during the previous April, at Roosevelt's request, Congress had appropriated $900,000 to construct a base there. It was the first step toward resolving the long-running debate over where to construct the main Pacific naval base. Many members of Congress had always been more enthusiastic about Hawaii than any site in the far-off Philippines. The following year, Congress made another large appropriation, and the Joint Board finally agreed that Pearl Harbor should become the nation's principal naval base in the Pacific.

It is interesting to note in the fleet the presence of four very junior officers whose later careers were famously bound up with Pearl Harbor. By December, 1941, Ensign Husband E. Kimmel would be Admiral Kimmel, in command of the Pacific Fleet. He would shoulder most of the blame—unfairly, many of his colleagues believed—for the debacle the navy suffered at the hands of the Japanese at Pearl Harbor. Ensign Harold Stark in 1941 would be Admiral Stark and Kimmel's superior as Chief of Naval Operations. He, too, would be blamed for the losses at Pearl Harbor and his reputation permanently damaged. The careers and reputations of the other two junior officers would be remembered very differently. Ensign William F. Halsey and Midshipman Raymond Spruance would become two of the navy's most famous and respected fleet commanders in the Pacific war against the Japanese.

In Honolulu, there were luaus and all the ceremonies and social events that had become routine in the fleet's ports of call. After a week in the islands, the fleet sailed forth on July 22 to begin the longest leg of the entire cruise, 3,850 miles to Auckland, New Zealand.

Several months before the fleet departed Hampton Roads, Roosevelt had come to the conclusion that he must abandon the one-ship-a-year battleship replacement policy he had announced in 1905, and acceler-ate construction of new battleships. One reason for his decision was the sudden appearance of *Dreadnought*. Its sea trials in late 1906 had been a resounding success, and it was obvious that "dreadnoughts" were the battleships of the future.

Even after it joined the fleet, Jacky Fisher and the Royal Navy con-tinued to keep the revolutionary battleship isolated from the prying eyes of naval attachés. During a visit to Britain in connection with his duties as inspector of target practice, William Sims approached Fisher to re-quest permission to tour *Dreadnought*. Fisher told him, "You can't see her at all. Nobody can see her. Even our own officers can't. The German naval attaché bothers me all the time. Everybody wants to see her— and I won't let them." Then, catching Sims's eye, Fisher told him in a loud whisper, "See Jellicoe!" He did, and arrangements were made for Sims to visit Portsmouth in civilian clothes, as if on a holiday tour. He was quietly whisked aboard the ship for a "gum-shoe inspection" which became the subject of a detailed report. Roosevelt knew that American battleships of pre-dreadnought design must be replaced by new dread-noughts if the American navy was to remain a modern fighting force. So the pace of replacement must be speeded up.

Another reason for his change of mind was the failure of the Hague Peace Conference even to discuss limitations of battleship size or num-bers. The naval race between Britain and Germany was in high gear, and the Japanese navy dominated the western Pacific. The United States needed a two-ocean navy, which meant more battleships.

In his annual message to Congress issued in early December, 1907, Roosevelt called for renewal of naval expansion. He noted the failure of the Hague Peace Conference and wrote, "To build one battleship of the best and most advanced type every year is not enough. In my judge-ment, we should this year provide for four battleships." He devoted con-siderable space in the message to the navy, calling for establishment of bases in the Pacific, construction of more smaller ships like destroyers and auxiliaries, and a change in the system for promoting senior officers to allow promising younger officers a chance to move up the ladder faster. The influence of both Mahan and Sims on Roosevelt's thinking was apparent in the message.

Unfortunately for Roosevelt and his campaign, Henry Reuterdahl's article hit the newstands less than two weeks after Roosevelt sent his message to Congress. The ensuing debate about the shortcomings of American battleships did nothing to promote Roosevelt's objectives. Also militating against him was the financial panic of the previous October and November that had shaken Wall Street and made many members of Congress reluctant to authorize large military expenditures. Roosevelt mounted a publicity campaign particularly directed at Senator Hale and his supporters, who strongly opposed a return to a policy of naval expansion. Hale's hearings in February about the Reuterdahl article did not, of course, help Roosevelt's cause. In the course of questioning a witness who was describing battleship shortcomings, one senator remarked that if the navy's battleships were so deficient, perhaps Congress ought to stop wasting money on them.

In April, Roosevelt sent Congress a special message pleading for four battleships, and the issue came to a climax late in the month when the Senate voted on the annual naval authorization bill. The result was a compromise: two battleships were authorized for the year, with the understanding that two ships would be authorized annually in future years. Construction would also begin on a naval base at Pearl Harbor. The new ships, like the single ships authorized in 1906 and 1907, would be dreadnoughts.

The publicity surrounding the battle fleet's cruise had helped the president's cause, as had the bustling preparations being made in California in April to welcome the fleet. In Congress, Roosevelt had solid support from the west coast representatives and senators. Most newspapers decided that neither side in the debate had won a clear-cut victory, but Roosevelt was satisfied. In a letter to the American ambassador to France, he wrote: "Congress will not stand for the four battleships. To be frank, I did not suppose that they would; but I knew I would not get through two and have those two hurried up unless I made a violent effort for four." He had gained as much assurance as it was possible to get from Congress's annual authorization and appropriation process

that the navy would remain a modern fighting force for the foreseeable future.

When the fleet arrived in Auckland on August 9, the exuberance of their
reception exceeded anything they had experienced in South America.
Franklin Matthews, a journalist traveling with the fleet, wrote, "California went mad; New Zealand not only went fleet mad but it developed
a new disease—fleetitis." Admiral Sperry thought the reception was
more enthusiastic than any they had encountered on the American
west coast.

But the people of Sydney and Melbourne in Australia were even less
restrained, if that was possible. The extravagance of the Australian welcome led to speculation that it revealed political undertones: a weaken-
ing of bonds with England, which the Australians hoped would be replaced with closer ties with the United States; a hope for increased
immigration from the United States to fill up the empty continent with
Caucasians to forestall an influx of Asians and keep Australia "white;"
and a desire for reassurance of American support against possible Japanese aggression. Australian newspapers openly and repeatedly discussed such implications. A newspaper in Melbourne editorialized, "We
are unfeignedly glad that America has invaded the Pacific. It is a move
that cannot help but lessen our danger of Asiatic aggression and
strengthen the grounds of our national security."

After coaling at Albany, a small port city in western Australia, the
fleet steamed north to its next stop, Manila, where it arrived October 2.
Unfortunately, a cholera epidemic was raging, and no liberty was
granted to the crews, to the disappointment of the Filipinos who had
been waiting to welcome the Americans.

When it had been announced the previous March that the fleet
would sail around the world, the Japanese government promptly issued
an invitation for a visit to Japan. In view of the strained relations with
Japan over immigration and the San Francisco school problem, the invitation posed a rather tricky and delicate diplomatic problem. The
American ambassador in Tokyo was wary of having a fleet of American
battleships descend upon Japan, even if they came in response to an
invitation from the Japanese. He was even more worried about having
thousands of sailors on liberty, perhaps causing an incident that could
escalate and further strain relations. He recommended that only half

the fleet make a visit. The question was discussed in a cabinet meeting in Washington before Roosevelt announced that the invitation would be accepted, and the whole fleet would make the visit.

The fleet arrived in Yokohama on October 18 to a welcome that officers and crews agreed was the warmest of the entire cruise. Tens of thousands of Japanese school children had learned to sing American songs to welcome their guests. The American ambassador reported that the magnificence of the reception exceeded even that accorded to Admiral Togo when he and his fleet returned from the victory at Tsushima. There could be no doubt that the spontaneous outpouring of warmth and hospitality demonstrated that the strained relations between the two countries were at an end. The ambassador reported that "the effects of the visit will be material and far-reaching for good." Roosevelt later wrote that the reception in Japan was "the most noteworthy incident of the cruise."

After a week in Yokohama, the fleet departed for its next stop, China. The invitation issued by the Manchu government of the venerable Empress Dowager Tzu-hsi had also posed a diplomatic problem for Washington, one even more tricky than in the case of Japan. The cornerstone of American policy toward China was John Hay's Open Door, a commitment to maintain China's territorial integrity against the inroads of imperialism, and keep the entire country open equally to the trade of all countries. But Japan and Russia controlled Manchuria, and those two countries, along with Germany and France, continued to seek spheres of interest in China, as all four nations strove to "cut up the Chinese melon" among themselves.

The United States opposed these imperialist inroads, but it was in no position to take military action on the Asian mainland to oppose them. Diplomatic maneuvers and "moral suasion" were as far as the United States was prepared to go in defending the Open Door.

China had followed Japan's lead in issuing an invitation for the fleet to make a visit. The prospect aroused excitement among both Chinese and the large foreign expatriate community in the treaty ports. The port selected for the visit, Chefoo, lay on the northern coast of the Shantung peninsula, not far from Manchuria, the cockpit of imperial clashes between Japan and Russia.

The American minister to China, William Rockhill, was an expert on China who was fluent in the language and had been the real author of John Hay's Open Door Notes. He was also a personal friend of Theodore Roosevelt. Rockhill sent a message from Peking arguing against the fleet making a visit. A visit by sixteen American battleships, especially to Chefoo, near Manchuria, would probably be misinterpreted by the Chinese government, he warned. They would read into the visit a commitment by the United States to defend the Open Door with force, if necessary. They would regard it as a warning to Japan and Russia, whereas the United States intended no such meaning.

Elihu Root, the secretary of state, agreed with Rockhill's reasoning, and Roosevelt could see its logic. But with the fleet already in eastern Asia, and having visited Japan, the invitation from the Chinese could not be rejected completely. A compromise was reached. The fleet would visit Amoy, in central China, far from Manchuria, and only half the fleet would make the visit. The other half would return to the Philippines to prepare for target practice.

The compromise arrangements put a damper on the visit. Amoy was perhaps the dirtiest, most disease-ridden port on the China coast. The Chinese government, determined to make the best of a bad situation, at great expense built a special, separate city several miles from Amoy for all the ceremonies and other activities. The American visitors never even entered Amoy itself. The American consul in Amoy did his best to make the occasion a success, but the artificial atmosphere in the isolated settlement erected for the visit prevented any repetition of the warmth and enthusiasm extended by the Australians and the Japanese. The visit was deemed a success, and the cordial relations that the United States enjoyed with China continued. But it was something of a disappointment after the incredible outpourings of warmth and friendship encountered in New Zealand, Australia, and Japan.

The fleet reunited in the Philippines for target practice, and on December 1, 1908, it departed Manila, homeward bound via the Suez Canal. The remainder of the cruise was an anticlimax after the succession of triumphant port visits in South America and Asia. The ships passed near Singapore as they navigated the Straits of Malacca, but they did not stop. Singapore was not yet the major British naval base it would become in the 1920s. A gaggle of fishing boats and private yachts came out to watch the passing parade of battleships. After a stop in Ceylon for coal, they crossed through the Suez Canal to enter the Mediterranean.

At the northern terminus of the canal at Port Said, the squadrons

Roosevelt addressing the officers and men of *Connecticut* in Hampton Roads on February 22, 1909, upon the Great White Fleet's return from its world cruise.

separated to permit visits to several ports in Europe, North Africa, and Turkey during the short time they would remain in the Mediterranean. A volcanic eruption in Sicily had devastated the city of Messina, and the Americans were able to provide assistance to the humanitarian relief efforts. The ships were reunited at Gibraltar on February 1 for the last leg of the cruise across the Atlantic. Everyone wanted to be sure the arrival back in the United States occurred before Theodore Roosevelt left office. There was strong sentiment for having the ships arrive in New York, where a massive, well-publicized "welcome home" celebration could be arranged. But Roosevelt insisted that they return to Hampton Roads, the navy's principal base on the east coast, whence they had departed more than a year before.

On February 22, 1909, the Great White Fleet entered Chesapeake Bay in triumph. Again, as in 1907, the hotels were filled with visitors from all over the country who had come to welcome the officers and crews home. The weather was not as inviting as it had been for the departure. Gray, overcast skies and drizzle did not, however, dampen the enthusiasm of the reception. *Mayflower* was on hand with Roosevelt aboard. When the ships had anchored, the president immediately went aboard *Connecticut* to congratulate Admiral Sperry, the ship's officers, and crew. They assembled on the foredeck to hear the president speak. Climbing on to the barbette encircling the forward turret from which he would speak, Roosevelt slipped and nearly suffered a bad fall that could have caused a severe injury. But he was caught by several sailors and hoisted to his improvised dais. He delivered a rousing speech congratulating everyone for the successful venture. "Other nations may do as you have done," he told the assembled sailors, "but they'll have to follow you."

The cruise was widely hailed as the technological and diplomatic triumph that it was. However, critics then and later pointed to several circumstances that, they argued, took away much of the triumphal gloss. In the absence of a worldwide system of American coaling stations, the navy had sent a fleet of colliers ahead to pre-position coal supplies all over the world. Moreover, since the navy lacked a sufficient number of its own colliers, foreign ships had to be chartered. It was an arrangement that probably could not be adopted in case of war. The departure from Hampton Roads had been timed to permit transit of the Straits of Magellan during the southern hemisphere's summer months. The fleet thus would avoid the freezing storms of the winter months in those latitudes. If the fleet had to move quickly to the west coast in time of war, critics pointed out, it would not have the luxury of timing its voyage in that fashion. The ships themselves had been tested, but as *ships* only, not as *battleships*. Finally, the critics argued, the brave show the fleet put on was deceptive, because the battleships had already been rendered obsolete by *Dreadnought*. The ships were not the powerful, up-to-date instruments of war they appeared to be.

The criticisms were valid, but the triumph was real and well-earned nonetheless. Diplomatically, the voyage had advanced the country's foreign policy objectives, especially in Australia and Japan. Roosevelt later wrote that the cruise was "the most important service that I rendered to peace." The cruise was a technological triumph, because no comparable fleet had ever before made such a voyage. They had steamed 42,227 miles in fourteen months without a major breakdown. When they arrived back in Hampton Roads, the ships' top speed had been reduced by growths on their hulls. They required scraping and other

minor refitting, but they were in fighting trim, ready for battle if necessary. In 1910, when Roosevelt visited Berlin on his way home after his
long African safari, Admiral von Tirpitz confessed to him that when he
had heard that a fleet of American battleships intended to sail around
the world, he had predicted that it could not be done.

The skill acquired by the crews testified to the success of the cruise
even more powerfully than the performance of the ships. Their professional skills had been honed by months of drills between port visits and
the target practice at Magdalena Bay and Manila, as well as the continuous operation of their ships as part of a fleet. The crews arrived home
in a much higher state of readiness than when they departed and quite
possibly were the best-trained, most seasoned navy sailors in the world.
The cruise was as much a triumph of the training and testing of the
officers and men of the American navy as it was a diplomatic and technological success.

On March 4, 1909, less than two weeks after he welcomed the fleet
home, Roosevelt sat on a platform erected in front of the east facade of
the Capitol and watched his successor, William Howard Taft, sworn in
as president. Some of the crew members of the returned battle fleet
marched in the inaugural parade. The ships were being dispersed
among shipyards up and down the east coast to be dry-docked for
scraping and refitting, many to be fitted with tall latticed masts to support fire control stations. They would also be shorn of the gilded scroll
work that decorated their bows and sterns, and they would be painted
the business-like gray that has been the color of American warships in
both peace and war ever since. The Great White Fleet was no more.

On his last full day in office, the outgoing president wrote a "Dear
Will" letter to the president-elect that revealed Roosevelt's intense continuing concern for the navy as well as Alfred Mahan's lasting influence
on his thinking. The battle fleet, Roosevelt cautioned Taft, must never
be divided. The letter was prompted by growing sentiment in Congress
that battleships should be stationed on both coasts. One west coast senator had even introduced legislation to that effect, which had been defeated.

Also on Roosevelt's last full day in the White House, Congress fulfilled the agreement it had reached the year before and authorized construction of two battleships. Christened *Wyoming* and *Arkansas*, they

would displace twenty-six thousand tons, be powered by turbine engines with a speed of twenty-one knots, and carry main batteries of twelve twelve-inch guns. If the battleships of the Great White Fleet were not the equals of *Dreadnought,* their immediate successors, for which Theodore Roosevelt had fought during his last year in office, would equal and even surpass it.

As Roosevelt's successor was sworn into office, probably no one, including Roosevelt himself, reflected upon the astonishing transformation that had occurred in the American navy in little more than a generation. In 1880, the biggest and most powerful ships of the American navy were pre–Civil War first-rate sailing ships, hybrid steam frigates that relied more upon sail than steam, and Civil War–era monitors armed with smooth-bore cannons. At sea, they were incommunicado. When Roosevelt left office in 1909, the nation had embarked, at his insistence, on building twenty-six-thousand-ton behemoth dreadnoughts, equipped with radio and capable of firing a broadside of twelve twelve-inch guns at ranges of several miles. When they were commissioned in 1912, these final contributions of Theodore Roosevelt to the United States Navy were the largest, most powerful warships afloat. They boasted a bigger displacement and a larger main battery than anything in Britain's Royal Navy.

In the latter half of the twentieth century, it has become a fashionable cliché to say that we suffer from "future shock"—the stress of accelerating changes in our lives caused by rapid technological innovation. Overlooked and forgotten are the equally revolutionary changes that beset many earlier generations. The transformation that occurred in the navies of the world during the thirty years before 1909 was as radical and disconcerting to those who experienced it as anything that has occurred in the design and employment of warships during an equivalent period since. In a very real sense, the creation of the steel and steam navy and its most awesome element, the dreadnought battleship, was a revolution of startling rapidity and sweeping scope. Theodore Roosevelt, as much or more than anyone else, led the way.

Virtually nothing remains of the armada of cruisers and battleships built during Roosevelt's era. *Indiana,* the first battleship, and its sister *Massachusetts* were declared obsolete and sold for scrap in 1920. The third of the trio of 1890 battleships, the redoubtable *Oregon,* was spared and installed at Portland, Oregon, as a naval museum. But it lived on only to suffer an even more ignominious fate later. In 1942, in a misplaced burst of patriotic zeal, the government stripped the old ship of its superstructure, turrets, guns, and armor, to melt them down for the war effort. After the war, the hulk was towed to Guam for use as an ammunition barge. It was driven ashore in a typhoon, and there it remained until 1956, when what was left of McKinley's Bulldog was sold to a Japanese salvage company for scrap.

The *Connecticut*-class battleships, proudest ornaments of the Great White Fleet, were all declared obsolete in 1923 and 1924 and sold for the scrap. Most of their immediate successors, the early dreadnoughts, were scrapped in the 1920s and 1930s. However, one of them, *Utah*— which had been one of the battleships that sparked debate at the 1908 conference at Newport—survived to be on hand at Pearl Harbor when the Japanese attacked in 1941. It received two aerial torpedo hits and sank, with a loss of fifty-eight crew members. Some of the ship was salvaged, and it was removed from the navy's rolls in 1944. The remnants of the wreck still lie on the bottom of Pearl Harbor.

Only one survivor of the steel and steam navy remains proudly intact and afloat. Dewey's flagship, *Olympia*, is moored at Penn's Landing at Philadelphia as a naval museum open to the public.

Epilogue
"The Machine Has Worked"

—⊰⊱—

The circumnavigation of the Great White Fleet constituted a milestone in the development of the American navy, and it marked the end of an era, but it did not signal an end to the process of growth and innovation that had been in progress for thirty years. Within a few years, the pre-dreadnought battleships of the famous fleet would be replaced by the bigger, faster, more powerful dreadnoughts already under construction. And when the fleet arrived home at Hampton Roads, ideas had already begun to percolate about aircraft that in turn would, within forty years, render those behemoths obsolete. Technological innovation, so foreign to the navy of 1880 and resisted by so many of its officers, was by 1909 considered the norm by their professional descendents.

It is not surprising that the potential of heavier-than-air machines as instruments of warfare, especially of naval warfare, was perceived by only a handful of far-seeing people in the first decade of this century. What is surprising is that anyone at all could conceive of those frail, underpowered devices of wood and fabric as being useful in war. One of the first such people was, characteristically, Theodore Roosevelt. In 1896, Professor Samuel P. Langley of the Smithsonian Institution conducted successful flying experiments using a steam-powered model "aerodrome." In March, 1898, Assistant Secretary of the Navy Roosevelt wrote to Secretary John D. Long about the experiments. "The machine has worked," he told Long. "It seems to me worthwhile for this government to try whether it will not work on a large enough scale to be of use in event of war."

He was a decade ahead of his time. Eight months after the return of the Great White Fleet, on November 9, 1909, Lieutenant George Sweet became the first naval officer to go aloft in an aircraft. The plane had been constructed by Orville and Wilbur Wright. It belonged to the army and was the only one the government possessed. A year later, on

November 14, 1910, the first takeoff from aboard a ship occurred. The ship was *Birmingham,* a cruiser, on the bow of which an inclined platform temporarily was erected as a primitive flight deck. Eugene Ely, a civilian pilot employed by the pioneering aircraft designer Glenn Curtiss, revved the engine of his biplane and wobbled into the air as *Birmingham* lay at anchor in Hampton Roads. He landed five minutes later near some beachfront cottages.

Only three months later, on January 18, 1911, another first in aviation history occurred when an airplane both landed on and took off from an American naval ship. The venue this time was San Francisco Bay and the ship was the armored cruiser *Pennsylvania,* with a temporary flight-deck platform rigged on its stern. The pilot again was the intrepid Ely. He took off from an airfield on shore and was able to land on the ship when hooks dangling from his plane snagged lines that were stretched across the deck and anchored by fifty-pound sandbags—essentially the same landing system used on today's supercarriers. An hour later Ely took off and returned to the shore. Although probably no one, including Ely, realized it at the time, the death knell of the mighty battleship had sounded.

Histories of the United States Navy during the first half of the twentieth century often depict the naval leadership as a group of reactionary, obstinate "battleship admirals," resisting to the bitter end the introduction of the aircraft carrier. There were, to be sure, many such admirals, as there had been admirals in the 1870s who resisted the introduction of steam and clung tenaciously to sail. But there were plenty of others who early on saw the potential of naval aviation. One such was William Sims.

Following World War I, Sims was a rear-admiral serving as president of the Naval War College. During his tenure, the War College enjoyed one of the most productive and influential periods of its existence. In view of his pioneering work to improve battleship design and gunnery, Sims might logically have become one of the most reactionary of the "battleship admirals." But he included aircraft carriers in the College's war games. In future wars, he wrote, the fleet with the strongest carrier task force "will sweep the enemy fleet clean of its airplanes and proceed to bomb the battleships, and torpedo them with torpedo planes."

In 1921, army Brigadier-General Billy Mitchell conducted a series of spectacular and heavily-publicized tests in and around Chesapeake

Bay that were designed to prove that battleships were vulnerable to attack by aircraft. The most spectacular test occurred in July when the German dreadnought *Ostfriesland,* a survivor of the battle of Jutland, was subjected to attacks by Mitchell's army bombers. For two days the ship survived a series of attacks in which ever-larger bombs were employed. Teams of experts examined the ship after each attack. Only after an attack by seven planes, each carrying a specially constructed one-ton bomb, did the old battleship go to the bottom.

The navy was reluctant to accept the test's results as proof of the validity of Mitchell's arguments. The ship, critics pointed out, was an unmanned hulk lying dead in the water, unable to maneuver to avoid the bombs or defend itself. The attackers knew its exact position, the weather was clear, and they flew at an altitude of only a few thousand feet. Mitchell's supporters argued that an unmanned hulk without volatile fuel or ammunition aboard was harder to sink than a fully loaded and manned ship. The critics, it must be admitted, had a point. It seems unlikely that military aircraft, as they existed in 1921, would have been capable of sinking a battleship under combat conditions.

So despite the arguments of Billy Mitchell and other equally radical proponents of air power, the world's principal naval powers—notably Britain, the United States, and Japan—continued to build battleships right through the years of World War II. The first sinking of battleships by aircraft under wartime conditions occurred in November, 1940. Three Italian battleships were sunk at their moorings at the Italian naval base at Taranto, in a surprise night attack by British torpedo planes. The first battleship to be sunk while underway in combat with aircraft was the German superdreadnought, *Bismarck,* that went to the bottom of the Atlantic on May 27, 1941. But *Bismarck,* operating alone, was overwhelmed by a fleet of British ships and aircraft, using bombs, torpedoes, and gunfire. The greatest damage was done by gunfire from battleships. The ship finally sank because it was scuttled by its crew, although some experts who have examined the wreckage on the bottom of the Atlantic have argued that it would have sunk soon anyway, even if the scuttling charges had not been set off.

The first sinking of a battleship while underway in combat solely with aircraft occurred in December, 1941, only three days after the Japanese attack on Pearl Harbor. A new British battleship, *Prince of Wales,* along with a battle cruiser, *Repulse,* went to the bottom off the coast of Malaya as a result of attacks by shore-based Japanese bombers and torpedo planes. Thus, the destruction of *Prince of Wales* provided the first unambiguous proof that a modern battleship could be sunk by aircraft under combat conditions. However, the two British warships were not protected by air cover of any kind (nor was *Bismarck* or the Italian battleships). Contrary to Billy Mitchell's arguments, aerial torpedoes launched from naval aircraft, rather than bombs, proved to be the main cause of their sinkings.

The Japanese attack on Pearl Harbor in December, 1941, demonstrated that the Japanese navy had achieved a very advanced and sophisticated level of expertise in aircraft carrier operations—more advanced, perhaps, than any other navy had attained at that time. What is perhaps surprising is that Japan chose to use that expertise—risking the bulk of its carriers, planes, and trained personnel—in an attack intended primarily to sink battleships. Out of respect for the targets' ability to survive and fight back, the attack was planned to occur when the ships were moored and stationary. Worth noting, too, is the fact that all the battleships that the Japanese sank, except *Arizona* and *Oklahoma*, were refloated and repaired in time to take part in combat operations later in the war against the Japanese.

The United States Navy continued to build battleships after World War I, but it did not ignore the aircraft carrier. In 1919, Congress authorized construction of the navy's first aircraft carrier when it voted funds to convert a collier, *Jupiter,* into a ship to conduct experiments in seaborne aviation. Recommissioned *Langley,* it commenced operations in 1922. Many of the navy's most important early breakthroughs in carrier operations were accomplished aboard *Langley.* Not built to be a combatant, the ship nevertheless survived to take part in combat operations in the early months of World War II. When war was declared, *Langley* lay at Cavite in the Philippines. It steamed south to take part in operations off Australia and among the islands of the Dutch East Indies. On February 22, 1942, while ferrying P-40s from Australia to Java, it was attacked by Japanese aircraft and sunk with a loss of sixteen crew members.

In 1922, the same year *Jupiter* was recommissioned *Langley,* the navy's first authentic combat aircraft carriers, *Lexington* and *Saratoga,* were authorized. Both were built on hulls intended to be battle cruisers, whose construction was cancelled as a result of the Washington Naval Limitation Treaty signed in 1922. Commissioned in 1927, both went on to illustrious combat careers in World War II. *Lexington* took part in early operations against the Japanese in the Southwest Pacific. On May 8, 1942, it was sunk by Japanese carrier planes during the battle of the Coral Sea. *Saratoga* just missed taking part in the battle of Midway in June, 1942, but it was in the thick of numerous other Pacific battles, including the invasions of Guadalcanal, Tarawa, and Iwo Jima. It survived the war only to be sunk in 1946 during "Operation Crossroads" at Bikini atoll to test the effect of the atomic bomb on naval vessels.

When the United States entered World War II, *Lexington* and *Saratoga* were not the navy's only aircraft carriers. More had been built during the 1930s. *Yorktown, Enterprise, Hornet,* and *Wasp* were also part of the fleet. By an extraordinary stroke of luck, none of them was in Pearl Harbor when the Japanese attacked, and all were therefore able to take part in the early battles of the Pacific war that blunted the Japanese advance. *Ranger,* completed in the 1920s and the first American ship built as an aircraft carrier from the keel up, spent the early years of the war in the Atlantic. However, it moved to the Pacific to take part in the later battles.

April 18, 1942, marked an aviation milestone of sorts, when sixteen army B-25 twin-engined bombers took off from *Hornet*'s flight deck in mid-ocean and bombed Tokyo. Army planes were used, because no navy plane had the range needed for the mission. Most aviators at the time probably thought it impossible for planes of that size to take off from a carrier at sea.

The replacement of the battleship by the aircraft carrier as the principal vessel of the battle fleet is usually interpreted as a significant change of direction in naval history. But it can also be seen as continuity, a continuation of the strategic doctrine espoused by Alfred Mahan that the proper role of the navy is offensive. The aircraft carrier replaced the battleship because its airplanes could reach farther with more devastating effect than the battleship's guns. That the navy is an offensive force to control the sea, project power, and destroy the enemy's navy is a principle taken for granted today. It is difficult to conceive that only a little more than one hundred years ago, this was a revolutionary idea that ran counter to what most Americans thought their navy should be or do.

The jets scream off the flight deck as they are catapulted into the cloudy Adriatic sky. Soon, they will be flying a support mission over Bosnia. The U.S.S. *Theodore Roosevelt* and its escort vessels maneuver in the restricted waters of the Adriatic Sea to prepare to receive a flight of fighters that departed a few hours earlier.

More than one thousand feet long and displacing ninety thousand tons, the *Theodore Roosevelt* dwarfs the twenty-six-thousand-ton dreadnought battleships, *Wyoming* and *Arkansas,* that constituted its namesake's final contribution to the American battle fleet. It is a floating city that is home to a population of nearly seven thousand men and women. The huge aircraft carrier has no guns to speak of, but its armament—its planes and missiles—reaches farther with more lethal effect than anything envisioned by naval architects in the days of the Great White Fleet. It bristles with a forest of electronic antennae connected to devices capable of performing feats undreamed of by Bob Evans or William Sims.

The giant aircraft carrier was built at the Newport News Shipbuilding and Drydock Company, where seven of the Great White Fleet's battleships were built. On hand for its commissioning in October, 1986, were Mr. and Mrs. Theodore Roosevelt III, Mr. and Mrs. Archibald Roosevelt, Theodore Roosevelt IV, Theodore Roosevelt V, and several other members of the family. It was reputedly the largest gathering of the Roosevelts in a generation.

Tucked away on the nuclear-powered supercarrier are reminders of the ship's namesake and his Great White Fleet. Aboard, for example, is a silver goblet from U.S.S. *Louisiana,* the battleship on which Roosevelt sailed to visit the unfinished Panama Canal. It was one of the four battleships of the Great White Fleet's First Squadron. Also aboard is a Colt .44 revolver and a Remington .30 rifle that belonged to Roosevelt. Especially intriguing is a piece of sheet music for "The Strenuous Life March and Two-Step." They are all part of a collection of nearly forty pieces of Roosevelt memorabilia that the ship carries in its Theodore Roosevelt Museum. The collection is testimony to the high regard the navy continues to feel for the most ardent navalist who ever occupied the White House.

As the jets scream off the U.S.S. *Theodore Roosevelt*'s flight deck, it is not difficult to imagine Theodore Roosevelt watching from the bridge. Throughout his presidency, Roosevelt often visited ships of the battle fleet. He would sail out of Oyster Bay aboard *Mayflower* to watch target practice and maneuvers by ships of the Atlantic Fleet. No other president, not even Franklin Roosevelt, has devoted so much time to the navy, not only in the corridors of power in Washington, but actually aboard its ships, among its officers and men. Always, he sought to investigate for himself the navy's latest technological innovations and to reassure its people that their efforts were appreciated.

On the bridge of the big aircraft carrier, Roosevelt would no doubt stride back and forth, his eyes shining behind the thick pince-nez, his neck craning this way and that so as not to miss any detail of the tangle of orderly activity in progress below and around him. Later, he would probably eat supper with the crew and meet with the captain and his officers in the wardroom. There would be no polite chit-chat or vague words of praise from the president at these gatherings. He would shoot forth dozens of pointed, detailed questions about what he had seen, and there had better be equally pointed, detailed answers if he were to be satisfied. When he departed the ship's quarterdeck, everyone—most of all, Roosevelt himself—would undoubtedly feel simply "bully." The officers and crew would realize that their visitor had not come aboard for ceremonial or selfish political reasons. He had done so because he wanted to become acquainted with them and understand what they do.

It is heartening and reassuring to know that the spirit of Theodore Roosevelt lives on in one of the most powerful warships ever to fly the American flag. He deserves nothing less.

BIBLIOGRAPHIC NOTES

GENERAL WORKS

The literature about Theodore Roosevelt is not as extensive as the literature about the United States Navy, but it probably comes close. In both cases, the bulk of it is extraneous to the subject of this book. Standard histories of the navy usually deal briefly and rather superficially with the years between 1880 and 1909, except for the Spanish-American War. Biographies of Roosevelt usually make clear his devotion to the navy. But they must deal with such a multitude of important issues and events in which he was a principal participant that they rarely address in any detail his important contributions to the navy's expansion and maturation. However, there have been several specialized studies devoted to aspects of the navy's history during the period covered by this book, and one or two that focus on Roosevelt's contributions to the development of the navy. I am especially indebted to the authors of those works on which I have drawn for this account.

Especially notable among the standard histories of the navy I have consulted are Harold and Margaret Sprout's classic study, *The Rise of American Seapower, 1776–1918* (Princeton: Princeton University Press, 1939); and Stephen Howarth's *To Shining Sea: A History of the United States Navy, 1775–1991* (New York: Random House, 1991), which is both more recent and more engaging than the Sprouts' book. Edward L. Beach's *The United States Navy: A 200-Year History* (Boston: Houghton, Mifflin Co., 1986) is anecdotal and delightful to read. Its focus on personalities reflects the author's background as a novelist as well as a naval officer. Nathan Miller's *The United States Navy: An Illustrated History* (New York: American Heritage, 1977) is excellent for both its illustrations and its text.

John D. Alden's *The American Steel Navy* (Annapolis: The Naval Institute Press, 1972) covers precisely the same period as this book. It is deservedly regarded as a classic. Its many fascinating photographs, reproduced with stunning beauty, tend to draw attention away from its equally excellent, if rather brief, text. Paolo E. Coletta's *A Survey of U.S. Naval Affairs, 1865–1917* (Lanham: University Press of America, 1987) offers brief but important information about most of the significant personalities and events of the era. Coletta also edited the two-volume *American Secretaries of the Navy* (Annapolis: Naval Institute Press, 1980), which contains informative profiles of all the secretaries and sketches of the principal events during their tenures of office. Walter Millis's *Arms and Men: A Study in American Military History* (New York: G. P. Putnam's Sons, 1956) is an iconoclastic study, often not admiring of the army or navy, that relates the development of the nation's military and naval forces to its economic, social, and political history.

From among the many full biographies of Roosevelt, I have drawn especially upon William H. Harbaugh, *The Life and Times of Theodore Roosevelt* (New York: Oxford University Press, 1975); Henry F. Pringle, *Theodore Roosevelt: A Biography* (New York: Harcourt, Brace & Co., 1931); and Joseph Bucklin Bishop, *Theodore Roosevelt and His Time* (New York: Charles Scribner's Sons, 1920). Pringle's book was recently reissued, and Bishop was a close friend of Roosevelt. Roosevelt's *An Autobiography* (New York: MacMillan, 1913) is more useful in revealing his attitudes, personality, and character than as a source of information about his life. Hermann Hagedorn's *The Roosevelt Family of Sagamore Hill* (New York: The Macmillan Company, 1954) is a charming book that focusses on his relationship with his family and recounts Roosevelt's life by tracing events that occurred at Sagamore Hill. Nathan Miller's *Theodore Roosevelt: A Life* (New York: William Morrow and Co., 1992) is a one-volume biography that benefits from recent scholarship.

Howard K. Beale's *Theodore Roosevelt and the Rise of America to World Power* (Baltimore: Johns Hopkins University Press, 1956) is basic to any study of Roosevelt's foreign policy and its inevitable connection with the navy. Massively documented, it is a formidable work of scholarship, to be admired even if one does not always agree with Beale's interpretation of Roosevelt's personality and philosophy of foreign policy. Indispensable to any study of Theodore Roosevelt are *The Letters of Theodore Roosevelt* (Cambridge: Harvard University Press, 1951–54), edited in eight volumes by Elting E. Morison and John Morton Blum, and Roosevelt's papers in the Manuscript Division of the Library of Congress. John Morton Blum's *The Republican Roosevelt* (New Haven: Harvard University Press, 1954) is a study, rather than a biography, which is excellent for its insights, though there is little in it about the navy.

PROLOGUE

The preparations for and departure of the fleet were covered extensively in the press, notably *The New York Times* and *The Washington Post*, throughout the first half of December, 1907. A concise but informative account of the building and significance of *Dreadnought* is contained in Robert G. Albion's *Five Centuries of Famous Ships* (New York: McGraw-Hill Book Company, 1978). (See also notes for chapter 8.)

CHAPTER I
"TEEDY'S DRAWING LITTLE SHIPS!"

A good contemporary description of the pitiful condition of the navy in 1880 is in "Navy of the United States," in *Harper's New Monthly Magazine*, November, 1880, pages 760–769. Beach's *The United States Navy: A 200-Year History* provides a good portrait of the post–Civil War years of decline. Walter R. Herrick's *The American Naval Revolution* (Baton Rouge: Louisiana State University, 1966) is a scholarly study of the transformation from the years of decline to the full flowering of the coal and steel navy.

The best biography of Roosevelt is Edmund Morris's *The Rise of Theodore Roosevelt* (New York: Ballantine Books, 1979). Unfortunately, it ends at his accession to the presidency. Thoroughly researched, detailed, and immensely readable, it is the best source of information about Roosevelt's formative years and early public life. Owen Wister's *Roosevelt: The Story of a Friendship* (New York: The Macmillan Company, 1930) is an episodic, affectionate portrait by the author of *The Virginian* who was Roosevelt's classmate at Harvard. David McCullough's *Mornings on Horseback* (New York: Simon and Schuster, 1981) is an account of Roosevelt's early life until 1886 with attention to how his character and personality developed.

The personalities and events connected with the fascinating story of the ABCD ships are described in several biographies and studies. Thomas Hunt's *Life of William H. Hunt* (Brattleboro, Vermont: E. I. Hildreth and Company, 1922) and Leon Burr Richardson's *William E. Chandler, Republican* (New York: Dodd, Mead & Company, 1940) are admiring biographies that devote considerable space to the inception of the steel navy. Chandler's papers in the Library of Congress contain his correspondence with John Roach. *John Roach: Maritime Entrepreneur,* by Leonard Alexander Swann, Jr. (Annapolis: United States Naval Institute, 1965), rescued Roach's reputation as an innovator and pioneer builder of iron and steel ships, after he had been pilloried for decades as a unscrupulous rascal. George Frederick Howe's *Chester A. Arthur: A Quarter-Century of Machine Politics* (New York: Frederick Unger Publishing Co., 1934) deals briefly with rejuvenation of the navy, as does Justus D. Doenecke's *The Presidencies of James A. Garfield and Chester Alan Arthur* (Lawrence: The Regents' Press of Kansas, 1981). Allan Nevins in *Grover Cleveland: A Study In Courage* (New York: Dodd, Mead and Company, 1933) attacks Roach and Chandler while defending Cleveland and William Whitney in the disputes over the ABCD ships. Mark Hirsch's *William Whitney: Modern Warwick* (New York: Dodd, Mead & Company, 1948) is an admiring portrait that includes considerable information about Whitney's tenure in the navy department.

H. Wayne Morgan's *From Hayes to McKinley* (Syracuse: Syracuse University Press, 1969) is a scholarly but readable history of the politics of the Gilded Age, the background against which the "New Navy" emerged.

CHAPTER 2

"POOR LITTLE POORHOUSE"

The standard biography of Luce is Albert Gleaves's *Life and Letters of Rear Admiral Stephen B. Luce* (New York: G. P. Putnam's Sons, 1925). *The Writings of Stephen B. Luce,* by John B. Hattendorf and John D. Hayes (Newport: Naval War College Press, 1975), complements it. Luce's papers are in the Manuscript Division of the Library of Congress. Ronald Spector's *Professors of War: The Naval War College and the Development of the Naval Profession* (Newport: Naval War College Press, 1977) is based upon material in the Naval War College Naval Historical Collection. A brief account of the founding of the War College is in "Stephen Bleecker Luce and the Naval War College," by Kay Russell (*Naval War College Review,* April-May, 1979, pages 20–41).

An excellent review of the rapid-fire technological developments of the nineteenth century and their impact on warship design is contained in Siegfried Breyer's *Battleships and Battle Cruisers, 1905–1970* (Garden City: Doubleday & Co., 1973). Arthur J. Marder's *The Anatomy of British Sea Power* (New York: Alfred A. Knopf, 1940) is a classic history of the development of the British steam-and-steel navy between 1880 and 1905. It includes a review of the nineteenth century technological innovations.

CHAPTER 3
"A VERY GOOD BOOK"

Mahan's autobiography, *From Sail To Steam: Recollections of Naval Life* (New York: Harper & Brothers Publishers, 1907), is mostly about his life before he joined Luce at the War College. It ends with his retirement from the navy, and it deals very cursorily with the important years 1890–1895. The best biography of Mahan is Robert Seager's two-volume *Alfred Thayer Mahan: The Man and His Letters* (Annapolis: Naval Institute Press, 1980). Thoroughly researched, eminently readable, and balanced in its judgments, it is a model biography. The older standard biography, William Puleston's *Mahan: The Life and Work of Captain Alfred Thayer Mahan, U.S.N.* (New Haven: Yale University Press, 1939), is much less impressive. The three-volume *Letters And Papers Of Alfred Thayer Mahan,* edited by Robert Seager and Doris D. Maguire (Annapolis: Naval Institute Press, 1975), reveals Mahan's prolific pen. Theodore Roosevelt's eulogy for Mahan is contained in "A Great Public Servant," in *Outlook,* January 13, 1915, pages 85–86.

Mahan and his writings have sparked a considerable amount of scholarly literature. William E. Livezey's *Mahan on Sea Power* (Norman: University of Oklahoma Press, 1981) is an investigation and assessment of Mahan's ideas, arranged by topic. It is thorough, balanced, and especially useful for assessing Mahan's influence today. Margaret T. Sprout's "Mahan: Evangelist Of Sea Power," in *Makers Of Modern Strategy,* edited by Edward M. Earle (Princeton: Princeton University Press, 1943), provides a brief, excellent review of his life, works, and influence during his lifetime and since. Richard W. Turk's *The Ambiguous Relationship: Theodore Roosevelt and Alfred Thayer Mahan* (Westport, Connecticut: Greenwood Press, 1987) is notable principally for containing the full texts of all the extant correspondence exchanged between Mahan and Roosevelt. Peter Karsten's *The Naval Aristocracy* (New York: The Free Press, 1972) is revisionist history designed to show that Mahan and most of his prominent naval officer colleagues do not deserve the reputations they have enjoyed. Long on opinion buttressed by selective documentation and innuendo, and short on objectivity and balance, it is notable mainly as an example of the revisionist attacks that have been made on Mahan and his writings. Karsten's "The Nature Of 'Influence': Roosevelt, Mahan and the Concept of Sea Power," in *American Quarterly*, October, 1971, pages 585–600, attempts unsuccessfully to demonstrate that Roosevelt influenced Mahan rather than the other way around.

CHAPTER 4
"THE DISASTROUS RISE OF MISPLACED POWER"

Benjamin Franklin Cooling's *Gray Steel and Blue Water Navy* (Hamden, Connecticut: Archon Books, 1979) deals with the relationship of private business, notably steel manufacturing, to the development of the "new navy" of steel and steam, and the consequent birth of the "military-industrial complex." Bernard Brodie's *Sea Power in the Machine Age* (Princeton: Princeton University Press, 1941) is a classic study of the increasing complexity of technological development in the steel and steam navy. Exhaustively researched, it is a work of impressive scholarship. Peter Padfield's *The Battleship Era* (London: Granada Publishing, Ltd., 1972) is an excellent comprehensive history from the creation of the first iron-clads to the end of World War II. It includes extensive technical information about armor, gunnery, and propulsion, written in understandable layman's language.

United States Battleships, edited by Alan F. Pater (Beverly Hills, California: Monitor Book Company, 1968), provides a brief but informative "biography," including a photograph, of every American battleship beginning with *Maine* and *Texas* and going through to World War II. Volume one of John Davis Long's two-volume *The New American Navy* (New York: The Outlook Co., 1903) recounts the development of the "new navy" in the 1880s and early 1890s. The author had the unusual experience as secretary of the navy of serving both "over" and under Theodore Roosevelt.

Benjamin Franklin Cooling's *Benjamin Franklin Tracy: Father of the Modern American Fighting Navy* (Hamden, Connecticut: Archon Books, 1973) is the biography of the navy secretary responsible for the first American battleships. *A Sailor's Log* (New York: D. Appleton & Co., 1901) is the first volume of Robley D. Evans's memoirs, which takes his story to the end of the Spanish-American War. The writing style nicely reflects Evans's personality and temperament. Edwin A. Falk's *Fighting Bob Evans* (New York: Cape & Smith, 1932) complements Evans's memoirs.

William H. McNeill's *The Pursuit of Power* (Chicago: University of Chicago Press, 1982) is a sweeping and incisive history of the interaction of technology, arms production, and society. In particular, a chapter entitled "Intensified Military-Industrial Interaction, 1884–1914" offers an insightful analysis of the origin and growth of the "military-industrial complex" in Britain, especially in connection with naval developments.

CHAPTER 5
"I HAVE THE NAVY IN GOOD SHAPE"

Roosevelt's conversation with Maria Storer is recounted in her article, "How Theodore Roosevelt Was Appointed Assistant Secretary of the Navy," in *Harper's Weekly,* June 1, 1912. Edmund Morris's *The Rise of Theodore Roosevelt* includes an excellent chapter on Roosevelt's adventures as assistant secretary.

George Dewey's *The Autobiography of George Dewey, Admiral of the Navy* (New York: Charles Scribner's Sons, 1913) takes the story of his life only to the end of the Spanish-American War and thus omits many of his most important years in the navy. Ronald Spector's *Admiral of the New Empire: The Life and Career of George Dewey* (Baton Rouge: Louisiana State University Press, 1974) is an excellent biography. Lawrence Shaw Mayo's *America of Yesterday As Reflected in the Diary of John D. Long* (Boston: Atlantic Monthly Press, 1923) includes Long's contemporary account of war preparations.

There is a great deal of published literature about the destruction of the *Maine.* The ship's commanding officer, Captain Charles D. Sigsbee, gave his version in *The Maine: An Account of Her Destruction in Havana Harbor* (New York: The Century Company, 1899). Hyman G. Rickover's account, *How The Battleship "Maine" Was Destroyed* (Washington, D.C.: Government Printing Office, 1976), was reissued in 1995. Michael Blow's *A Ship To Remember: The "Maine" and the Spanish-American War* (New York: William Morrow and Company, 1992) is a very readable account of the entire war with particular attention to *Maine.* It includes a detailed review of all the evidence.

A brief but excellent account of the battle of the Yalu is included in Edward Shippen's *Naval Battles of the World* (Philadelphia: P. W. Ziegler Co., 1905), pages 482–501. Another brief but more recently published description is contained in Bernard Edwards's *Salvo! Classic Naval Gun Actions* (Annapolis: Naval Institute Press, 1995).

Margaret Leech's *In the Days of McKinley* (New York: Harper's Bros., 1959) is an absorbing account of McKinley's presidency, including the events leading to the war, although the portrait that emerges of McKinley himself is probably more flattering than he deserves.

CHAPTER 6
"A FOURTH OF JULY PRESENT"

The story of *Oregon* is told in Sanford Sternlicht's *McKinley's Bulldog* (Chicago: Nelson-Hall, 1977). Charles E. Clark's *My Fifty Years in the Navy* (Boston: Little, Brown and Co., 1917) includes his experiences as commanding officer of *Oregon.* The incredible voyage is recounted in "The Race of the *Oregon,*" in *Oregon Historical Quarterly,* Volume seventy-six, September, 1975, pages 269–299.

The Spanish-American War has not generated nearly as much literature as the

Civil War or either of the two World Wars. Nevertheless, the amount is considerable, especially in the form of accounts and memoirs published early in this century. I have consulted Herbert W. Wilson's *The Downfall of Spain: Naval History of the Spanish-American War* (London: Sampson, Low, Marston and Company, Ltd., 1900), a detailed account of the naval war written by a British scholar immediately after the war ended. David F. Trask's *The War with Spain in 1898* (New York: Macmillan, 1981) is perhaps the best, most complete account of the entire conflict. Frank Freidel's *The Splendid Little War* (Boston: Little, Brown & Co., 1958) is notable for its wealth of illustrations and abundance of quotations from accounts by participants. Volume two of John D. Long's *The New American Navy* provides the perspective of Washington and the navy department. Walter Millis's *The Martial Spirit: A Study of Our War with Spain* (New York: Houghton Mifflin Co., 1931), like his *Arms and Men*, is iconoclastic and hypercritical of the military. Nathan Sargent's *Admiral Dewey and the Manila Campaign* (Washington: Naval Historical Foundation, 1947) is brief but detailed and thoroughly documented.

Richard S. West's *Admirals of American Empire* (Indianapolis: Bobbs-Merrill Co., 1948) is a good joint biography of Mahan, Dewey, Sampson, and Schley. William Goode's *With Sampson through the War* (New York: Doubleday & McClure, 1899) defends Sampson, while George E. Graham's *Schley and Santiago* (Chicago: Conkey Co., 1902) defends Schley in the famous controversy. Schley gives his own version in *Forty-five Years under the Flag* (New York: Appleton, Century, Croft, 1904). Sampson gives his account of the battle of Santiago in "The Atlantic Fleet in the Spanish War," in *Century Magazine*, LVII (1899), pages 886–913.

CHAPTER 7
"OUR MARKSMANSHIP IS CRUSHINGLY INFERIOR"

Frederick W. Holls's *The Peace Conference at The Hague* (New York: The Macmillan Company, 1900) is an account of the first peace conference. Biographies of Mahan include information that focuses, of course, on his role.

Elting E. Morison's *Admiral Sims and the Modern American Navy* (New York: Houghton Mifflin Company, 1942) is an outstanding biography that provides extensive, detailed information about Sims's innovations and his relationship with Roosevelt. S. S. McClure's "Admiral Sims" in *McClure's Magazine*, November, 1922, pages 26–31, includes admiring statements about Sims by two senior British admirals, Percy Scott and John Jellicoe. In three articles in *McClure's Magazine* (November and December, 1922, and January, 1923), Sims himself gave an account of his relationship with Roosevelt and his impressions of the president.

The evolution of long-range central fire control, a formidably technical subject, has been touched upon in a few publications for the general reader. Arthur Marder's *The Anatomy of British Sea Power* includes material on continuous aiming and the development of central fire control until 1905. The story of Arthur Pollen and his ill-fated invention is treated in Jon T. Sumida's "British Capital Ships and Fire Control in the *Dreadnought* Era: Sir John Fisher, Arthur Hungerford Pollen and the Battle Cruiser," in *Journal of Modern History*, Vol. 51 (1979), pages 205–230. Peter Padfield's *Aim Straight: A Biography of Admiral Sir Percy Scott* (London: Granada Publishing, Ltd., 1966) is an excellent biography of the creator of continuous aiming, who exerted such influence on William Sims.

CHAPTER 8
"THE ONLY LOGICAL BATTERY FOR A FIGHTING SHIP"

George T. Davis's *A Navy Second to None* (New York: Harcourt, Brace & Co., 1940) has become a classic. It is an outstanding account of the expansion of the navy in the late nineteenth and early twentieth centuries. William Reynolds Braisted's *The United States Navy in the Pacific, 1897–1909* (Austin, Texas: University of Texas Press, 1958) is another classic study, with excellent documentation that focusses on the dilemma faced by the navy in the wake of the Spanish-American War when it was expected to defend the new colonial acquisitions in the Pacific. *American Battleships, 1886–1923,* by John C. Reilly, Jr. (Annapolis: Naval Institute Press, 1980), contains numerous photographs and excellent, though very technical, text about all the pre-dreadnought battleships. John Roberts's *U.S. Battleships: An Illustrated History* (Annapolis: Naval Institute Press, 1985) is quite technical and covers all the ships from *Texas* and *Maine* to the *Iowa*-class of World War II.

Theodore Roosevelt and the Rise of the Modern Navy, by Gordon C. O'Gara (Princeton: Princeton University Press, 1943), is very brief and deals only with Roosevelt's years as president. It can be useful as an outline of the principal events between 1901–1909 affecting the navy. The biographies of Sims and Mahan cited above include accounts of the debates about the all-big-gun battleship.

Published literature about Jacky Fisher and *Dreadnought* is extensive, including several biographies, Fisher's own memoirs, and a three-volume collection of his correspondence. A good, readable account of both the man's life and the building of the ship is contained in Robert Massie's *Dreadnought: Britain, Germany and the Coming of the Great War* (New York: Random House, 1991). David Howarth's *The Dreadnoughts* (Alexandria, Va.: Time-Life Books, 1979) provides an excellent, if brief, text and numerous illustrations. It includes concise but useful information on the development of central fire control, and a gripping account of the battle of Jutland. John Roberts's *The Battleship "Dreadnought"* (Annapolis: The Naval Institute Press, 1992) is technical and contains numerous photographs and detailed drawings.

The voyage of the Russian Baltic Fleet and the battle of Tsushima have been recounted and analyzed in numerous publications. Richard Hough, a respected British naval historian, is the author of *The Fleet That Had To Die* (London: Macmillan, 1958), which is both thorough and readable. Denis and Peggy Warner's *The Tide at Sunrise: A History of the Russo-Japanese War, 1904–1905* (New York: Charterhouse, 1974) contains excellent chapters on the voyage and the battle. Oliver

Warner's *Great Sea Battles* (London: George Weidenfeld and Nicolson, Ltd., 1963) contains a brief account of the battle, as does David Howarth's *The Dreadnoughts*.

CHAPTER 9

"THEY SHOULD REALIZE I AM NOT AFRAID OF THEM"

Roosevelt's mediation to end the Russo-Japanese War is recounted in Tyler Dennett's *Roosevelt and the Russo-Japanese War: A Critical Study of American Policy in Eastern Asia, 1902–1905* (New York: Doubleday, Page & Co., 1925). The debates over the site for the major Pacific naval base are covered in some detail in Davis's and Braisted's works, cited above.

A thoroughly documented and eminently readable account of the construction of the Panama Canal can be found in *A Path Between The Seas*, by David McCullough (New York: Simon and Schuster, 1977).

Two thoroughly researched, scholarly studies of the San Francisco school board crisis with Japan and the decision to send the battle fleet to the Pacific are Thomas A. Bailey's *Theodore Roosevelt and the Japanese-American Crisis* (Palo Alto: Stanford University Press, 1934) and Charles E. Neu's *An Uncertain Friendship: Theodore Roosevelt and Japan, 1906–1909* (Cambridge: Harvard University Press, 1967). The latter is especially useful in providing the Japanese perspective, and both books include extensive information about American naval policy and strategy during the last half of Roosevelt's administration.

CHAPTER 10

"THE MOST IMPORTANT SERVICE THAT I RENDERED TO PEACE"

The best account of the world cruise is James Reckner's *Teddy Roosevelt's Great White Fleet* (Annapolis: Naval Institute Press, 1988). It is thoroughly documented, objective, and detailed. Although mainly an account of the cruise itself, it includes excellent if brief accounts of the historical context and the debates over battleship design that occurred while the fleet was at sea. Much less useful is Robert A. Hart's *The Great White Fleet* (Boston: Little, Brown & Co., 1965). Although copiously documented, it is shot through with generalizations and innuendoes that range from misleading to dead wrong. Its tone of undergraduate snigger belies any claim to objectivity or seriousness of purpose. Thomas A. Bailey's "The World Cruise of the American Battleship Fleet, 1907–1909," in *Pacific Historical Review* (Vol. I, No. 4, December, 1932, pages 389–422), is a brief account that focuses on the diplomatic context and implications. Two volumes by Franklin Mathews, *With the Battle Fleet* and *Back to Hampton Roads* (both New York: B. W. Huebsch, 1909) have the virtue of being first-hand accounts by someone who sailed with the fleet. Their defects are superficiality and an unrelenting rosiness of tone that becomes cloying. Theodore

Roosevelt in his *Autobiography* devotes several pages to his version of the cruise's origins and significance.

The second volume of Bob Evans's memoirs, *An Admiral's Log* (New York: D. Appleton & Co., 1910), covers his life from the end of the Spanish-American war to his retirement, including material on the cruise as far as San Francisco.

EPILOGUE
"THE MACHINE HAS WORKED"

The Billy Mitchell bombing demonstrations and their aftermath are examined in Burke Davis's *The Billy Mitchell Affair* (New York: Random House, 1967). The destruction of *Bismarck* has been recounted in numerous publications. A virtually hour-by-hour account of its last voyage is given in Burkard Baron von Mullenheim-Rechberg's *Battleship Bismarck: A Survivor's Story* (Annapolis: Naval Institute Press, 1980). The author was the ship's gunnery officer and the highest ranking survivor. Richard Hough's *The Hunting of Force Z* (London: Fontana Books, 1964) provides a gripping account of the destruction of *Prince of Wales* and *Repulse*. It includes an excellent capsule history of the rise and decline of the battleship. *The Eclipse of the Big Gun: The Warship, 1906–1945*, edited by Robert Gardiner (Annapolis: Naval Institute Press, 1992), reviews the decline of the battleship and the rise of the aircraft carrier by tracing the development of types of ships in the world's major navies until the end of World War II. The story of the development of the American aircraft carrier is given in Norman Friedman's *United States Aircraft Carriers: An Illustrated Design History* (Annapolis: Naval Institute Press, 1983).

INDEX

ABOUT THE AUTHOR

Kenneth Wimmel is a retired Foreign Service officer and a graduate of the Naval War College. He served in the navy for four years as a shipboard radio operator. His first book, entitled *The Alluring Target: In Search of the Secrets of Central Asia,* was published in 1996. Mr. Wimmel lives with his wife and daughter in Bethesda, Maryland, where he devotes his time to writing on historical subjects.